THE BOOK OF MORMON

Miracle

— *25* REASONS TO BELIEVE —

THE BOOK OF MORMON

Miracle

—— *25* REASONS TO BELIEVE ——

RANDAL A. WRIGHT

CFI
An Imprint of Cedar Fort, Inc.
Springville, Utah

Praise for
Book of Mormon Miracle

"With that . . . unique style of common sense, wit, and spiritual insight that makes his classes at BYU Education Week and elsewhere so popular, Randal Wright gives reason after reason to believe the special record is the miracle it is claimed to be. This engaging book presents information that cannot be easily dismissed by honest minded readers, and that will add to the testimonies of those who already have a spiritual witness of the truthfulness of the Book of Mormon."

—Gary McFadyen, vice president of marketing, American Mutual Benefits; founder of HoldOn Communications; Campus Education Week Speaker

"Randal has written a book that is enjoyable to read and accessible to readers of any age or background. This book makes a strong, clear, undeniable case for the truthfulness of what Joseph Smith affirmed about the divine origins of the Book of Mormon while also refuting simplistic criticisms that have been parroted over the years."

—Nate Sharp, PhD; associate professor, Mays Business School at Texas A&M University; founder of www.aggielandmormons.org

"Randal has provided us with irrefutable evidence that a simple farm boy from New York translated this ancient record by the Spirit and power of God. Period. He offers compelling logic while continually pointing to the source of all truth—the words of the Lord and His prophets."

—Tara Collins, founder of Make Change; international volunteer project developer

"Randal Wright's newest book arms Book of Mormon apologists with a wealth of essential observations on the ancient origins and the unique content of the Book of Mormon. . . . If you're looking for another reason to believe that the Book of Mormon truly is a divine work of scripture, this book will give you twenty-five!"

—Brandon Carlton, MBA, JD, LLM; national tax principal at Ernst & Young; adjunct professor, Georgetown University Law Center

"As a geoscientist, I want all the evidences I can possibly find before I believe. Randal Wright provides evidences and convincing arguments on the authenticity of the Book of Mormon. I learned many things that I did not know before and loved how they are presented. My testimony was strengthened! I highly recommend this book to anyone who wants to find out the truthfulness of the Book Mormon for themselves."

—Shihong Chi, PhD; senior geophysical advisor, ION Geophysical; postdoctoral research fellow at Earth Resources Laboratory, Massachusetts Institute of Technology

"The central thesis of this book is that Joseph Smith, or even a legion of other well-educated writers, could not possibly have written the Book of Mormon. That point is effectively made in some rather original ways. Though the author effectively uses logical arguments, he does not rely on them primarily to make [his] point. He still points the reader to the power of the Book of Mormon to change lives, and the importance of obtaining a testimony in the direct manner Moroni challenges every reader to do."

—Chad Richardson, PhD; Emeritus professor of sociology and department chair; director of Borderlands Research Center, University of Texas-Pan American; author

"Randal's style of beautiful, simply communicated information and understanding [helps] us to think our way through the pages of *The Book of Mormon Miracle*. His way of teaching allows readers to take his illustrations to heart, as it helps us better appreciate and love the Book of Mormon. His choice to begin each chapter with a perfect quote [and] then elaborate on it is inspiring."

—Vickey Pahnke Taylor, MS; songwriter, producer, and vocalist; frequent speaker at BYU Education Week and Best of Especially for Youth; founder of www.goodnessmatters.com

"Randal Wright is not only a tremendous speaker, but his writing is equally inspiring! One only needs to listen to or read his messages to grasp the significant meanings and concepts that motivate the soul!"

—Jay Osmond, vocalist and drummer for the Osmond Brothers; voted one of the top ten drummers in the United States; author of *Stages: An Autobiography*

ISBN 13: 978-1-4621-1469-6

Published by CFI, an imprint of Cedar Fort, Inc.
2373 W. 700 S., Springville, UT 84663
Distributed by Cedar Fort, Inc., www.cedarfort.com

LIBRARY OF CONGRESS CATALOGING-IN-PUBLICATION DATA

Wright, Randal A., author.
The Book of Mormon miracle : 25 reasons to believe / Randal A. Wright.
    pages cm
Summary: Discusses twenty-five reasons why Joseph Smith, an uneducated farm boy from rural New York, could not have written the Book of Mormon.
ISBN 978-1-4621-1469-6 (alk. paper)
1. Book of Mormon--Authorship. 2. Book of Mormon--Criticism, interpretation, etc. I. Title.

BX8627.W75 2014
289.3'22--dc23

2014036459

Cover design by Shawnda T. Craig
Cover design © 2014 Lyle Mortimer
Edited and typeset by Kevin Haws

Printed in the United States of America

10 9 8 7 6 5 4 3 2 1

Printed on acid-free paper

Contents

Contents

Chapter 1: Introduction

One night at an institute class, a visitor walked in and sat down right after the lesson had begun. We were discussing the Book of Mormon and the organization of the Church. The visitor didn't say anything for awhile but then made a derogatory comment about the Church.

That put me in an awkward position. On one hand, I wanted to be kind to everyone who walked into the class, but at the same time, I always defended the Church. I acknowledged his comment, thanked him for his opinion, and then said something positive about the Church. At one point during the lesson, a student mentioned the testimonies of the witnesses to the Book of Mormon. Our visitor mockingly pointed out that most of the witnesses were related and therefore their testimonies were worthless. It was apparent to me that he had not come to participate in a positive class discussion but to cast doubts and attempt to raise a debate.

At that point I said, "If I were an atheist, I think I would belong to The Church of Jesus Christ of Latter-day Saints because of the tremendous blessings that come through membership. There is no other organization like it in the world." I also said if there were no God or no life after death, the last thing I would want to do is "eat, drink, and be merry" since living that lifestyle has been proven to lead to early death. I told the class that if this life was all there is, we should all try to live like the prophets and apostles of the Church because they live far longer and more productive lives than the average person.

Next, we discussed the temporal and social benefits of belonging to the Church. The following are some of the advantages the students pointed out:

- Scientifically proven health code to help people live longer, more productive lives
- High-quality programs for every age group, beginning at eighteen months of age
- Dedicated leaders and teachers who desire to help others learn and succeed
- Public speaking opportunities and leadership training
- Opportunities to provide service to the community and those in need
- Free use of beautiful buildings for socials, sports, wedding receptions, funerals, and so on
- Chance to associate often with high achievers who are trying to better themselves
- Instant friends and acceptance wherever you go in the world
- Networking system for those seeking jobs or wanting to upgrade employment
- Award programs that help youth learn to set and accomplish worthwhile goals
- Programs to help the needy, where all donations are used for that purpose
- Advice from world-class experts through conference talks and magazine articles
- Assistance for those who are sick, have new babies, or have had a death in the family
- Free support group for those struggling with addictions
- Free counseling given to those struggling with marriage or personal problems
- Free help for those moving in or out of an area
- Chance to share talents through speaking, choirs, and so on
- Teachers assigned to visit homes monthly to provide needed support
- Perpetual Education Fund to assist YSA in developing countries go to college
- Extremely low tuition rates at prestigious Church schools with world-class faculty
- Church welfare farms and canneries, all of which provide basic necessities for the needy

My testimony of the Church was greatly strengthened that evening as students listed such amazing benefits of membership. I felt incredibly fortunate that my family and I belonged to such an organization.

It was obvious, however, that our visitor was not impressed in the least. I felt quite certain that he would stay after class looking to debate anyone willing to stand up for the Church. That feeling proved to be true. He came to me after class and immediately began to mock the Church, our leaders, and the "gullible" members. I hoped no one else would stay around to listen to him, but several others did gather. I tried to be considerate, not knowing his background or why he had such negative feelings toward the Church. He was a walking encyclopedia of anti-Mormon criticisms of Joseph Smith, the Book of Mormon, and the Church.

In between his mocking rants, I asked him several questions to learn more about him. I found out that he was from a western state, had just moved to Austin, Texas, and that his parents were serving a mission for the Church. I also found out that he was currently unemployed and looking for a job. I assumed that he was a University of Texas graduate student but then learned he was thirty years old and about to start his first semester at a local community college. He was quite proud of the fact that he would be studying to be a developmental psychologist.

It seemed that almost everything that came out of his mouth about the Church was either misleading or outright false. Every time I clarified or corrected one of his statements, he quickly changed to another topic. He not only ridiculed early Church history, but he also criticized everything he could about the modern one. He mocked the *per capita* giving of Church members to humanitarian aid. He said the Church was being deceptive by counting those who were less active in membership statistics. I felt as if we were getting a little taste of what missionaries like Alma and Amulek must have heard in Ammonihah.

I tried to be respectful about his views, but at one point he crossed the line with me. I tried to stay calm. He looked at pictures of the First Presidency and the Quorum of the Twelve that were hanging on the wall in our classroom and sarcastically called them the "geriatric good old boys club." I love the Brethren and have tremendous respect for them and their willingness to do anything in their power to build up the kingdom. I decided at that point that it was time to ask him a few questions. I asked him if he really believed that Elder Russell M. Nelson, an internationally renowned heart surgeon whose innovative medical procedures have saved countless lives, would walk away from his career to join some "good old boys club." He said, "Yes." I found it ironic that an unemployed thirty-year-old with zero college education would be mocking a brilliant PhD medical doctor.

I then asked where he thought the Book of Mormon came from. He told me that Joseph Smith wrote it. I hoped that would be his answer. I asked if he really believed that a twenty-four-year-old uneducated farm boy could have written that book. I felt sure he would say that Sidney Rigdon had helped him write it, but he didn't. He said that Joseph Smith wrote it himself by heavily plagiarizing the Bible and other books of his day.

It so happened that at that time I was doing a computer search for three- to seven-word phrases from the Book of Mormon to see how many were unique to this book of scripture and how many could have been copied from the Bible. I knew from my preliminary research that there were thousands of phrases that Joseph Smith could not have copied from any other source, including the Bible. I'm speaking of original phrases such as "made white through the blood of Christ" (Alma 5:27) and "that precious gift of eternal life" (Helaman 5:8).

After hearing him declare that Joseph Smith wrote the Book of Mormon, I changed the subject back to his employment. He again said he was looking for a job because he was short on cash. That was just what I wanted him to say. I then said, "Well, it's your lucky day because I have a job for you!" He seemed interested in what I had to offer. I told him that he was obviously bright, so the job should be easy for him. When he asked what I needed him to do, I told him to write a short story the same length as the first chapter of the Book of Mormon, for which I would pay him two hundred dollars.

He seemed to tense up a little but asked me what the content should include. I told him his story should be based on an Ethiopian family who lived in 600 BC. One day, the father has a dream that the area is going to be destroyed, so he takes his family and leaves. They travel to the shores of the Red Sea where they build a ship and sail to Australia and become some of the Australian aborigines.

The visitor's countenance changed. He appeared to become rather nervous. I then explained he could write about anything he wanted, but it needed to have a religious theme and be written in King James Bible language. The only other requirement would be that he had to invent five original names for his main characters and use ten original three- to seven-word phrases that had never appeared in print. He also had to agree that he would not use a search engine to see if his names or phrases had been used before.

At that point, he began to pace back and forth and stammer, "I, I don't see what that would prove!"

I said he didn't need to prove anything. I reminded him that he was looking for a job and I was offering him a quick way to make two hundred dollars for what should have been no more than a couple of hours of work. I added that other than the five original names and ten unique phrases, he could copy anything else he wanted from other sources. I gave him one week to complete the story and told him that I wanted to make copies of his story and let the class read it to see what they thought.

He said, "I don't see the purpose of this. It'd be meaningless."

It was interesting just how quickly the cocky, sarcastic critic became a nervous and evasive young man who appeared to want to run from the situation. He repeated again that he didn't see what the assignment would prove. I reminded him that he said uneducated Joseph Smith wrote the 588 pages of the Book of Mormon, with its 180 original names and thousands of original phrases.

Within a short time, he told me that he really needed to be going. As he walked away, I again offered to pay him if he would bring his story to class the next week. If you are wondering, I was dead serious about paying him. Unfortunately, I never saw this young man again.

Our conversation caused me to think how critics spend enormous amounts of time trying to bring down the Book of Mormon and the Church, which tries to teach its members to be "honest, true, chaste, benevolent, virtuous, and in doing good to all men" (Articles of Faith 1:13). At the same time, we face serious social challenges in America. We have terrible problems with divorce, suicide, single parenting, racism, bullying, crime, gangs, abortion, child abuse, drug abuse, and much more. Why not spend precious time trying to help with the social issues that are threatening to destroy our civilization rather than attacking the Book of Mormon and its believers?

Yet it has been that way since the Book of Mormon first appeared on the scene and the Church was organized. President Gordon B. Hinckley said this about those like our class visitor who believe Joseph Smith was a fraud who wrote the Book of Mormon: "Joseph Smith couldn't have written the Book of Mormon. These people who wear out their lives trying to find some other cause for the coming forth of the Book of Mormon are doing just that—wearing out their lives."[1]

I did not always have a strong testimony of the gospel. My testimony came many years ago by reading the Book of Mormon with real intent, pondering what I read. I do not know how many times I have read it over the years, but I did read it once a month in 2013. During those twelve times, I never tired of it. In fact, many days I found myself having a hard time putting the book down because I was fascinated by something new I had learned. No other book could hold my attention to that degree twelve times in one year. I also noticed that the more I read, the more I wanted to do my part to try and help alleviate the world's social ills.

I think that if a set of ancient gold plates with engraved writing on them were uncovered in Israel by a research team of archeologists from Harvard University, it would be international news. If a team of PhD linguists found the record covering a period from 600 BC to 421 AD and published it as a book, it would generate tremendous interest.

However, when a similar thing happened in upstate New York involving an uneducated farm boy who said an angel was also involved, the work was immediately branded as fraudulent or was ignored by the majority of people. Even when eleven witnesses stepped forward, putting their names and reputations on the line to testify that they had seen the plates, it did not generate widespread interest or belief.

It is not so different today. In our fast-paced society, people are busy. Most do not have time to read every book that comes along, even if it is listed as a best seller. At the end of 2013, the Library of Congress in Washington, D.C. housed 158,007,115 total items, including books, manuscripts, pamphlets, photographs, and other artifacts. If we were to read or examine each one at a rate of one per day, it would take about 432,896 years to complete the task. We do need to be selective in what we choose to read. Isn't a book that is rated excellent and life-changing by millions of people worthy of the twenty-four hours it would take the average person to read it? What is there to lose? On the other hand, what do we have to gain if it is true? After all, it claims to be from God, to be written for our day, and to contain answers to life's most important questions.

Imagine having a book readily available with so many great promises and truths if we simply read it with real intent. After many years of personal study, I believe that the Book of Mormon is a miracle, whether Joseph Smith wrote it or translated it. Obviously, if Moroni delivered the plates and Joseph Smith translated them from an ancient language, it would be a miracle. And if an uneducated farm boy wrote the book, which has changed the lives of millions for good, it would also be a miracle. If that were not the case, then surely some critic in the past 185 years would have stepped forward and duplicated the feat by now. Strangely, no one has even tried.

Whichever camp people favor, a miracle was involved in the coming forth of the Book of Mormon. I find it far easier to believe that the book was translated by "the gift and power of God" rather than believe Joseph wrote it, or that he wrote it with the help of some unknown assistant. I can at least comprehend that he translated it. As hard as I have tried to grasp the idea that he composed the book in sixty-three working days, I cannot do it.

I have not written this book to try and prove the truthfulness of the Book of Mormon. I agree with Hugh Nibley, who said, "The evidence that will prove or disprove the Book of Mormon does not exist."[2] No matter what the evidence is, some will not be convinced. Even if the Church were to put the plates on display, doubters would say there is no way those plates were produced in 600 BC. If the Angel Moroni were to give a presentation at the Joseph Smith Building, some would say something like, "Big deal. It is obviously an illusion. David Copperfield made the Statue of Liberty disappear."

This book was written to share things that have built up my testimony of the Book of Mormon in the last few years. My desire in writing this book is to create enough interest in the reader that he or she will read the Book of Mormon with real intent and ask

God if it is true. The English theologian and philosopher Austin Farrer said, "Though argument does not create conviction, lack of it destroys belief. What seems to be proved may not be embraced; but what no one shows the ability to defend is quickly abandoned. Rational argument does not create belief, but it maintains a climate in which belief may flourish."[3]

Included in these pages are a few of my "rational arguments." I will mention twenty-five of the numerous reasons why I believe the Book of Mormon to be exactly what it claims to be: the truth. Though it is not meant to be a scholarly work, I hope these will lead to—as Austin Farrer called it—"a climate in which belief may flourish."

Notes

1. Gordon B. Hinckley, from Priesthood Session, Boston Massachusetts Regional Conference, April 22, 1995 (*Church News*, January 6, 1996).
2. Hugh W. Nibley, *Since Cumorah* (Salt Lake City: Deseret Book, 1987), 14.
3. Austin Farrer, "The Christian Apologist," in *Light on C. S. Lewis*, ed. Jocelyn Gibb (New York: Harcourt, Brace & World, 1965), 26.

Chapter 2: All of Joseph Smith's Family Believed

"He [Joseph] arose and told us how the angel appeared to him, what he told him. . . . He continued talking to us [for] sometime. The whole family were melted to tears, and believed all he said. Knowing that he was very young, that he had not enjoyed the advantages of a common education; and knowing too, his whole character and disposition, they were convinced that he was totally incapable of arising before his aged parents, his brothers and sisters, and so solemnly giving utterance to anything but the truth."[1]

—William Smith

It seems to be the case in life that individuals who consistently exaggerate or say dishonest things are exposed in time. This is especially true in families where members are in close contact with each over extended periods of time. Family members often know each other's tendencies and weaknesses all too well and can tell when someone is not being truthful.

Think for a moment about your own family. Now, imagine one of them coming to you and telling you that he was in the woods praying when an evil influence came over him that was so powerful it affected him to the point that he couldn't even talk and thought he was going to die. However, just at his lowest point, God the Father and Jesus Christ appeared. Would you believe him? A few years later, he comes to you again and said that during the night an angel of light appeared by his bed and told him that God had a special work for him to do. Apparently, he would find some ancient gold plates that God wanted him to translate, and his name would be known for both good and evil throughout the entire world. Again, would you believe him? This is like the situation in which the immediate family of Joseph Smith found themselves.

Joseph Smith said in his famous King Follett Sermon, "I don't blame any one for not believing my history. If I had not experienced what I have, I would not have believed it myself."[2] Joseph said he would not have believed it himself, and yet every member of his immediate family believed everything he said. Not only did they believe him with their words, but also with their actions. I doubt that his family had any idea of the storm that would erupt after word got out about Joseph's visions. The rumors, mockery, and persecutions began quickly.

Brigham Young gave us a glimpse of what it was like for Joseph (and his family) to live from that point on. He said, "If a thousand hounds were on this Temple Block, let loose on one rabbit, it would not be a bad illustration of the situation at times of the Prophet Joseph. He was hunted unremittingly."[3] It seems logical that if Joseph Smith were making up his story, he would have backed off when the persecution and mocking became that intense. But he never once retracted or changed his story.

If Joseph were making up his story, how did he convince every member of his immediate family to believe him and stand by him throughout his life when it caused them so much grief and heartache? The only thing that makes sense is they knew he was telling the truth.

At one point, William Smith, Joseph's younger brother, explained why the family had such faith in what Joseph told them: "We all had the most implicit confidence in what he said. He was a truthful boy. Father and mother believed him, why should not the children? I suppose if he had told crooked stories about other things we might have doubted his word about the plates, but Joseph was a truthful boy. That father and mother believed his report and suffered persecution for that belief shows that he was truthful. No, we never doubted his word for one minute."[4]

The entire family never questioned his word, even though believing him came at a tremendous price for the entire Smith family. The family's reputation as honest, respectable citizens was tainted forever. In the eyes of many of their former friends and neighbors, the family's belief in the "gold bible" meant that they were either involved in a gigantic hoax with their son or they were just ignorant and easily deceived. William put it this way: "We never knew we were bad folks until Joseph told his vision. We were considered respectable till then, but at once people began to circulate falsehoods and stories in a wonderful way."[5]

Much of the abuse was directed toward Joseph himself. Joseph described his difficult situation:

> And though I was hated and persecuted for saying that I had seen a vision, yet it was true; and while they were persecuting me, reviling me, and speaking all manner of evil against me falsely for so saying, I was led to say in my heart: Why persecute me for telling the truth? I have actually seen a vision; and who am I that I can withstand God, or why does the world think to make me deny what I have actually seen? For I had seen a vision; I knew it, and I knew that God knew it, and I could not deny it, neither dared I do it; at least I knew that by so doing I would offend God, and come under condemnation." (Joseph Smith—History 1:25)

Joseph Smith also recognized the negative impact his story had on his family. He added, "The excitement, however, still continued, and rumor with her thousand tongues was all the time employed in circulating falsehoods about my father's family, and about myself. If I were to relate a thousandth part of them, it would fill up volumes" (Joseph Smith—History 1:61). What kind of son and brother would do this to his family unless he was telling the truth?

Through the years, the rumors and accusations intensified. At one point, Oliver Cowdery felt compelled to defend the Smith family. He wrote, "It has been industriously circulated that they were dishonest, deceitful and vile. On this I have the testimony of responsible persons, who have said and will say, that this is basely false; and besides, a personal acquaintance for seven years, has demonstrated that . . . their names are like[ly] to (indeed they will) be handed down to posterity, and had among the righteous. They are industrious, honest, virtuous and liberal to all. This is their character."[6]

The steadfastness and loyalty of Joseph's entire family through intense persecution and blatant misrepresentation support the belief that he was telling the truth. By examining individual members of the Smith family, we can see by their words and actions that they each believed what Joseph told them.

Joseph Smith Sr.

His father, Joseph Smith Sr., was the son of Asael and Mary Smith. Asael apparently had a feeling that one of his descendants would have a tremendous religious mission to accomplish. He said, "It has been borne in upon my soul that one of my descendants will promulgate a work to revolutionize the world of religious faith."[7] I wonder if Asael realized at the time that he would hear the news of the work that would revolutionize the world while he was still alive.

The angel Moroni's appearance to Joseph Smith three times during the night of September 21, 1823, took up most of the night. The next day, Joseph went to work with his father but did not feel well, so he was told to return home. At this point, he had not mentioned his vision to his father. While walking home, he crossed a fence, but his strength failed him and he fell unconscious to the ground. The next thing he remembered was Moroni appearing to him again and relating everything he had told Joseph the night before. The angel told Joseph to inform his father about the vision and the commandments he had received.

Joseph described what happened next: "I obeyed; I returned to my father in the field, and rehearsed the whole matter to him. He replied to me that it was of God, and told me to go and do as commanded by the messenger" (Joseph Smith—History 1:50).

Thus, Joseph Smith Sr. became the first person Joseph told of his visit from Moroni. He also became the first person to believe Joseph was telling the truth. He was later given the privilege of seeing and handling the plates and becoming one of the Eight Witnesses.

Joseph Smith Sr. was baptized on April 6, 1830, the day the Church was organized. When Joseph Jr. witnessed his father coming up out of the water, he is reported to have said, "Oh! My God, I have lived to see my own father baptized into the true church of Jesus Christ."[8]

Shortly after the Book of Mormon was published and the Church was organized, Joseph Sr. and his son Don Carlos left Kirtland, Ohio, on a mission. They carried copies of the Book of Mormon and traveled to Massachusetts. This mission was to personally share the details of the Restoration with Joseph Sr.'s elderly parents and his siblings. Because of the powerful testimony Joseph Smith Sr. bore, all of his siblings eventually came into the Church except his brother Jesse and his sister Susan.

Asael Smith died two months after this visit. George A. Smith said, "My grandfather Asael fully believed the Book of Mormon, which he read nearly through, although in his eighty-eighth year, without the aid of glasses."[9] In October 1830, "F[at]her Asael Smith . . . on his deathbed declared his full and firm belief in the everlasting gospel and also regretted that he was not baptized when Joseph his son was there."[10] A few years later, Asael's wife Mary Duty Smith traveled to Kirtland, Ohio, with her missionary grandson Elias Smith to see her children and grandchildren. She had completely accepted the gospel and fully intended to be baptized; however, she died just ten days after arriving in Kirtland.

Joseph Smith Sr. served as the first patriarch in this dispensation and traveled extensively throughout the Church giving patriarchal blessings. He had a strong testimony of the Book of Mormon and faithfully followed his prophet son throughout his life. After enduring severe persecution in Missouri, he fled to Illinois, arriving in the spring of 1839, and became one of the founders of Nauvoo. Having never fully recovered from the harsh exposure he suffered in the winter exodus from Missouri, he died in September of 1840. At his funeral, his friend Elder Robert B. Thompson said this:

> If ever there was a man who had claims on the affections of the community, it was our beloved but now deceased Patriarch . . . for truly we can say with the king of Israel, "A prince and a great man has fallen in Israel." A man endeared to us by every feeling calculated to entwine around and adhere to the human heart, by almost indissoluble bonds. A man faithful to his God and to the Church in every situation and under all circumstances through which he was called to pass. . . . He . . . was chosen by the Almighty to be one of the witnesses to the Book of Mormon. From that time, his only aim was the promotion of truth—his soul was taken up with the things of the Kingdom; his bowels yearned over the children of men; and it was more than his meat and his drink to do the will of his Father, who is in heaven.[11]

Clearly, Joseph Smith Sr.'s life confirmed his belief in his son's work, including the Book of Mormon. His belief was so strong that he counseled young Joseph to follow the heavenly directions as he himself was able to do throughout his life.

Lucy Mack Smith

Like her husband, Lucy Mack Smith accepted the testimony of her son from the beginning. She gave this interesting insight into what it was like at the Smith home after Joseph began receiving his divine manifestations:

> During our evening conversations, Joseph would occasionally give us some of the most amusing recitals that could be imagined. He would describe the ancient inhabitants of this continent, their dress, mode of travelings, and the animals upon which they rode; their cities, their buildings, with every particular; their mode of warfare; and also their religious worship. This he would do with as much ease, seemingly, as if he had spent his whole life among them.[12]

Lucy Mack Smith was also a bold missionary. Early on, she wrote letters to her relatives telling them about the Restoration of the gospel.

Once, when she was in a large crowd, a man called out to her, "Is the Book of Mormon true?" She replied for all to hear, "That book was brought forth by the power of God, and translated by the gift of the Holy Ghost; and, if I could make my voice sound as loud as the trumpet of Michael, the Archangel, I would declare the truth from land to land, and from sea to sea, and the echo should reach every isle, until every member of the family of Adam should be left without excuse."[13]

In 1842, Joseph paid tribute to his mother, saying, "My mother also is one of the noblest and best of all women. May God grant to prolong her days and mine, that we may live to enjoy each other's society long."[14]

Lucy Mack Smith's confidence in her son's words and work far surpasses an ordinary mother's love and support. She was totally and deeply devoted to him, his revelations, and the Book of Mormon. She encouraged him, advocated for him, and suffered for him as she taught others the truths Joseph had taught her.

Alvin Smith

Alvin was the oldest child of Joseph Sr. and Lucy Mack Smith. He died at twenty-five from mercury poisoning, given to him by a doctor to cure a bout of "bilious colic" just two months after the angel Moroni appeared to his younger brother. He fully believed Joseph and was excited about the work he was called to do. Lucy Mack Smith shared this:

> Knowing he was dying, Alvin called his brothers and sisters to him and spoke to each of them. To Joseph, who was almost 18 years old and had not yet received the gold plates, Alvin said, "I want you to be a good boy and do everything that lies in your power to obtain the records. Be faithful in receiving instruction and keeping every commandment that is given you. Your brother Alvin must now leave you, but remember the example which he has set for you, and set a good example for the children that are younger than you."[15]

Joseph Smith later said this of his brother: "Alvin, my oldest brother—I remember well the pangs of sorrow that swelled my youthful bosom and almost burst my tender heart when he died. He was the oldest and the noblest of my father's family. He was one of the noblest of the sons of men. . . . He was one of the soberest of men, and when he died the angel of the Lord visited him in his last moments."[16]

Alvin was not alive for long after the angel Moroni came to Joseph and therefore did not have the opportunity to act upon what was in the records. Nevertheless, his last words to Joseph emphatically reaffirmed his belief in the truth of Joseph's vision.

Hyrum Smith

As one of the Eight Witnesses to the Book of Mormon, Hyrum testified to the world in writing that he personally saw and handled the plates from which the Book of Mormon was translated.

Later, Hyrum was unjustly confined in Liberty Jail. His account of that confinement shows the depth of his testimony. It was an extremely trying time for Hyrum because the year before he was incarcerated, his wife Jerusha and daughter Mary passed away. He was left with five motherless children, the oldest being only eleven years old and the youngest eleven days old. He later married Mary Fielding. She gave birth to their son Joseph F. Smith while Hyrum was imprisoned. Hyrum writes of this period of life:

> In the fall of 1838, I was imprisoned with my brethren for about six months . . . and suffered much for want of proper food, and from the nauseous cell in which I was confined. . . . How inadequate is language to express the feelings of my mind, knowing that I was innocent of crime, and that I had been dragged from my family at a time, when my assistance was most needed; that I had been abused and thrust into a dungeon, and confined for months on account of my faith, and the "testimony of Jesus Christ." However I thank God that I felt a determination to die, rather than deny the things which my eyes had seen, which my hands had handled, and which I had bore testimony to. . . . I can assure my beloved brethren that I was enabled to bear as strong a testimony, when nothing but death presented itself, as ever I did in my life . . . I yet feel a determination to do the will of God, in spite of persecutions, imprisonments or death.[17]

Hyrum proved that this stated determination to do the will of God was not just idle talk. Knowing the extreme danger they were in as Carthage loomed before them, Joseph strongly suggested that Hyrum take his family and travel to Cincinnati rather than come to Carthage with him. Hyrum replied that he could not leave him.

The love that Hyrum and Joseph had for each other is legendary. They were fiercely loyal, no matter what the circumstances. Joseph said this of his older brother: "I could pray in my heart that all my brethren were like unto my beloved brother Hyrum, who possesses the mildness of a lamb, and the integrity of a Job, and in short, the meekness and humility of Christ; and I love him with that love that is stronger than death, for I never had occasion to rebuke him, nor he me."[18]

Even as mobs conspired against them, the Book of Mormon filled their minds. When Hyrum and Joseph started for Carthage to face martyrdom, Hyrum read a few verses from the twelfth chapter of Ether in the Book of Mormon to comfort his brother and turned the page down. Dan Jones recorded the events of the night before they were killed in Carthage Jail: "During the evening the Patriarch [Hyrum] read and commented upon copious extracts from the Book of Mormon."[19]

After Hyrum's death, the *Times and Seasons* printed this touching eulogy: "He lived so far beyond the ordinary walk of man, that even the tongue of the vilest slanderer could not touch his reputation. He lived godly and he died godly."[20]

Hyrum's life and death demonstrated his unfailing faith in and knowledge of the Restoration. His belief was strong at the beginning and perfect at the end. His guileless life magnified his work.

Sophronia Smith

Little is known about Sophronia, third child and oldest daughter of Joseph Sr. and Lucy Mack Smith. She was thirteen years old when her family moved to Palmyra, New York. She married Calvin Stoddard and had two children before he died in 1836 while living in Kirtland, Ohio. She married a second time to William McCleary, and they moved to Missouri in 1838 and Illinois in 1839. She was living among the Saints in Hancock County, Illinois, at the time of her brothers' deaths.

Sophronia received the following blessing from her father:

> I pronounce the blessing of thy father Jacob upon thee, and thou shalt have a name and a place in thy father's family, because of thy tears and prayers, for thou hast prevailed unto the obtaining this blessing: Thou shalt yet be comforted, for the days of thy tribulation shall have an end, and the time of thy rejoicing shall come; and thou shalt be blessed with an abundance of the good things of this life. Thou art blessed and shall be blessed, and saved in the kingdom of heaven. Amen.[21]

Sophronia's belief in Joseph and his words was evidently sufficient enough for her to live with the Saints and receive a patriarchal blessing.

Samuel Smith

Samuel was also one of the Eight Witnesses of the Book of Mormon. In the spring of 1832, he reaffirmed that experience when he told a group of people that he was a witness of it: "He knew his brother Joseph had the plates, for the Prophet had shown them to him; and he had handled them and seen the engravings thereon."[22]

Samuel was baptized on May 25, 1829, the third person in this dispensation to receive that ordinance, following Joseph Smith and Oliver Cowdery. The next spring, on April 6, 1830, he became one of the six original members of the Church. Two months later, Joseph set Samuel apart as the Church's first official missionary.

On the first day of his mission, he visited four homes and walked twenty-five miles. He found that no one was interested in hearing his message. That night, he asked an innkeeper if he would like to buy a copy of the Book of Mormon. When Samuel told the man that his brother had translated it from gold plates that had been buried in the ground, the man called him a liar and told him to get out of his inn. That night, the discouraged missionary slept on the ground.

The next day, he was able to share the Book of Mormon with John Greene, a Methodist minister, whose wife, Rhoda, was the sister of Brigham Young. That fateful encounter eventually led to the baptism of both John and Rhoda Greene. Samuel later sold a copy of the Book of Mormon to Phineas Young, also a Methodist minister and the brother of Brigham Young. Even though Samuel didn't baptize anyone during his early missionary efforts and only shared a few copies of the Book of Mormon, the end result was amazing. Just those two copies brought many faithful members into the Church, including future prophet Brigham Young, along with his parents and brothers and sisters, as well as future Apostle Heber C. Kimball.

During his meeting with Phineas Young, Samuel Smith bore his testimony of the Book of Mormon's truthfulness. He maintained that same testimony until the day he died in 1844. He said, "The Book of Mormon, or, as it is called by some, the Golden Bible . . . is a revelation from God. . . . If you will read this book with a prayerful heart and ask God to give you a witness, you will know the truth of the work. . . . I am one of the witnesses. . . . I know the book is a revelation from God, translated by the power of the Holy Ghost, and that my brother, Joseph Smith, Jr., is a Prophet, Seer, and Revelator."[23]

Samuel's witness of the Book of Mormon impacted many lives, some near him and others many generations beyond, as did his missionary labors. His written witness as one of the Eight Witnesses of the Book of Mormon affirms his testimony throughout the world to all who hold the book in their hands.

William Smith

William was nearly six years younger than Joseph. He was with the family during many significant events connected to the coming forth of the Book of Mormon. Fortunately for us, he recorded those experiences, as well as the emotions that permeated those events. His record states, "[Following the visitations of Moroni to Joseph Smith,] we were all gathered. He [Joseph] arose and told us how the angel appeared to him. . . . All of us, therefore, believed him and anxiously awaited the result of his visit to the hill Cumorah, in search of the plates containing the record of which the angel told him."[24]

William gave meaningful insight into those events. He explained why the family readily believed Joseph. He also provided a detailed description of the plates when they were first brought to the home: "We handled them [the plates] and could tell what they were. They were not quite as large as this Bible. Could tell whether they were round or square. Could raise the leaves this way (raising a few leaves of the Bible before him). One could easily tell that they were not stone, hewn out to deceive, or even a block of wood."[25]

William's record of handling the plates shows his willingness and excitement to be a witness. It was clearly important to him to share the belief and trust the family had in Joseph's proclamations and actions.

Katharine Smith

Katharine was fifteen years old when Joseph received the Book of Mormon plates. She recalled the event with these words:

> I well remember the trials my brother had, before he obtained the records. After he had the vision, he went frequently to the hill, and upon returning would tell us, "I have seen the records, also the brass plates and the sword of Laban with the breast plate and interpreters." He would ask father why he could not get them? The time had not yet come, but when it did arrive he was commanded to go on the 22d day of September 1827 at 2 o'clock.[26]

Katharine left one of the most powerful testimonies concerning the influence of the Book of Mormon. She said, "Many times when I have read its sacred pages, I have wept like a child, while the Spirit has borne witness with my spirit to its truth."[27] Catherine's experience with the Book of Mormon could serve as a model for anyone who chooses to read the book with real intent.

Don Carlos Smith

Older brothers are often models and examples for their younger brothers. Beyond mere sibling respect and admiration, Don Carlos embraced Joseph's accounts of his experiences and revelations. There can be no doubt that Don Carlos was fully committed to the restored gospel and had a strong testimony of the Book of Mormon.

The Prophet paid the following tribute to his youngest brother:

Saturday, August 7—My youngest brother, Don Carlos Smith, died at his residence in Nauvoo this morning, at twenty minutes past two o'clock, in the 26th year of his age. He was born 25th March, 1816, was one of the first to receive my testimony, and was ordained to the Priesthood when only 14 years of age.

The evening after the plates of the Book of Mormon were shown to the eight witnesses, a meeting was held, when all the witnesses, as also Don Carlos bore testimony to the truth of the latter-day dispensation.

He accompanied father to visit grandfather, Asael Smith, and relatives in St. Lawrence County, New York, in August, 1830. During that mission he convinced Solomon Humphrey, a licentiate of the Baptist order, of the truth of the work. He was one of the 24 Elders who laid the corner stones of the Kirtland Temple. . . . On the 30th July, 1835, he married Agnes Coolbrith, in Kirtland, Ohio. On the 15th January, 1836, he was ordained President of the High Priests' quorum.

He took a mission with Wilber Denton in the spring and summer of 1836, in Pennsylvania and New York. . . . Early in the spring of 1838 he took a mission through the states of Virginia, Pennsylvania and Ohio. . . . On the 26th September he started on a mission to the states of Tennessee and Kentucky, to collect means to buy out the claims and property of the mobbers in Daviess county, Missouri.

During his absence, his wife and two little children were driven by the mob from his habitation, and she was compelled to carry her children three miles, through snow three inches deep, and wade through Grand river, which was waist deep, during the inclement weather. He returned about the 25th of December, after a very tedious mission, having traveled 1,500 miles, 650 of which were on foot.[28]

The faith, loyalty, and trust that Don Carlos had in his older brother were reciprocated. Don Carlos was given many important responsibilities in the Church. He was trusted to carry the message of the gospel and the Book of Mormon, through great personal sacrifice, far beyond his home. He loved his brother and willingly followed him.

Lucy Smith

Lucy was the youngest child in the Smith family. She was born on July 18, 1821, in Palmyra, New York, and was only six years old when Joseph obtained the plates. At thirteen, she received a patriarchal blessing from her father. In that blessing, she was told, "Thou shalt have dreams and visions: the holy angels shall minister unto thee. My child, I seal a father's blessing upon thee: thou art the fruit of my loins, even in my old age, and thou art numbered among the chosen seed. Thou art sealed up to eternal life; even so. Amen."[29]

While we do not know a great deal about Lucy, we do know that she married Arthur Millikin in Nauvoo when she was eighteen years old. Lucy's name also appears on early temple records as assisting her mother with baptisms for the dead for the Mack side of the family. She served as proxy in the baptism of her Aunt Lovina, her mother's oldest sister.

Lucy's acts of service to her family demonstrate her faith in the work that her brother Joseph brought forth. The little information we have about her is sufficient to highlight her enduring belief.

Family United in Belief

If Joseph Smith had lied about the events surrounding the coming forth of the Book of Mormon, he totally fooled every member of his immediate family. I find that extremely difficult to believe. To deceive his family, he would have had to do far more than just tell them about the First Vision and the appearance of the angel Moroni. Remember, Joseph Sr., Hyrum, and Samuel were personal witnesses "that Joseph Smith, Jun., the translator of this work, has shown unto us the plates of which hath been spoken, which have the appearance of gold; and as many of the leaves as the said Smith has translated we did handle with our hands. . . . And we lie not, God bearing witness of it" ("The Testimony of the Eight Witnesses," Book of Mormon).

What could possibly motivate these three immediate family members to lie before *God* if they had not seen the plates? If Joseph really had gold plates, where on earth did he get them? Can you imagine trying to secretly produce metal plates and then engrave them with ancient-looking characters? It seems logical that someone in the family would have heard him pounding on metal around the house. There is also the huge challenge of finding some metal that looks like gold from which to somehow make plates.

Family members do often try to protect one other. However, few people are as blunt or accusatory as family members when one of their own is doing something wrong. Is it even conceivable to think that the Bible-believing Smith family knew that their son was really a fraud and were trying to protect him? If so, what could possibly be their motive for doing so? What they got for their belief was mockery, rejection, and persecution from day one. If any member of the family doubted Joseph's story in the least, then surely at some point in their lives they would have expressed that doubt to a spouse, a family member, friend, or a child. That never happened.

If Joseph were truly a fraud, doesn't it seem logical that he would have told everyone that he was that rather than go to his death? What overpowering motive could entice a man to leave behind a wife who was four months pregnant and four children, ages thirteen, twelve, seven, and five? A lie? That seems highly unlikely.

Reason to Believe

I have tried to think logically why Joseph Smith would watch his wife, children, parents, brothers, sisters, and thousands of followers suffer untold abuse and persecution if it were all a lie. No matter how much I try to think of possible motives, none come to mind. When I consider the idea of him trying to actually produce plates with the appearance of gold to show his father and two brothers, I can't think of how he could have possibly pulled that off.

This leads me to believe that the only way to make sense of all of this is that Joseph was telling the truth. The undaunted loyalty of his family certainly underscores the veracity of Joseph's experiences and work.

Notes

1. William Smith, *William Smith on Mormonism* (Lamoni, Iowa: Herald Steam Book and Job Office, 1883), 9–11.

2. Joseph Smith, *History of The Church of Jesus Christ of Latter-day Saints*, ed. B. H. Roberts, 2nd ed. rev., 7 vols. (Salt Lake City: The Church of Jesus Christ of Latter-day Saints, 1932–1951) 6:317.

3. Brigham Young, *Discourses of Brigham Young*, ed. John A. Widtsoe (Salt Lake City: Deseret Book, 1954), 464.

4. "William B. Smith's Last Statement," *Zion's Ensign,* 1894, 6.

5. "Another Testimony," *Deseret Evening News,* 20 January 1891.

6. *Latter-day Saints' Messenger and Advocate.* Kirtland, Ohio, October 1835, 195–202.

7. Quoted in George Q. Cannon, *Life of Joseph Smith, the Prophet* (Salt Lake City: Deseret Book, 1988), 26.

8. Richard Lyman Bushman, *Joseph Smith: Rough Stone Rolling* (New York: Vintage Books. 2007), 110.

9. Smith, "Memoirs" 2, cited in Anderson, Joseph Smith's New England Heritage, 112–13.

10. Richard L. Anderson, *Joseph Smith's New England Heritage,* 215 (note 217).

11. *History of the Church,* 4:192.

12. Lucy Mack Smith, *Biographical Sketches of Joseph Smith The Prophet* (Liverpool: S. W. Richards, 1853), 82–83.

13. Lucy Mack Smith, *History of Joseph Smith* (Salt Lake City: Bookcraft, 1958), 204.

14. *Documentary History of the Church*, vol. 5, 26.

15. Alvin Smith, quoted in Lucy Mack Smith, "The History of Lucy Smith, Mother of the Prophet," 1844–1845 manuscript, book 4, Church Archives.

16. *History of the Church*, 5:126–27.

17. *Times and Seasons*, December 1839, 23.

18. *History of the Church*, 2:338.

19. "The Martyrdom of Joseph and Hyrum Smith," LDS Church Archives, 20 January 1855.

20. Andrew Jenson, "Hyrum Smith," *Latter-day Saint Biographical Encyclopedia* (Salt Lake City: Andrew Jenson History Company, 1901–1936), 1:71.

21. Oliver Cowdery, clerk and recorder. Kirtland, Ohio, December 9, 1834. *Patriarchal Blessing Book* 1:3.

22. Daniel Tyler, *Scraps of Biography* (Salt Lake City, Juvenile Instructor Office 1883), 23.

23. William Smith, *William Smith on Mormonism: This Book Contains a True Account of the Origin of the Book of Mormon. A Sketch of the History, Experience, and Ministry of Elder William Smith* (Lamoni, IA: Herald Steam Book and Job Office, 1883), 9–11.

24. William Smith, *William Smith on Mormonism* (Lamoni, Iowa: Herald Steam Book and Job Office, 1883), 9–11.

25. Richard Lloyd Anderson, *Investigating the Book of Mormon Witnesses* (Salt Lake City: Deseret Book, 1981), 24.

26. Dan Vogel, ed., *Early Mormon Documents* (Salt Lake City: Signature Books, 1996), 1:521.

27. Katherine Smith Salisbury, "Dear Sisters," *Saints' Herald*, 33 (1 May 1886), 260.

28. *History of the Church*, 4:393–99.

29. Oliver Cowdery, clerk and recorder. Kirtland, Ohio, December 9, 1834. *Patriarchal Blessing Book* 1:8.

Chapter 3: Gold Plates and Other Sacred Objects

"Behold, I say unto you, that you must rely upon my word, which if you do with full purpose of heart, you shall have a view of the plates, and also of the breastplate, the sword of Laban, the Urim and Thummim, which were given to the brother of Jared upon the mount, when he talked with the Lord face to face, and the miraculous directors which were given to Lehi while in the wilderness, on the borders of the Red Sea."

—Doctrine and Covenants 17:1

Exactly four years after seventeen-year-old Joseph Smith was first shown the ancient Nephite records by the angel Moroni, the time finally arrived for him to actually take possession of them. The day after viewing the plates for the first time, "the angel of the Lord says that we must be careful not to proclaim these things or to mention them abroad, for we do not any of us know the weakness of the world, which is so sinful, and that when we get the plates they will want to kill us for the sake of the gold, if they know we have them."[1]

Somehow, word of this leaked out, and several individuals were already plotting how to get the plates from the Prophet when he went to retrieve them.

It seems probable that members of the Smith family thought it all right to mention details to certain trusted friends. It is evident that Martin Harris, Joseph Knight Sr., Joseph Knight Jr., Josiah Stowell, and perhaps others were in on the secret far in advance of the actual event.

Lucy Mack Smith wrote about the night of September 21, 1827, about midnight when Joseph came to her and asked if she had a chest that had a lock and key. When she answered no, she must have been worried about him, despite his reassurance to her that everything would be fine. She obviously knew that more than just trusted friends were aware of the date, for she said, "Joseph's wife passed through the room with her bonnet and riding dress; and in a few minutes they left together, taking Mr. Knight's horse and wagon. I spent the night in prayer and supplication to God."[2]

While no detailed record exists telling what happened that night, we do know a few things. Joseph received more instruction and warning by the angel Moroni when he took possession of the plates. According to his mother, who obviously got her information from Joseph, Moroni told him:

> Now you have got the record into your own hands, and you are but a man, therefore you will have to be watchful and faithful to your trust, or you will be overpowered by wicked men, for they will lay every plan and scheme that is possible to get them away from you. And if you do not take heed continually, they will succeed. While they were in my hands I could keep them, and no man had power to take them away, but now I give them up to you. Beware, and look well to your ways, and you shall have power to retain them until the time for them to be translated.[3]

Joseph added more explanation about the instruction he received when he wrote, "The same heavenly messenger delivered them up to me with this charge: that I should be responsible for them; that if I should let them go carelessly, or through any neglect of mine, I should be cut off; but that if I would use all my endeavors to preserve them, until he, the messenger, should call for them, they should be protected" (Joseph Smith—History 1:59).

Joseph quickly discovered the difficulties that came with having possession of the plates. He said, "I soon found out the reason why I had received such strict charges to keep them safe, and why it was that the messenger had said that when I had done what was required at my hand, he would call for them. For no sooner was it known that I had them, than the most strenuous exertions were used to get them from me. Every stratagem that could be invented was resorted to for that purpose" (Joseph Smith—History 1:60).

Joseph Knight divulged what happened the next morning:

> [In] the forepart of September [1827], I went to Rochester on business and returned by Palmyra to be there by the 22nd of September. . . . That night we went to bed and in the morning I got up and my horse and carriage were gone. . . . After a while he [Joseph Smith] came home [with] the horse. All came into the house to breakfast but nothing [was] said about where they had been. After breakfast Joseph called me into the other room. . . . He set his foot on the bed, leaned his head on his hand and said. . . . "It is ten times better than I expected." Then he went on to tell length and width and thickness of the plates; and said he, "They appear to be gold."[4]

Both Lucy Mack Smith and Martin Harris said the plates were hidden in a hollow tree at first. Joseph had a chest built to secure the plates, and afterward he felt it was time to bring the plates home. His mother described what happened to him on his journey:

> As he was jumping over a log, a man sprang up from behind and gave him a heavy blow with a gun. Joseph turned around and knocked him to the ground, and then ran at the top of his speed. About half a mile further, he was attacked again in precisely the same way. He soon brought this one down also and ran on again, but before he got home, he was accosted the third time with a severe stroke with a gun.[5]

Martin Harris added, "While on his way home with the plates, he [Joseph] was met by what appeared to be a man, who demanded the plates, and struck him with a club on his side, which was all black and blue. Joseph knocked the man down, and then ran for home, and was much out of breath."[6] While fighting off the third attacker, Joseph dislocated his thumb but made it home safely.

Word that Joseph had the plates spread quickly and people began dropping by the Smith home, some offering money to view them. When he refused to show them, the mocking, persecution, and abuse increased dramatically from those who doubted his story.

At some point after the plates were brought home, Lucy Mack Smith went to visit Martin Harris. She told him that Joseph had the plates and wanted to talk to him. He records what happened during that visit:

> While at Mr. Smith's I hefted the plates, and I knew from the heft that they were lead or gold, and I knew that Joseph had not credit enough to buy so much lead. I left Mr. Smith's about eleven o'clock and went home. I retired to my bedroom and prayed God to show me concerning these things, and I covenanted that if it was his work and he would show me so, I would put forth my best ability to bring it before the world. He then showed me that it was his work, and that it was designed to bring in the fullness of his gospel to the gentiles to fulfill his word, that the first shall be last and the last first. He showed this to me by the still small voice spoken in the soul. Then I was satisfied that it was the Lord's work, and I was under a covenant to bring it forth.[7]

If Joseph Smith made all of this up, he certainly managed to create a complicated and intriguing story. To this point, the plot had multiple twists and turns, with more and more people involved as the story unfolded.

With word spreading that Joseph had the plates, he was faced with a gigantic problem. Up until this point, Joseph's word of visions, angels, gold plates, and other sacred objects was between immediate family members and close trusted friends. It was only "talk." Now that he had the plates in his possession, he needed to convince those closest to him that he had them, without actually showing them to anyone unless the Lord commanded him to do so. This happened as his family and now his wealthy neighbor and financier became believers.

When Joseph Smith was growing up, the Smith's were tenant farmers with little in the way of material possessions. Because of their circumstances, you would think that, if Joseph were trying to deceive people with talk of being called of God to a special work, the last thing in the world he would use would be gold plates! Not only would they have been impossible to produce, but also most would not believe that a book was translated from ancient metal plates delivered by an angel.

In Joseph Smith's day, he was mocked for his description of the plates more than anything else. However, critics today no longer laugh as loudly about writing on metal plates. There have been over a hundred discoveries of ancient metal plates. Daniel C. Peterson said,

Although the Prophet's critics found his claim of angelic visits and gold plates ridiculous, we now know that the writing of religious texts on metal plates (sometimes on gold), was an authentic ancient practice. Indeed, the ancient practice now is known to have occurred at precisely the era and place from which Book of Mormon peoples came. In fact, with the Copper Scroll and other materials from the Dead Sea, we have an almost exact parallel: like the ancient Nephite plates, these materials were sealed up in a hillside just prior to military disaster, to preserve them for a future time.[8]

Perhaps his critics did not read their Bibles closely enough to catch an Old Testament verse that says, "And thou shalt make a plate of pure gold, and grave upon it, like the engravings of a signet, Holiness to the Lord" (Exodus 28:36).

Let's consider for a moment the evidence that Joseph Smith really did have the plates—along with other ancient relics—in his possession.

The Plates

Joseph Smith alone saw and handled the plates at first, but other people were given the opportunity to see and touch the plates as time went on. They described the plates, recorded the circumstances of seeing them, and volunteered written witness of their reality. The following are some of the statements of the witnesses:

Martin Harris: "These were seven inches wide by eight inches in length, and were of the thickness of plates of tin; and when piled one above the other, they were altogether about four inches thick; and they were put together on the back by three silver rings, so that they would open like a book."[9]

William Smith: "We handled them [the plates] and could tell what they were. They were not quite as large as this Bible. Could tell whether they were round or square. Could raise the leaves this way (raising a few leaves of the Bible before him). One could easily tell that they were not a stone, hewn out to deceive, or even a block of wood. Being a mixture of gold and copper, they were much heavier than stone, and very much heavier than wood."[10]

Oliver Cowdery: "I beheld with my eyes, and handled with my hands, the gold plates from which it was transcribed. . . . That book is true."[11]

Hyrum Smith: "I thank God that I felt a determination to die, rather than deny the things which my eyes had seen, which my hands had handled [the plates], and which I had bore testimony to, wherever my lot had been cast."[12]

Emma Smith: "The plates lay in a box under our bed for months and on the [table in our home] without any attempt at concealment, wrapped in a small linen table cloth, which I had given him to fold them in. I once felt . . . the plates as they thus lay on the table, tracing their outline and shape. They seemed to be pliable like thick paper, and would rustle with a metallic sound when the edges were moved by the thumb, as one does sometimes thumb the edges of a book."[13]

Lucy Mack Smith: "I have myself seen and handled the golden plates; they are about eight inches long, and six wide; some of them are sealed together and are not to be opened, and some of them are loose. They are all connected by a ring which passes through a hole at the end of each plate, and are covered with letters beautifully engraved."[14]

Oliver Cowdery, Martin Harris, and David Whitmer: "And we declare with words of soberness, that an angel of God came down from heaven, and he brought and laid before our eyes, that we beheld and saw the plates, and the engravings thereon; and we know that it is by the grace of God the Father, and our Lord Jesus Christ, that we beheld and bear record that these things are true" ("Testimony of Three Witnesses," Book of Mormon).

Christian Whitmer, Jacob Whitmer, Peter Whitmer Jr., John Whitmer, Hiram Page, Joseph Smith Sr., Hyrum Smith, Samuel Smith: "Be it known unto all nations, kindreds, tongues, and people, unto whom this work shall come: That Joseph Smith, Jun., the translator of this work, has shown unto us the plates of which hath been spoken, which have the appearance of gold; and as many of the leaves as the said Smith has translated we did handle with our hands; and we also saw the engravings thereon, all of which has the appearance of ancient work, and of curious workmanship. And this we bear record with words of soberness, that the said Smith has shown unto us, for we have seen and hefted, and know of a surety that the said Smith has got the plates of which we have spoken. And we give our names unto the world, to witness unto the world that which we have seen. And we lie not, God bearing witness of it" ("Testimony of Eight Witnesses," Book of Mormon).

All those who saw and handled the plates observed and then reported what was salient to them. They observed not only what the plates looked like, but also their weight and the sound they made when moved. Many went beyond a simple physical description and explained the emotional impact of seeing the plates.

The Urim and Thummim

The Urim and Thummim were used in ancient times as a means of facilitating revelation, or as a conduit for revelation. Obviously they were such precious objects that Moroni carefully hid them with the plates. Joseph Smith used these stones as he translated the engravings on the gold plates. The following are statements of evidence that the Urim and Thummim were with the plates and were used for translation:

Leviticus 8:8: "And he put the breastplate upon him: also he put in the breastplate the Urim and the Thummim."

1906 Jewish Encyclopedia: "Objects connected with the breastplate of the high priest, and used as a kind of divine oracle. Since the days of the Alexandrian translators of the Old Testament it has been asserted that Urim and Thummim mean 'revelation and truth,' or 'lights and perfections.'"[15]

Oliver Cowdery: "I wrote, with my own pen, the entire Book of Mormon (save a few pages), as it fell from the lips of the Prophet Joseph Smith, as he translated it by the gift and power of God, by the means of the Urim and Thummim, or, as it is called by that book, 'holy interpreters.'"[16]

Joseph Smith: "Also, that there were two stones in silver bows—and these stones, fastened to a breastplate, constituted what is called the Urim and Thummim—deposited with the plates; and the possession and use of these stones were what constituted 'seers' in ancient or former times; and that God had prepared them for the purpose of translating the book" (Joseph Smith—History 1:35).

Martin Harris: "The two stones set in a bow of silver were about two inches in diameter, perfectly round, and about five-eighths of an inch thick at the centre; but not so thick at the edges where they came into the bow. They were joined by a round bar of silver, about three-eighths of an inch in diameter, and about four inches long, which, with the two stones, would make eight inches. The stones were white, like polished marble, with a few gray streaks."[17]

William Smith: "A silver bow ran over one stone, under the other, arround [sic] over that one and under the first in the shape of a horizontal figure 8. . . . They were much too large for Joseph and he could only see through one at a time using sometimes one and sometimes the other. These stones were attached to the breastplate by a rod which was fastened at the outer shoulde[r] edge of the breastplate and to the edge of the silver bow."[18]

Lucy Mack Smith: "I have seen and felt also the Urim and Thummim. They resemble two large bright diamonds set in a bow like a pair of spectacles. My son puts these over his eyes when he reads unknown languages, and they enable him to interpret them in English. I have likewise carried in my hands the sacred breastplate. It is composed of pure gold, and is made to fit the breast very exactly."[19]

These statements from witnesses allow others to visualize the Urim and Thummim. In addition, some witnesses were able to explain the way Joseph Smith used them and told of the wonder of that experience as heavenly knowledge flowed into Joseph's mind and through his voice.

The Breastplate

The breastplate associated with the Urim and Thummim was designed to protect and support the Urim and Thummim rather than protect against weapons and injuries during battle. Other people besides Joseph Smith saw the breastplate and knew how it was used. The following are comments and other facts about the breastplate:

Bible Dictionary: "The high priest in the law of Moses wore a breastplate as part of his sacred attire. This was called the 'breastplate of judgment' (Exodus 28:13–30; 39:8–21). It was made of linen, very colorfully arranged, bearing 12 precious stones and the Urim and Thummim."

Lucy Mack Smith: "It was concave on one side and convex on the other, and extended from the neck downwards as far as the center of the stomach of a man of extraordinary size. It had four straps of the same material for the purpose of fastening it to the breast, two of which ran back to go over the shoulders, and the other two were designed to fasten to the hips. They were just the width of two of my fingers (for I measured them), and they had holes in the end of them to be convenient in fastening."[20]

William Smith: "A pocket was prepared in the breastplate on the left side, immediately over the heart. When not in use the Urim and Thummim was placed in this pocket, the rod being of just the right length to allow it to be so deposited. This instrument could, however, be detached from the breastplate . . . when away from home, but [Joseph] always used it in connection with the breastplate when receiving official communications, and usually so when translating as it permitted him to have both hands free to hold the plates."[21]

This breastplate of ancient times held the Urim and Thummim. The witnesses provided detailed descriptions and declared that the breastplate was more than just an interesting object. It was essential to the work that Joseph Smith accomplished.

The Sword of Laban and the Liahona

The plates, the Urim and Thummim, and the breastplate were integral to the translation. Along with these were at least two other artifacts that had tremendous significance to the people of the Book of Mormon. Both the sword of Laban and the Liahona represent the love and aid of God in the quest for righteousness. They were also great reminders of how vital obedience was to the Nephites' success and happiness. That these items were preserved with the plates sends a significant message to the world today about God's dealings with His children when they are obedient. The following are statements from witnesses of these precious artifacts:

Nephi: "The hilt thereof was of pure gold, and the workmanship thereof was exceedingly fine, and I saw that the blade thereof was of the most precious steel" (1 Nephi 4:9).

Nephi: "And it came to pass that as my father arose in the morning, and went forth to the tent door, to his great astonishment he beheld upon the ground a round ball of curious workmanship; and it was of fine brass. And within the ball were two spindles; and the one pointed the way whither we should go into the wilderness" (1 Nephi 16:10).

Martin Harris: "Just as sure as you see the sun shining, just as sure am I that I stood in the presence of an angel of God with Joseph Smith, and saw him hold the gold plates in his hands. I also saw the Urim and Thummim, the breastplate, and the sword of Laban."[22]

John Hyde: "Joseph Smith says he found, with these [Moroni's] plates, . . . the sword of Laban. He also recorded that when Joseph finally got the plates on September 22, 1827, that besides the plates, he had, according to his third story, a breast-plate of brass, Laban's sword, the crystal interpreters, [and] the 'brass ball with spindles' director of Lehi."[23]

Katharine Salisbury (Joseph's Sister): "I remember well the trials my brother had, before he obtained the records. After he had the vision, he went frequently to the hill, and upon returning he would tell us, 'I have seen the records, also the brass plates and the sword of Laban with the breast plate and the interpreters.'"[24]

David Whitmer: "We not only saw the plates of the Book of Mormon but also the brass plates, the plates of the Book of Ether, the plates containing the records of the wickedness and secret combinations of the people of the world down to the time of their being engraved, and many other plates. . . . There appeared as it were, a table with many records or plates upon it, besides the plates of the Book of Mormon, also the Sword of Laban, the Directors i.e., the ball which Lehi had—and the Interpreters [Urim and Thummim]. I saw them just as plain as I see this bed (striking the bed beside him with his hand), and I heard the voice of the Lord, as distinctly as I ever heard anything in my life declaring that the records of the plates of the Book of Mormon were translated by the gift and power of God."[25]

Reason to Believe

Try to imagine a New York farm boy sitting around dreaming up a gigantic scheme involving an angel and the history of a group from Israel inscribed on metal plates with Egyptian-looking characters. Why metal? Why not papyrus? Did anyone in Palmyra, New York—or the United States, for that matter—write on metal plates? Then he throws in a Urim and Thummin that has to be connected to a breastplate, whatever that means. If Joseph Smith were a fraud, as critics have claimed, it seems strange that he would go to the Bible for ideas on how to deceive people. I wonder if any of the ministers of his day wore breastplates with two clear stones attached to give him the idea? The whole story is extremely far-fetched if he was making it up. Then of course there was an ancient GPS system and a sword made of precious steel with a hilt of pure gold. What a tale!

There is one small—or should we say massive—problem with this story if it is not true: How on earth does Joseph get a group of witnesses to testify before God that they actually saw these items, a testimony that they never denied for the rest of their lives, despite mockery and persecution? These are what they saw:

- An angel
- Gold plates with ancient writing
- The Urim and Thummim
- A breastplate
- A gold-hilted sword
- A fine brass ball with two spindles

Think of how Joseph Smith, or anyone else, could have possibly convinced others to sign their names to a statement going to the world that says they had seen an angel and these items. Who played the role of an angel? Where did Joseph get the metal for the plates, breastplate, sword, and brass ball? Where did he get the gold? If he found the metal and was pounding on it around the house, don't you think someone would have noticed? If you find the metal, where did he learn (or even find the time to learn) reformed Egyptian engraving?

Recently, I saw a statement from a critic who said the only people who claimed to have actually seen the gold plates were eleven close friends of Joseph (many of them related to each other). He then said most of the witnesses later abandoned the Prophet and left his movement.

This logic makes no sense to me. The first reason given is that he found witnesses to publicly lie under an oath to God because they were either close friends or relatives of Joseph Smith. The next statement says you can't believe these witnesses because they were no longer his friends and abandoned him and left the movement. Which is it? If they abandoned him because they did not believe, why did they not expose him? Why would they ruin their good names and testify that they saw and heard the things they testified of for a fraud?

I liked how the critic said Joseph *only* had eleven eyewitnesses besides him who saw the plates. Can you imagine if you had *only* eleven reputable witnesses in a court of law all independently testifying to the exact same thing? The fact that so many witnesses testified until death that they actually saw the items mentioned previously leads me to believe that they told the truth. The fact that most of the witnesses later abandoned Joseph and left his movement yet continued to testify of what they had seen and heard is even more amazing.

Now, critics want me to believe that once Joseph Smith pulled all of this off, he came up with a 588-page book about ancient America and verbally dictated it in about sixty-three working days with no written notes. I believe logic would say that what he said was true.

Notes

1. Lucy Mack Smith, *The Revised and Enhanced History of Joseph Smith by His Mother,* ed. Scot Facer Proctor and Maurine Jensen Proctor (Salt Lake City: Deseret Book, 1996), 111.
2. Lucy Mack Smith, *History of Joseph Smith,* rev. George A Smith and Elias Smith (Salt Lake City: Improvement Era, 1902), 100.
3. Lucy Smith, *History of Joseph Smith,* ed. Preston Nibley (Salt Lake City: Bookcraft, 1958), 145.
4. Dean Jessee, "Joseph Knight's Recollection of Early Mormon History," *Brigham Young University Studies,* Fall 1976, 30–39.
5. Lucy Smith, *History of Joseph Smith,* ed. Preston Nibley (Salt Lake City: Bookcraft, 1958), 144.
6. "Mormonism," *Tiffany's Monthly,* Joel Tiffany, June 1859, 166.
7. "Mormonism—No. II," *Tiffany's Monthly,* Joel Tiffany, ed., May 1859, 170.
8. Daniel C. Peterson, "Mounting Evidence for the Book of Mormon," *Ensign,* January 2000, 19.
9. "Mormonism—No. II," *Tiffany's Monthly,* Joel Tiffany, ed., 5(4), August 1859, 165.
10. "The Old Soldier's Testimony," *The Saints' Herald,* vol. 31, no. 40 (4 October 1884), 643–44.

11. "Last Days of Oliver Cowdery," *Deseret News*, April 13, 1859, 48.

12. Hyrum Smith, "A History of the Persecution of the Church of Jesus Christ, of Latter Day Saints in Missouri," *Times and Seasons*, (Commerce, IL: Dec. 1839), 23.

13. "Last Testimony of Sister Emma," *The Saints' Herald,* October 1, 1879, 290.

14. Henry Caswall, "The City of the Mormons; or, Three Days at Nauvoo," *Prophet of the 19th Century* (London: J. G. F. & J. Rivington, 1843), 2nd ed. revised and enlarged, 1842, 26.

15. "Urim and Thummim," www.jewishencylopedia.com.

16. "Last Days of Oliver Cowdery," *Deseret News*, April 13, 1859, 48.

17. "Mormonism—No. II," *Tiffany's Monthly*, 5(4), Joel Tiffany, ed., August 1859, 165.

18. Terryl Givens, *By the Hand of Mormon: The American Scripture that Launched a New World Religion* (Oxford: Oxford University Press, 2002), 22.

19. Henry Caswall, *The City of the Mormons; or, Three Days at Nauvoo in 1842* (London: J. G. F. & J. Rivington, 1843), 2nd ed. revised and enlarged, 26.

20. Lucy Smith, *History of Joseph Smith,* ed. Preston Nibley (Salt Lake City: Bookcraft, 1958), 111.

21. William Smith, *Rod of Iron,* vol. 1, no. 3, February 1924, 7.

22. William Pilkington to Vern C. Poulter, 28 February 1930, Provo, Utah: Special Collections, Harold B. Lee Library, Brigham Young University.

23. John Hyde, *Mormonism: Its Leaders and Designs* (New York: Fetridge, 1857), 215, 244.

24. Katharine (Catherine) Salisbury, "Dear Sisters," *The Saints' Herald,* 33 (1 May 1886), 260.

25. Sidney B. Sperry, "1878 interview between Orson Pratt and David Whitmer," *Book of Mormon Compendium* (Salt Lake City: Deseret Book, 1968), 55–56.

Chapter 4: So Few Changes

"I told the brethren that the Book of Mormon was the most correct of any book on earth, and the keystone of our religion, and a man would get nearer to God by abiding by its precepts, than by any other book."[1]
—Joseph Smith

Back when the Book of Mormon was first published in March 1830, its influence was immediate and dramatic. That influence has fueled the growth of the Church since the beginning. While our missionaries tell the events surrounding the Restoration of the gospel, it is the Book of Mormon that usually leads to true conversion. President Heber J. Grant said, "The Book of Mormon is the great, the grand, the most wonderful missionary that we have."[2]

At the end of 1830, there were 280 members of the Church. By 1835, there were 8,835 members. The reason for pointing out the Church's growth during this five-year period is because it verifies the dramatic impact that the first edition of the Book of Mormon had on people. In a personal way, many have related how the Book of Mormon has affected their lives. The following are statements by three individuals who read the book and got "nearer to God by abiding by its precepts, than by any other book."

Parley P. Pratt: "The Spirit of the Lord came upon me, while I read, and enlightened my mind, convinced my judgment, and riveted the truth upon my understanding, so that I knew that the book was true, just as well as a man knows the daylight from the dark night."[3]

Brigham Young: "I knew it was true, as well as I knew that I could see with my eyes, or feel by the touch of my fingers, or be sensible of the demonstration of any sense."[4]

Wilford Woodruff: "As I [began to read the Book of Mormon], the Spirit bore witness that the record which it contained was true. It opened my eyes to see, my ears to hear, and my heart to understand. It also opened my doors to entertain the servants of God."[5]

Despite the incredibly dramatic influence the Book of Mormon had on readers, critics were quick to find and point out that the first edition had spelling errors and incorrect grammar. The argument was that if the Book of Mormon were an inspired translation and the "most correct of any book on earth," there should be no corrections whatsoever. This line of reasoning continues today, and countless websites point out those changes made to the text. There can be no question that adjustments have been made to spelling, punctuation, and grammar throughout the years, but the vast majority of these are insignificant and were mainly done by editors and publishers.

It is important to understand that Joseph Smith did not write the Book of Mormon. Not only did he not come up with the story, he did not physically write it either. He used scribes to write down the manuscript as he verbally dictated it. Martin Harris drafted the first 116 pages, or the record of Lehi, but that manuscript was lost because of carelessness. Emma and others were also scribes for portions of the translation, but twenty-two-year-old Oliver Cowdery recorded most of what twenty-three-year-old Joseph Smith dictated, which is known as the "original manuscript." Oliver said this about the experience:

> I wrote, with my own pen, the entire Book of Mormon (save a few pages), as it fell from the lips of the Prophet Joseph Smith, as he translated it by the gift and power of God, by the means of the Urim and Thummim, or, as it is called by that book, "holy interpreters." I beheld with my eye and handled with my hands the gold plates from which it was translated. I also beheld the interpreters. That book is true. . . . It contains the everlasting gospel and came in fulfillment of the revelations of John where he says [that] he saw an angel come with the everlasting gospel to preach to every nation, tongue and people.[6]

I can't imagine how difficult it would be for Oliver to listen to Joseph dictate hour after hour while he wrote the entire manuscript by hand. There were no paragraphs and almost no punctuation—just straight dictation as fast as they could go.

The original manuscript was apparently started no later than April 1829 and was completed in June 1829. Imagine the likelihood of making spelling errors as you consider the unusual names and places. Then, to prevent any loss of the manuscript, Oliver and two other scribes replicated another copy of it for the printing, which began in July 1829 and was completed early in 1830. Researchers comparing the original manuscript with the printer's manuscript found that about three minor scribal errors were made per page in this second copy.

When the time came to actually print the Book of Mormon, a frontier newspaper publisher named Egbert B. Grandin was called upon. John Gilbert, a twenty-seven-year-old typesetter, was given the task of typesetting, punctuating, and dividing the text into paragraphs for what would become a 588-page book. The manuscript was given to him in segments, but it was one solid paragraph from beginning to end.

Gilbert began his work in August 1829 and completed it in early March 1830. He read the manuscript one sentence at a time, memorized the spelling, and set the type one letter at a time. He punctuated as he went. Gilbert proofread the face of the type as it was placed upside down and reversed, ready for printing. Nearly all of the names and places within the text would have been entirely unfamiliar to him. It couldn't have been easy to create a printed page from a handwritten manuscript with no punctuation.

It is also worth noting that Joseph Smith was not involved in the printing process at all. John H. Gilbert said, "Joseph Smith, Jr., had nothing to do whatever with the printing or furnishing copy for the printers, being but once in the office during the printing of the Bible [Book of Mormon], and then not over fifteen or twenty minutes."[7]

So let's review the process. An uneducated farm boy named Joseph Smith, who couldn't write a well-worded letter according to his wife, dictated the translation of an ancient record that became a 588-page book. He had no notes and often used a hat to block distractions while translating. His scribes wrote down the text, the unfamiliar names, places, and expressions in long hand. Upon completion of the first manuscript, these scribes made a duplicate copy that consisted of one continuous paragraph with no punctuation. This copy was taken to a typesetter, who then set the type one letter at a time, punctuated it, and divided the text into paragraphs as he went.

When the first edition came out, errors in spelling and grammar were found. When this occurred, Joseph Smith wrote to W. W. Phelps and said, "As soon as we can get time, we will review the manuscripts of the Book of Mormon, after which they will be forwarded to you."[8] When all things involved are considered, the fact that so few errors occurred in the first edition was really quite a miracle.

Most of the corrections to the first edition were minor and can be easily explained. For one thing, American English spelling had not been standardized by 1829. This required multiple changes in both the English Bible and the Book of Mormon. Oliver Cowdery's handwriting also presented challenges for John Gilbert. What appeared to be misspellings in some cases were in actuality correct spellings. Oliver also wrote what he heard. That could explain several mistakes with regard to names, places, and phrases.

For example, the word *strait* usually refers to a naturally formed, narrow waterway that connects two larger bodies of water, or it means strict and rigorous. The word *straight* means continuing in the same direction without deviating. The words have two different meanings but are pronounced the same way. In several places, Oliver wrote *straight,* which had to be changed to *strait* in later editions.

A few corrections to clarify meanings were made by Joseph in the two other editions published in his lifetime. Among the most notable are:

- "the Son of" was added to identify Jesus Christ (1 Nephi 11:18; 1 Nephi 11:21; 1 Nephi 11:32; 1 Nephi 13:40)
- "or out of the waters of baptism" was added to describe the house of Israel (1 Nephi 20:1)
- "white" was changed to "pure" to describe the condition of righteous converts (2 Nephi 30:6)

But again, according to critics, there should not have been any reason to make corrections. They often use a statement by Joseph Smith to back up this claim. When describing his experience with the three witnesses, the Prophet said, "We heard a voice from out of the bright light above us, saying, 'These plates have been revealed by the power of God, and they have been translated by the power of

God. The translation of them which you have seen is correct, and I command you to bear record of what you now see and hear.'"[9]

Several critical websites state that thousands of changes to the Book of Mormon have been made. Some members of the Church have had their testimonies shaken when they see that there were corrections to the 1830 first edition. When I see that number, my reaction is different. I wonder how in the world they were so accurate with this complicated document. It strengthened my testimony immensely to read the 1830 replica and see how little has really changed. I'm shocked that so few corrections needed to be made and that most of them were insignificant.

Perhaps those who are Bible believers should look a little more closely at the different editions of the Bible. Speaking of the King James Version of the Bible, Daniel B. Wallace, professor of New Testament Studies at Dallas Theological Seminary, said, "It has undergone three revisions, incorporating more than 100,000 changes. Even with all these changes, much of the evidence from new manuscript discoveries has not been incorporated. . . . Furthermore, there are over 300 words in the KJV that no longer mean what they meant in 1611."[10]

It appears that neither spelling nor punctuation have that much to do with the influence that both the Bible and Book of Mormon have had on millions of individuals. It also appears that both can be "correct," even with a comma missing. Perhaps Joseph F. Smith summed it up best with this interesting observation: "There is not a word or doctrine, of admonition, of instruction within its [the Book of Mormon] lids, but what agrees in sentiment and veracity with those of Christ and His Apostles, as contained in the Bible. Neither is there a word of counsel, of admonition or reproof within its lids, but what is calculated to make a bad man a good man, and good man a better man, if he will hearken to it."[11]

It might be interesting to look at some of the corrections that were made to the 1830 edition of the Book of Mormon. Remember that John H. Gilbert put the 1830 edition into paragraphs, but no verses were set in that edition. I will show one paragraph at a time from the first 15 verses of the first chapter of 1 Nephi. The 1830 edition is in the first column and the corresponding verses in the 1981 edition are in the second. Changes are in bold face and explanatory notes are in brackets at the end of the quotation.

1830 Edition Compared to the 1981 Edition

1830 Edition	1981 Edition
I, Nephi, having been born of goodly parents, therefore I was taught somewhat in all the learning of my father; and having seen many afflictions in the course of my days -- nevertheless, having been highly favored of the Lord in all my days; yea, having had a great knowledge of the goodness and the mysteries of God, therefore I make a record of my proceedings in my days; yea, I make a record in the language of my father, which consists of the learning of the Jews and the language of the Egyptians. And I know that the record which I make, to be true; and I make it with mine own hand; and I make it according to my knowledge.	1 I, Nephi, having been born of goodly parents, therefore I was taught somewhat in all the learning of my father; and having seen many afflictions in the course of my days, nevertheless, having been highly favored of the Lord in all my days; yea, having had a great knowledge of the goodness and the mysteries of God, therefore I make a record of my proceedings in my days. 2 **Yea**, I make a record in the language of my father, which consists of the learning of the Jews and the language of the Egyptians. 3 And I know that the record which I make **is** true; and I make it with mine own hand; and I make it according to my knowledge.
For it came to pass in the commencement of the first year of the reign of Zedekiah, king of Judah, (my father Lehi having dwelt at Jerusalem in all his days;) and in that same year there came many prophets, prophesying unto the people, that they must repent, or the great city Jerusalem must be destroyed.	4 For it came to pass in the commencement of the first year of the reign of Zedekiah, king of Judah, (my father, Lehi, having dwelt at Jerusalem in all his days); and in that same year there came many prophets, prophesying unto the people that they must repent, or the great city Jerusalem must be destroyed.

1830 Edition	1981 Edition
Wherefore it came to pass, that my father Lehi, as he went forth, prayed unto the Lord, yea, even with all his heart, in behalf of his people.	5 Wherefore it came to pass that my father, Lehi, as he went forth prayed unto the Lord, yea, even with all his heart, in behalf of his people. [Commas removed after *pass* and *forth*.]
And it came to pass, as he prayed unto the Lord, there came a pillar of fire and dwelt upon a rock before him; and he saw and heard, he did quake and tremble exceedingly.	6 And it came to pass as he prayed unto the Lord, there came a pillar of fire and dwelt upon a rock before him; and he saw and heard **much; and because of the things which he saw and heard** he did quake and tremble exceedingly. [This phrase was left out of the 1830 edition.]
And it came to pass that he returned to his own house at Jerusalem; and he cast himself upon his bed, being overcome with the spirit and the things which he had seen; and being thus overcome with the spirit, he was carried away in a vision, even that he saw the Heavens open; and he thought he saw God sitting upon his throne, surrounded with numberless concourses of angels in the attitude of singing and praising their God.	7 And it came to pass that he returned to his own house at Jerusalem; and he cast himself upon his bed, being overcome with the **S**pirit and the things which he had seen. 8 **A**nd being thus overcome with the Spirit, he was carried away in a vision, even that he saw the **h**eavens open, and he thought he saw God sitting upon his throne, surrounded with numberless concourses of angels in the attitude of singing and praising their God.

1830 Edition	1981 Edition
And it came to pass that he saw one descending out of the midst of Heaven, and he beheld that his lustre was above that of the sun at noon-day; and he also saw twelve others following him, and their brightness did exceed that of the stars in the firmament; and they came down and went forth upon the face of the earth; and the first came and stood before my father, and gave unto him a Book, and bade him that he should read.	9 And it came to pass that he saw **O**ne descending out of the midst of **h**eaven, and he beheld that his lust**er** was above that of the sun at noon-day. 10 **A**nd he also saw twelve others following him, and their brightness did exceed that of the stars in the firmament. 11 **A**nd they came down and went forth upon the face of the earth; and the first came and stood before my father, and gave unto him a **b**ook, and bade him that he should read.
And it came to pass as he read, he was filled with the spirit of the Lord, and he read saying, Wo, wo unto Jerusalem! for I have seen thine abominations; yea, and many things did my father read concerning Jerusalem -- that it should be destroyed, and the inhabitants thereof, many should perish by the sword, and many should be carried away captive into Babylon.	12 And it came to pass that as he read, he was filled with the **S**pirit of the Lord. 13 **A**nd he read, saying: Wo, wo, unto Jerusalem, for I have seen thine abominations! **Y**ea, and many things did my father read concerning Jerusalem—that it should be destroyed, and the inhabitants thereof; many should perish by the sword, and many should be carried away captive into Babylon.

1830 Edition	1981 Edition
And it came to pass that when my father had read and saw many great and marvellous things, he did exclaim many things unto the Lord; such as, Great and marvellous are thy works, O Lord God Almighty! Thy throne is high in the Heavens, and the power and goodness, and mercy is over all the inhabitants of the earth; and because thou art merciful, thou wilt not suffer those who come unto thee that they shall perish! And after this manner was the language of my father in the praising of his God; for his soul did rejoice, and his whole heart was filled, because of the things which he had seen; yea, which the Lord had shewn unto him.	14 And it came to pass that when my father had read and **seen** many great and marvelous things, he did exclaim many things unto the Lord; such as: Great and marvelous are thy works, O Lord God Almighty! Thy throne is high in the **h**eavens, and **thy** power**,** and goodness, and mercy **are** over all the inhabitants of the earth; and, because thou art merciful, thou wilt not suffer those who come unto thee that they shall perish! [Extra *l* taken out of *marvelous*.] 15 And after this manner was the language of my father in the praising of his God; for his soul did rejoice, and his whole heart was filled, because of the things which he had seen**,** yea, which the Lord had shown unto him.

The content and meaning stayed intact with the few changes made. The main differences generally involved changing paragraphs to verses, adjusting capitalization and punctuation, and correcting grammar.

Joseph Smith was committed to having the Book of Mormon say and read the way the Lord revealed it to him. From the time the first edition came out until the end of his life, the Prophet made note of anything that needed clarification. On January 15, 1842, he recorded, "I commenced reading the Book of Mormon, at page 54, . . . (the previous pages having been corrected), for the purpose of correcting the stereotype plates of some errors which escaped notice in the first edition."[12]

Reason to Believe

It is a rare writer who does not end up having to make significant revisions and edits to his or her work. While visiting the Ransom Center Museum at the University of Texas in Austin a few years ago, I viewed the manuscript of a famous book called *Main Street* by Sinclair Lewis. The center was displaying a first page draft of chapter one of this book that was published back in 1920, which brought the Yale University graduate immediate acclaim. Ten years later, Sinclair Lewis became the first American writer to ever receive a Nobel Prize in Literature.

Looking over the page, I counted 246 words on the twenty-one lines of typed text. Of all those I was shocked that seventy-six words had been scratched out. In some cases, words written in above the scratched-out words were also scratched out. Counting the changes in *Main Street* the same way critics count those in the Book of Mormon, I saw ninety-one changes in words and punctuation marks on the first page. The Book of Mormon averages 505 words per page, which is a little over two times the number of words that were on that first page of *Main Street*. At that rate, Sinclair Lewis would have had 99,196 changes in a book as large as the Book of Mormon.

When the book was printed, however, the first page bore little resemblance to his corrected page. Either he found a far better way to write his novel, or the editors at Harcourt, Brace & Howe helped him a lot, because almost everything reads differently.

Let's think about this. On the one hand, we have a Yale University graduate who can't write the first page of a novel about the backbiting and hypocrisy that goes on in Gopher Prairie, Minnesota, without a massive number of revisions. In fact, it doesn't appear that he wrote even one sentence on the first page without changes. After revisions, rewrites, and possibly a good editor, he gained instant fame and later a Nobel Prize in Literature.

On the other hand, an uneducated farm boy verbally dictated a manuscript that is infinitely more complicated than *Main Street* in about sixty-three days. He did it without notes and never even had his scribes read it back to him. It turned into a 588-page, Christ-centered book filled with thousands of original phrases, brilliant doctrinal speeches, and unique names. It has had a remarkable influence for good on its sincere readers. With no rewrites and no editors, he totally depended on scribes and typesetters to get the punctuation, grammar, and spelling right. Overall, they did a remarkable job. For his efforts he received mocking, ridicule, persecution, and ultimately death. And while the world will never give him a Nobel Prize for Literature, he certainly deserves one for what he has done for the world at the very least. That the Book of Mormon has had so few changes made to it gives me one more reason to believe it is true.

Notes

1. Joseph Smith, *History of The Church of Jesus Christ of Latter-day Saints*, ed. B. H. Roberts, 2nd ed. rev., 7 vols. (Salt Lake City: The Church of Jesus Christ of Latter-day Saints, 1932–1951), 4:461.
2. Heber J. Grant, Conference Report, April 1937; *Improvement Era*, 39:660.
3. *Journal of Discourses,* 26 vols. (Liverpool: F. D. Richards & Sons, 1851–1886), 5:194.
4. Ibid., 3:91.
5. Matthias F. Cowley, *Wilford Woodruff: History of His Life and Labors* (Salt Lake City: Deseret Book, 1964), 34.
6. *Millennial Star,* August 20, 1859, 544.
7. Recollections of John H. Gilbert [Regarding printing Book of Mormon], 8 September 1892, Palmyra, New York, typescript, BYU.
8. *History of the Church,* 1:363.
9. Ibid., 1:54–55.
10. "Choosing a Bible Translation," christianity.com
11. *Journal of Discourses*, 25:100.
12. *History of the Church,* 4:494.

Chapter 5: Mormon as Editor, Compiler, and Abridger

"To presume that Joseph Smith invented the character Mormon as an editor, compiler, and abridger nearly 400 years after Christ who could then refer to records kept from the preceding thousand years is a great compliment! Then to have this Mormon produce a digest or abridgment of these thousand years of records, written by more than a score of official historians, would represent one of the most complicated literary inventions ever seen at that time."[1]

—G. Homer Durham

During the first general conference over which President Ezra Taft Benson presided, he delivered a talk on the Book of Mormon that many still remember. That day, he gave members this challenge: "There is a book we need to study daily, both as individuals and as families, namely the Book of Mormon. I love that book. It is the book that will get a person nearer to God by abiding by its precepts than any other book. . . . President Romney recommended studying it half an hour each day. I commend that practice to you."[2]

I have tried to follow his counsel of studying the Book of Mormon for a half an hour each day since that time. I can testify that it has been an extremely rewarding ritual. I cannot think of another book in existence that could hold my attention for thirty minutes a day for so many years. Not only has it held my attention, I actively look forward to studying it every day and often end up getting so engrossed that I don't even want to stop after the length of time designated. Several times I have gotten inexpensive copies of the book to mark specific themes. For example, one time through I marked every reference to the Godhead with a red pencil as I read. Another time, I took a new copy and attempted to understand the Lamanite point of view. After each completed reading, I indicate the theme used and then get a new copy for the next reading. It has been an amazing experience, for there are many thematic ways to study the Book of Mormon.

Perhaps the most rewarding experience ever was the time I read it looking for the speaker of the words I was reading. I used an unmarked copy as usual, but this time I didn't mark the text at all, but simply wrote in the margins the name of the person speaking. The first name written was that of Nephi beside verse one of 1 Nephi. I then drew a vertical line down until the next speaker began, which happened to be Lehi. That experience dramatically increased my testimony of the Book of Mormon. It was as if each person who spoke became real to me instead of just words in a book. I could also see that Nephi was a much different writer and personality than Jacob, as were all of the other writers. It was amazing to see how many individuals and groups spoke. I had never considered this before.

Another thing that happened while I attempted to identify each speaker within the book was the increase in gratitude and love I felt for Mormon. Here was a great prophet and leader who was surrounded by death, carnage, and repulsive wickedness and who spent a great deal of his life writing for people who would live 1,600 plus years in the future. He also began a brilliant research project as he examined hundreds of years of records looking for information that would help those who would read it in the future. He knew his own people would never even see what he wrote.

His technique was consistent and obvious. Like any good researcher, he preferred quoting original source material rather than summarizing it. If someone like Alma, Amulek, Abinadi, or Samuel the Lamanite gave an extremely insightful talk, he inserted their actual words. The same is true for father's blessings, letters, missionary exchanges with investigators, and other important statements. It would be wonderful if he could have added footnotes to cite the original sources. Can you imagine looking below direct quotations and seeing something like "Personal Journal of Alma, 64." The number of sources Mormon quotes from would rival any modern scholarly work of our day. However, if an important topic of discussion was too long—such as a war that lasted over an extended time—he skillfully summarized it in his own words.

I also began to realize how incredibly complicated the Book of Mormon really is. If Joseph Smith wrote it as many critics claim, then each time a different character spoke, he would have had to make a whole new, believable person.

After finishing my "identify the speaker" project, I discussed my experience with three friends (John Hilton III, Jennifer Brinkerhoff Platt, and Shon Hopkin) who were teaching in the religion department at Brigham Young University. When I showed them what I had done, they all expressed interest and agreed to do the same thing by perusing the entire Book of Mormon and writing the speaker's name in the margins of each page. I was shocked at how many more individuals and groups with speaking parts they found.

After each of us identified the voices in the Book of Mormon, we discovered 153 individuals or groups who had speaking parts. With the different writers identified, it became easy to reformat the Book of Mormon as if it were a modern book. It became obvious that the intent of the record keepers was to write a testament of Jesus Christ.

The following is a chapter from the Book of Alma that shows how the book might look in dialogue-like format, or if Mormon were writing in our day without footnotes added. Look carefully at how skillfully he narrates the story, quotes when he can, and summarizes when he needs to. In Alma 20, we see the words of the Lord and five individuals:

- *Mormon:* The prophet who abridges the thousand-year history of two nations
- *Ammon:* A sinner who repents and becomes a great missionary for Christ
- *King Lamoni:* A wicked Lamanite king who repents and is converted to Christ
- *The Lord*: The creator of heaven and earth, our Savior and Redeemer
- *Father of King Lamoni*: A wicked Lamanite king who repents and is converted

Alma Chapter 20

Mormon: 1 And it came to pass that when they had established a church in that land, that king Lamoni desired that Ammon should go with him to the land of Nephi, that he might show him unto his father.

2 And the voice of the Lord came to Ammon, saying:

The Lord: Thou shalt not go up to the land of Nephi, for behold, the king will seek thy life; but thou shalt go to the land of Middoni; for behold, thy brother Aaron, and also Muloki and Ammah are in prison.

Mormon: 3 Now it came to pass that when Ammon had heard this, he said unto Lamoni:

Ammon: Behold, my brother and brethren are in prison at Middoni, and I go that I may deliver them.

Mormon: 4 Now Lamoni said unto Ammon:

King Lamoni: I know, in the strength of the Lord thou canst do all things. But behold, I will go with thee to the land of Middoni; for the king of the land of Middoni, whose name is Antiomno, is a friend unto me; therefore I go to the land of Middoni, that I may flatter the king of the land, and he will cast thy brethren out of prison.

Mormon: Now Lamoni said unto him:

King Lamoni: Who told thee that thy brethren were in prison?

Mormon: 5 And Ammon said unto him:

Ammon: No one hath told me, save it be God; and he said unto me—

The Lord: Go and deliver thy brethren, for they are in prison in the land of Middoni.

Mormon: 6 Now when Lamoni had heard this he caused that his servants should make ready his horses and his chariots.

7 And he said unto Ammon:

King Lamoni: Come, I will go with thee down to the land of Middoni, and there I will plead with the king that he will cast thy brethren out of prison.

Mormon: 8 And it came to pass that as Ammon and Lamoni were journeying thither, they met the father of Lamoni, who was king over all the land.

9 And behold, the father of Lamoni said unto him:

Father of Lamoni: Why did ye not come to the feast on that great day when I made a feast unto my sons, and unto my people?

Mormon: 10 And he also said:

Father of Lamoni: Whither art thou going with this Nephite, who is one of the children of a liar?

Mormon: 11 And it came to pass that Lamoni rehearsed unto him whither he was going, for he feared to offend him.

12 And he also told him all the cause of his tarrying in his own kingdom, that he did not go unto his father to the feast which he had prepared.

13 And now when Lamoni had rehearsed unto him all these things, behold, to his astonishment, his father was angry with him, and said:

Father of Lamoni: Lamoni, thou art going to deliver these Nephites, who are sons of a liar. Behold, he robbed our fathers; and now his children are also come amongst us that they may, by their cunning and their lyings, deceive us, that they again may rob us of our property.

Mormon: 14 Now the father of Lamoni commanded him that he should slay Ammon with the sword. And he also commanded him that he should not go to the land of Middoni, but that he should return with him to the land of Ishmael.

15 But Lamoni said unto him:

King Lamoni: I will not slay Ammon, neither will I return to the land of Ishmael, but I go to the land of Middoni that I may release the brethren of Ammon, for I know that they are just men and holy prophets of the true God.

Mormon: 16 Now when his father had heard these words, he was angry with him, and he drew his sword that he might smite him to the earth.

17 But Ammon stood forth and said unto him:

Ammon: Behold, thou shalt not slay thy son; nevertheless, it were better that he should fall than thee, for behold, he has repented of his sins; but if thou shouldst fall at this time, in thine anger, thy soul could not be saved.

18 And again, it is expedient that thou shouldst forbear; for if thou shouldst slay thy son, he being an innocent man, his blood would cry from the ground to the Lord his God, for vengeance to come upon thee; and perhaps thou wouldst lose thy soul.

Mormon: 19 Now when Ammon had said these words unto him, he answered him, saying:

Father of Lamoni: I know that if I should slay my son, that I should shed innocent blood; for it is thou that hast sought to destroy him.

Mormon: 20 And he stretched forth his hand to slay Ammon. But Ammon withstood his blows, and also smote his arm that he could not use it.

21 Now when the king saw that Ammon could slay him, he began to plead with Ammon that he would spare his life.

22 But Ammon raised his sword, and said unto him:

Ammon: Behold, I will smite thee except thou wilt grant unto me that my brethren may be cast out of prison.

Mormon: 23 Now the king, fearing he should lose his life, said:

Father of Lamoni: If thou wilt spare me I will grant unto thee whatsoever thou wilt ask, even to half of the kingdom.

Mormon: 24 Now when Ammon saw that he had wrought upon the old king according to his desire, he said unto him:

Ammon: If thou wilt grant that my brethren may be cast out of prison, and also that Lamoni may retain his kingdom, and that ye be not displeased with him, but grant that he may do according to his own desires in whatsoever thing he thinketh, then will I spare thee; otherwise I will smite thee to the earth.

Mormon: 25 Now when Ammon had said these words, the king began to rejoice because of his life.

26 And when he saw that Ammon had no desire to destroy him, and when he also saw the great love he had for his son Lamoni, he was astonished exceedingly, and said:

Father of Lamoni: Because this is all that thou hast desired, that I would release thy brethren, and suffer that my son Lamoni should retain his kingdom, behold, I will grant unto you that my son may retain his kingdom from this time and forever; and I will govern him no more—

27 And I will also grant unto thee that thy brethren may be cast out of prison, and thou and thy brethren may come unto me, in my kingdom; for I shall greatly desire to see thee.

Mormon: For the king was greatly astonished at the words which he had spoken, and also at the words which had been spoken by his son Lamoni, therefore he was desirous to learn them.

28 And it came to pass that Ammon and Lamoni proceeded on their journey towards the land of Middoni. And Lamoni found favor in the eyes of the king of the land; therefore the brethren of Ammon were brought forth out of prison.

29 And when Ammon did meet them he was exceedingly sorrowful, for behold they were naked, and their skins were worn exceedingly because of being bound with strong cords. And they also had suffered hunger, thirst, and all kinds of afflictions; nevertheless they were patient in all their sufferings.

30 And, as it happened, it was their lot to have fallen into the hands of a more hardened and a more stiffnecked people; therefore they would not hearken unto their words, and they had cast them out, and had smitten them, and had driven them from house to house, and from place to place, even until they had arrived in the land of Middoni; and there they were taken and cast into prison, and bound with strong cords, and kept in prison for many days, and were delivered by Lamoni and Ammon.

Mormon narrates with simple language, giving essential yet vivid emotional details. The words of the other speakers highlight their personalities and characters and the narration and dialogue among the five individuals includes thirty-four voice changes that move seamlessly back and forth. Mormon definitely selected meaningful quotations so that he could effectively declare the spiritual message of the Book of Mormon. He presents the narrative with an emphasis on the people involved in such a way that his writing is both accessible and spiritually powerful to those who read his abridgement. Mormon, through his narration and inspired selection of quotations, goes beyond the noteworthy tasks of compiler and abridger.

This chapter of Alma is a great example of the inspired genius of Mormon. It also demonstrates how implausible it would be for young Joseph Smith to create such a complex masterpiece.

Reason to Believe

I cannot comprehend how Joseph Smith could have verbally quoted a book to Oliver Cowdery or come up with content for 153 different characters and groups, with totally different personalities and motives, and made them all entirely believable.

Mormon had a divine commission to prepare this book for people in our day through his inspired work of weaving his words of abridgement with the words he selected from significant people in ancient America to make the Book of Mormon another testament of Jesus Christ.

Notes

1. G. Homer Durham, "The Christ of the Book of Mormon," BYU Devotional Address, March 7, 1978.
2. Ezra Taft Benson, "A Sacred Responsibility," *Ensign*, May 1986, 78.

Chapter 6: The Lamanite Perspective

"The greatest obstacle that has ever opposed the spread of truth and the diffusion of correct principles is the traditions of the people. So potent is their influence and so much importance is there attached to them that truth is but seldom received, even when supported by the best of reasons and evidence, if it comes in contact with them. They are set up as a standard or criterion by which every new principle or idea must be measured and judged; and whether they be true or false, correct or incorrect, by its agreement or disagreement with them must it be accepted or rejected. Every advocate of truth, whether religious or scientific, has experienced this."[1]

—George Q. Cannon

Overall, the Book of Mormon is mainly the record of two groups called the Nephites and the Lamanites, with a side story of another group called the Jaredites. For the most part, those who kept and added to the records from 600 BC to 421 AD were Nephite prophets. Therefore, the vast majority of the record is written only from the Nephite perspective.

However, we can also learn plenty about the Lamanite perspective if we read closely. It is fascinating to me to compare the influence of Nephi and Laman. Both of them started traditions that were repeated over and over by different individuals and groups throughout the near thousand-year history. For example, Nephi kept a written record of the important spiritual events in his life for his posterity. After almost ten centuries, his direct descendant Moroni continued the tradition of recording sacred records. Laman apparently kept no written records and passed on that tradition to his descendants. Nephi was a "go and do what the Lord commanded" kind of person with a positive attitude. Laman, for the most part, seemed to resist what the Lord commanded and had a murmuring, complaining attitude that, in many cases, was passed on to his descendants.

One day while reading the following verse in the Book of Mormon, I realized again just how powerful traditions can be, for good or for evil. The scripture is Mosiah 10:17, which says, "And thus they [the Lamanites] have taught their children that they should hate them, and that they should murder them, and that they should rob and plunder them, and do all they could to destroy them; therefore they have an eternal hatred towards the children of Nephi." This was written about 422 years after Lehi left Jerusalem. I have wondered why the Lamanites would indoctrinate their children to hate the children of Nephi. Hundreds of thousands—maybe even millions—of Nephites, along with many Lamanites, were killed because of this wicked tradition.

I decided a few years ago to try to read the Book of Mormon from the Lamanite point of view. I wanted to make sense of where they were coming from. I could not understand the intense hatred for Nephi, one of my heroes. Since we do not have Lamanite records, I had to look closely to see if the Nephite record keepers recorded their enemy's views. So, with a determination to understand why Laman would teach his children, and therefore his descendants, to hate the Nephites, I bought a hardbound copy of the Book of Mormon and a red pencil. It turned out to be one of the most enlightening things I have ever done. I think I began to see more clearly why the Lamanites felt they had been robbed, even though I still disagree with their perspective.

I would like to share a little about why I believe the tradition of hate was started by Laman. As we begin, it is critical to point out that Nephi gained an unshakable testimony at an early age and never appears to doubt it afterward. 1 Nephi 2:16 says (emphasis added), "And it came to pass that I, Nephi, being exceedingly young, nevertheless being large in stature, and also *having great desires* to know of the mysteries of God, wherefore, I did cry unto the Lord; and behold *he did visit me*, and did *soften my heart* that I did believe all the words which had been spoken by my father; wherefore, *I did not rebel* against him like unto my brothers."

Lehi—like other prophets before and since—taught things that were difficult for the masses to accept. Most likely, those teachings went against what was popular with the world. Instead of immediately rejecting those teachings like his brothers, Nephi went to the Lord with a desire to gain a testimony of what Lehi taught. Notice that he says that the Lord visited him and later says, "for he [Jacob, his brother] verily saw my Redeemer, even as *I have seen him*" (2 Nephi 11:2). From that point on, he viewed the world with an eye of faith and the attitude of "I will go and do the things which the Lord hath commanded, for I know that the Lord giveth no commandments unto the children of men, save he shall prepare a way for them that they may accomplish the thing which he commandeth them" (1 Nephi 3:7). It helped Nephi to realize as a young man that the Lord would never command him to do anything that was not right or that was impossible to accomplish.

Lehi's two oldest sons were rebellious from the beginning of the Book of Mormon story. Nephi records, "And thus Laman and Lemuel, being the eldest, did murmur against their father. And they did murmur because they knew not the dealings of that God who had created them" (1 Nephi 2:12). So on the one hand, Nephi actually sought and saw the Lord, and on the other, Laman knew nothing of God's dealings. Laman looked at life as a natural man, devoid of the Spirit. He did not recognize that sometimes what the Lord commands a person to do might appear to be foolish and illogical in the short run. It takes spiritual maturity to realize that what He commands will prove to be absolutely brilliant in the long run. Picture Noah, for example, who built the ark on dry ground when it was not raining. It was hardly foolishness on his part. Those who do not have a testimony that God truly is involved in our lives must count on their own wisdom or the wisdom of the world to determine what is right or wrong. Once we realize that Laman took the Lord and revelation out of the equation, his actions make far more sense.

As the Book of Mormon story begins, we are told that Lehi received a vision that Jerusalem was to be destroyed if its inhabitants did not repent. Imagine the shock the family must have felt when Lehi came to them with this news. Nephi tells us that "the Lord commanded my father, even in a dream, that he should take his family and depart into the wilderness" (1 Nephi 2:2).

As I read, I tried to imagine myself in Laman's position in a modern setting. I imagined that I was the oldest unmarried son in a family with three younger brothers and some older married sisters. We lived in a beautiful home with acreage in a suburb of San Diego, California. I had worked for several years in my father's business, being groomed to take over when he died. I understood that I would get a larger share of the stock in the company but would also have the responsibility of providing jobs and supporting other family members as the oldest son. Everything was going well until my dad got called as a missionary.

Over time, I noticed he was spending less time with the business and more time preaching on street corners and knocking on people's doors. He seemed to be a bit fanatical in his religious views, and thus quickly lost the respect he once had as a successful businessman in our city. I tried to talk with him and make him see reason, but he would not listen. Over time, he offended almost everyone in San Diego with his comments, and people were becoming furious with him. He began to receive death threats that seemed serious.

Then one day, my father came in and said he had a dream in which the Lord told him that because the people of San Diego were so wicked, the city would soon be destroyed, so our family needed to leave. I could hardly believe that he was serious, but he started making preparations to leave our beautiful home and city. I asked him where we were going and he told me to the Mojave Desert, to live in tents. He said that we would be there until the Lord told us how to get to the promised land. When I asked how long we would be gone from home, he said, "We are never coming back."

What about the business? "We're shutting it down and leaving all of our material possessions behind."

What about our friends and family? "They were invited to come along with us, but they refuse to believe that San Diego is going to be destroyed."

What will we eat? "We will bring some weapons so we can hunt for food."

Who will we date and marry? "We'll let the Lord worry about that."

After mentally putting myself in that situation, I began to see why Laman would have been upset with the move because we know that he did not have a testimony of his father's call. I think that without a personal witness from the Lord that what your father was doing came from Him, many would likely join the murmuring camp of Laman. We now have the advantage of seeing the big picture and realizing that when the Lord asks us to do something difficult, He always gives us rewards that are greater than the sacrifice.

I'm sure the call to leave Jerusalem was extremely difficult for everyone in the family, including Lehi and Sariah. Laman obviously had the hardest time of all the boys because he was the birthright son. In that role, he was in line to receive special status with respect to inheritance rights and privileges. In the Jewish tradition, this means that he would become the head of the family upon the death of his father and would have charge of the family's possessions. He would also be responsible for the welfare of his mother, younger brothers, and any unmarried sisters in his family. To be the birthright son was not only a position of prestige but also a heavy responsibility. In Laman's case, he would have inherited more than his siblings as his father had land and abundance in gold, silver, and other riches.

To his credit, Laman did leave Jerusalem with his family when it was time to go. Perhaps he thought his father would come to his senses after a few days of trying to travel and sleep in the extreme heat and discomfort. It may be that he wanted to stay in his father's good graces because he did not want to risk having his birthright taken away.

However, once the family reached the borders of the Red Sea, both Laman and Leumel expressed their feelings about what their father was doing. Nephi says, "They did murmur in many things against their father, because he was a visionary man, and had led them out of the land of Jerusalem, to leave the land of their inheritance, and their gold, and their silver, and their precious things, to perish in the wilderness. And this they said he had done because of the foolish imaginations of his heart" (1 Nephi 2:11). Both boys apparently believed that the dream Lehi had was nothing more than foolish imaginations. If Lehi were only dreaming, then to leave behind their land and riches would make absolutely no sense. There was another concern they expressed, far more worrisome than material possessions. The two older boys apparently thought that they were going to die of starvation out in the wilderness.

Without a strong testimony, it likely appeared that what Lehi was told in his dream was extremely illogical. It is obvious that the older boys did not have the spiritual confirmation that what they were doing was right, as their father and brother had. Nephi points out that "neither did they believe that Jerusalem, that great city, could be destroyed according to the words of the prophets" (1 Nephi 2:13). He goes on to say that they were like the Jews who were at Jerusalem and had rebelled against prophets like Lehi, Jeremiah, and Ezekiel.

Since Nephi had gained a personal witness that what they were doing was commanded of them by the Lord, he often felt compelled to share his testimony with his older brothers. Sam, the third-oldest brother, accepted his testimony, but Laman and Lemuel usually rejected his words. It is hardly unusual to find older children having a hard time being corrected by younger siblings.

Once the family stopped near the Red Sea, Lehi had another dream where he learned that his sons needed to return to Jerusalem to the house of Laban in order to get "the record of the Jews and also a genealogy of my forefathers, and they are engraven upon plates of brass" (1 Nephi 3:3). Based on his previous attitude, I would think that Laman could care less about these family records. He also may have wondered why Lehi didn't just get the records before they left rather than making them go all the way back to obtain them. We do know that when Lehi was talking to Nephi about this journey his sons would make, he said, "Thy brothers murmur, saying it is a hard thing which I have required of them" (1 Nephi 3:5). But all four sons returned to Jerusalem to acquire the plates.

Once the boys arrived at Jerusalem, Nephi said, "And we cast lots—who of us should go in unto the house of Laban" (1 Nephi 3:11). Many believe that casting lots meant a set of objects, such as sticks or pebbles, was drawn or thrown from a container to make sure the decision was impartial and unbiased. With this method, no one could argue that a decision was the result of human intervention. The people of God frequently used casting lots to determine the Lord's will in a situation. That being the case, it seems more than coincidental that the lot fell on Laman. He was the birthright son. This allowed Lehi's oldest son the chance to prove he could be a leader of the family. It also might have been meant to show him that the Lord was involved in their mission.

Laman followed through with his assignment and went to the house of Laban to ask for the plates. The meeting, however, turned out to be less than faith promoting. Nephi says, "And behold, it came to pass that Laban was angry, and thrust him out from his presence; and he would not that he should have the records. Wherefore, he said unto him: Behold thou art a robber, and I will slay thee" (1 Nephi 3:13). At that point, Laman literally ran for his life. If casting lots revealed God's will, Laman most likely did not get the connection to those things that happened in his short visit with Laban.

Looking at it from his point of view, it would probably be hard for Laman to see Lehi's two dreams as inspired. Dream one resulted in the family's leaving behind relatives, friends, opportunities, and all of their material possessions to live in a tent in the wilderness with the constant threat of starvation. Dream two resulted in a difficult return trip to Jerusalem, only to fail in obtaining the records and nearly getting him killed.

After Laman's failure to get the plates, Nephi recorded that his brethren were about to return to their father in the wilderness. But Nephi had a testimony that they were on the Lord's errand, so they could not accept defeat. Being filled with the Spirit, he told his brothers, "As the Lord liveth, and as we live, we will not go down unto our father in the wilderness until we have accomplished the thing which the Lord hath commanded us" (1 Nephi 3:15). He explained the importance of having the records, so that they could preserve the language and the words of the prophets for their children. Next, he revealed his plan to get the plates. They would retrieve the gold, silver, and other riches their father had left behind in the family residence and use it to purchase the plates from Laban. For whatever reason, Laman and Lemuel went along with the plan.

Which of the boys had the most to lose from this new plan? I'm sure the last thing the birthright son wanted to do was trade their riches for a book of family history, especially when he hoped they would be returning. Nephi says he did "persuade my brethren, that they might be faithful in keeping the commandments of God" (1 Nephi 3:21).

All four boys returned to their family home to gather the riches, and then went to Laban's house to try to buy the plates of brass. Perhaps if everything had gone smoothly, Laman and Lemuel would have been convinced that Nephi was inspired. But what happened instead? "And it came to pass that when Laban saw our property, and that it was exceedingly great, he did lust after it, insomuch that he thrust us out, and sent his servants to slay us, that he might obtain our property" (1 Nephi 3:25). So far, both Lehi's and Nephi's plans had resulted in the family's leaving behind home, comfort, friends, relatives, and now the family treasures.

After losing their material possessions and narrowly escaping death, Laman and Lemuel went from murmuring to violence. They became so angry that they began beating both Nephi and Sam with a rod. At this point, an angel of the Lord appeared and said, "Why do ye smite your younger brother with a rod? Know ye not that the Lord hath chosen him to be a ruler over you, and this because of your iniquities? Behold ye shall go up to Jerusalem again, and the Lord will deliver Laban into your hands" (1 Nephi 3:29).

You would think that this angelic appearance would convince Laman and Lemuel that the Lord was leading both their father, Lehi, and their brother Nephi. However, that was not the case. It probably didn't help that the angel mentioned the fact that Nephi would be their ruler because of their iniquities. The older boys could not believe that Laban would be delivered into their hands. "And after the angel had departed, Laman and Lemuel again began to murmur, saying: How is it possible that the Lord will deliver Laban into our hands? Behold, he is a mighty man, and he can command fifty, yea, even he can slay fifty; then why not us?" (1 Nephi 3:31).

Nephi provided them with another speech, using the story of Moses leading the children of Israel through the Red Sea on dry ground. He reminded them that Pharaoh's army was drowned to show them that impossible odds could be overcome when the Lord is on your side. Why be worried about fifty if the Lord was with them? The older boys were still angry after Nephi's talk, but they again followed him to Jerusalem where they stayed outside the city walls while he went in alone—Nephi being led by the Spirit but not knowing beforehand exactly where to go or what he should do. (See 1 Nephi 4:6.)

Once Nephi was within the walls of the city, he came upon Laban, who had been drinking heavily and was passed out on a street. Nephi was constrained by the Spirit to kill Laban, but he was shocked by that prompting and resisted. The Spirit told him that the Lord had delivered Laban to him, just as the angel had promised. We know that Laban tried to have Laman killed simply because he requested the plates when all he had to do was simply say no. He stole Lehi's property and attempted to have all four boys killed when all they did was suggest a more than generous business deal. Based on his violent reactions, I have a feeling that this was not the first time Laban had ordered people killed. He was obviously extremely wicked, and the Lord chose to end his life rather than have him stand in the way and cause an entire civilization to dwindle in unbelief because they had no spiritual records.

Nephi followed the promptings of the Spirit and killed Laban. He then dressed in Laban's clothes and convinced his servant Zoram to open the treasury and accompany him outside the walls. Thinking he was following Laban, Zoram did as he was told.

As Nephi and Zoram came outside the city wall, the other boys ran, thinking Nephi to be Laban. When Nephi called after them, they recognized his voice and stopped. At that point, Zoram panicked and wanted to run, but Nephi grabbed him and promised that his life would be spared if he would come with them into the wilderness. Zoram agreed to do so.

Do you think that Laman and Lemuel realized that the Lord helped Nephi get the brass plates? You would think they would have gained a testimony on the spot. However, when they heard the circumstances of how the plates were secured, they were furious. The culmination of that evening's events meant they could *never* come back home again. The Jewish authorities would investigate the murder of a prominent citizen, the theft of important records engraved on metal plates containing their religious history, and the kidnapping of one of Laban's servants. They would obviously be the prime suspects because they had already tried to procure the plates on two other occasions. Now they were fugitives on the run because of Nephi's actions. Not exactly something that would build testimonies from those who already doubted.

They fled from Jerusalem with Zoram and the brass plates. They all returned to their parents in the wilderness. Next, we learn something that could have also had a negative impact on Laman and Lemuel. While her sons were gone, Sariah murmured and expressed her doubts about Lehi's dreams. Nephi records that "she also had complained against my father, telling him that he was a visionary man; saying: Behold thou hast led us forth from the land of our inheritance, and my sons are no more, and we perish in the wilderness" (1 Nephi 5:2). With her boys' safe return, Sariah bore testimony that she knew the Lord was involved in their departing Jerusalem. However, it could not have been good for her sons without testimonies to know that their mother at least temporarily shared some of their same doubts.

During this long stop in the wilderness, Lehi spent time searching the plates and shared what he learned. Laman and Lemuel especially had trouble understanding what their father taught concerning the natural branches of the olive tree and the Gentiles. With a desire to understand, Nephi pondered and prayed about the information provided by his father. He realized that the doctrinal principles taught by his father "were hard to be understood, save a man should inquire of the Lord; and they being hard in their hearts, therefore they did not look unto the Lord as they ought" (1 Nephi 15:3). Nephi asked Laman and Lemuel this question: "Have ye inquired of the Lord? And they said unto me: We have not; for the Lord maketh no such thing known unto us" (1 Nephi 15:8–9). It is easy to recognize that these two did not have a testimony and made no effort to get one.

Laman and Lemuel resented their younger brother preaching to them in a straightforward manner. Nephi was a great doctrinal teacher and—like his father and most prophets—he could be rather direct when condemning sin. When the older boys had a hard time understanding some of their father's teachings, they asked Nephi a series of questions. When he told them about the justice of God and how the wicked will be cut off from Him, the following exchange occurred:

1 Nephi 16

1 And now it came to pass that after I, Nephi, had made an end of speaking to my brethren, behold they said unto me: Thou hast declared unto us hard things, more than we are able to bear.

2 And it came to pass that I said unto them that I knew that I had spoken hard things against the wicked, according to the truth; and the righteous have I justified, and testified that they should be lifted up at the last day; wherefore, the guilty taketh the truth to be hard, for it cutteth them to the very center.

3 And now my brethren, if ye were righteous and were willing to hearken to the truth, and give heed unto it, that ye might walk uprightly before God, then ye would not murmur because of the truth.

This kind of exchange likely did not build brotherly love. They were obviously offended by the things Nephi said to them. We know that they complained to Lehi about the perceived harsh words they felt Nephi used. Lehi's response probably seemed to them that he favored Nephi and condemned them. He said to them, "And ye have murmured because he hath been plain unto you. Ye say that he hath used sharpness; ye say that he hath been angry with you; but behold, his sharpness was the sharpness of the power of the word of God, which was in him; and that which ye call anger was the truth, according to that which is in God, which he could not restrain, manifesting boldly concerning your iniquities" (2 Nephi 1:26).

The resentment and anger that Laman felt toward Nephi seemed to grow over time. Laman obviously felt he had been wronged. The Book of Mormon seems to indicate that Laman believed Nephi conspired to steal his birthright, or his right to rule. Perhaps he thought his father was in on it, that he wanted Nephi to have what Laman thought was his by right. He may have justified his attempts to kill Nephi since in most countries trying to take the right of leadership unjustly is a crime punishable by death. He appears to justify his plan to kill his father and Nephi by tying it to taking his right to rule. He also explained away the angel by saying Nephi used cunning arts to deceive them and it didn't really happen. Laman spoke to the sons of Ishmael about their situation:

1 Nephi 16

37 And Laman said unto Lemuel and also unto the sons of Ishmael: Behold, let us slay our father, and also our brother Nephi, who has taken it upon him to be our ruler and our teacher, who are his elder brethren.

38 Now, he says that the Lord has talked with him, and also that angels have ministered unto him. But behold, we know that he lies unto us; and he tells us these things, and he worketh many things by

his cunning arts, that he may deceive our eyes, thinking, perhaps, that he may lead us away into some strange wilderness; and after he has led us away, he has thought to make himself a king and a ruler over us, that he may do with us according to his will and pleasure. And after this manner did my brother Laman stir up their hearts to anger.

Because of these perceived offenses, Laman taught his children to hate the children of Nephi because he believed that they, Laman and his children, had been wronged. This must have been repeated so often that it became a Lamanite tradition. Brigham Young gave this insight about the power of traditions: "Whether surrounded with error or truth, the web woven around them in childhood's days lasts, and seldom wears threadbare. . . . The traditions of my earliest recollection are so forcible upon me that it seems impossible for me to get rid of them. And so it is with others; hence the necessity of correct training in childhood."[2] With that in mind, look closely at the following verses to learn why hundreds of thousands of both Nephites and Lamanites lost their lives.

Mosiah 10 (422 years after Lehi left Jerusalem)

12 They were a wild, and ferocious, and a blood-thirsty people, believing in the tradition of their fathers, which is this—Believing that they were driven out of the land of Jerusalem because of the iniquities of their fathers, and that they were wronged in the wilderness by their brethren, and they were also wronged while crossing the sea;

13 And again, that they were wronged while in the land of their first inheritance, after they had crossed the sea, and all this because that Nephi was more faithful in keeping the commandments of the Lord—therefore he was favored of the Lord, for the Lord heard his prayers and answered them, and he took the lead of their journey in the wilderness.

14 And his brethren were wroth with him because they understood not the dealings of the Lord; they were also wroth with him upon the waters because they hardened their hearts against the Lord.

15 And again, they were wroth with him when they had arrived in the promised land, because they said that he had taken the ruling of the people out of their hands; and they sought to kill him.

16 And again, they were wroth with him because he departed into the wilderness as the Lord had commanded him, and took the

records which were engraven on the plates of brass, for they said that he robbed them.

17 And thus they have taught their children that they should hate them, and that they should murder them, and that they should rob and plunder them, and do all they could to destroy them; therefore they have an eternal hatred towards the children of Nephi.

There can be no doubt that the Lamanites actually believed the Nephites had wronged them. From their perspective, I'm sure they felt they had plenty of evidence to back their grievances. They could look their children in the eye and believe they were telling the truth as they spoke of the iniquities of Lehi and Nephi. They also viewed the brass plates as the only material possession of worth that came out of Jerusalem, so it should rightfully have gone to the birthright son, Laman. Of course, from their perspective, Nephi stole the brass plates and ran away with his people. Surely these are the kinds of things that Laman passionately taught his posterity.

Consider other Book of Mormon examples that show the power of these unrighteous traditions that the Lamanites were taught and believed for the next thousand years. This indoctrination eventually led to the destruction of the entire Nephite civilization.

Lamoni's father clarifies their traditions of hate:

Alma 20 (510 years after Lehi leaves Jerusalem)

10 And he also said: Whither art thou going with this Nephite, who is one of the children of a liar?

11 And it came to pass that Lamoni rehearsed unto him whither he was going, for he feared to offend him.

12 And he also told him all the cause of his tarrying in his own kingdom, that he did not go unto his father to the feast which he had prepared.

13 And now when Lamoni had rehearsed unto him all these things, behold, to his astonishment, his father was angry with him, and said: Lamoni, thou art going to deliver these Nephites, who are sons of a liar. Behold, he robbed our fathers; and now his children are also come amongst us that they may, by their cunning and their lyings, deceive us, that they again may rob us of our property.

Justifying the Lamanite tradition of fighting and bloodshed, the king Ammoron explains their reasons for war:

Alma 54 (537 years after Lehi left Jerusalem)

16 I am Ammoron, the king of the Lamanites; I am the brother of Amalickiah whom ye have murdered. Behold, I will avenge his blood upon you, yea, and I will come upon you with my armies for I fear not your threatenings.

17 For behold, your fathers did wrong their brethren, insomuch that they did rob them of their right to the government when it rightly belonged unto them.

18 And now behold, if ye will lay down your arms, and subject yourselves to be governed by those to whom the government doth rightly belong, then will I cause that my people shall lay down their weapons and shall be at war no more . . .

23 I am Ammoron, and a descendant of Zoram, whom your fathers pressed and brought out of Jerusalem.

24 And behold now, I am a bold Lamanite; behold, this war hath been waged to avenge their wrongs, and to maintain and to obtain their rights to the government; and I close my epistle to Moroni.

One day, it would be interesting to ask Laman exactly what he lost because of the perceived wrongs Nephi inflicted upon him. I'm sure he would list the loss of the house, land, gold, silver, and other riches they left behind. At the top of the list appears to be the loss of his right to rule. And yet he actually *did* rule over his own family and other followers. The only people he didn't rule were those he hated anyway. Why not good riddance that they were gone?

Most of all, I would love to see him answer the question of what he gained by leaving Jerusalem. If he were truthful, he would have to say, "Well, we got our wives and children, the fertile land, gold, silver, wild game, livestock, timber, and water in all of North and South America." Laman and his many descendants spent their entire lives focused on what they lost and paid little attention to the fact that they had been blessed with infinitely more than all the riches left in Jerusalem.

Reason to Believe

The Book of Mormon is full of layers of meaning such as the Lamanite perspective to keep its readers engaged and fascinated for a lifetime. Here are a few lessons I learned when I tried to see things from a Lamanite point of view:

- Everyone should go to the Lord to gain a testimony of what the prophets teach.
- If children are taught to hate others, it is difficult to change these views.
- Most people can justify their positions, whether they are true or false.
- One passionate righteous or wicked leader can start traditions that last for generations.
- Totally false teachings are often viewed as truth if they are repeated often enough.
- When we are obedient to God's commandments, He gives us more than what we sacrifice.
- Often we focus so much on what other people have that we forget what we have.

The traditions of hate in the Book of Mormon go a long way in helping to explain the animosity between some groups in our own day. Joseph Smith could not have understood this much about the power of traditions at his young age. I don't believe he could have woven the Lamanite perspective throughout the book so authentically and seamlessly if he were not actually translating an ancient record. He lived a life of goodness and relative innocence, which precluded his ability to write authentically about such extensive hatred. Contrasting such powerful, destructive traditions and their ramifications with total faith and obedience would have been beyond the wisdom of such a young writer. Of course that is the case; Joseph Smith did not write the Book of Mormon. He translated it by the power of God.

Notes

1. George Q. Cannon, *Gospel Truth; Discourses and Writings of President George Q. Cannon*, comp. Jerreld L. Newquist. (Salt Lake City: Deseret Book, 1974), 294.
2. *Journal of Discourses,* 26 vols. (Liverpool: F. D. Richards & Sons, 1851–1886), 13:243, 252.

Chapter 7: Emphasis Placed on Jesus Christ

"For we labor diligently to write, to persuade our children, and also our brethren, to believe in Christ, and to be reconciled to God; for we know that it is by grace that we are saved, after all we can do. . . . And we talk of Christ, we rejoice in Christ, we preach of Christ, we prophesy of Christ, and we write according to our prophecies, that our children may know to what source they may look for a remission of their sins" (2 Nephi 25:23, 26).

—Nephi

Several years ago, I met Summer while speaking at a multi-stake priest and laurel conference in Toronto, Canada. She was a senior in high school and a beautiful girl both inside and out. She had a strong testimony of the Book of Mormon and the gospel. After reading a *New Era* article about a girl who hung a picture of Christ in her locker at school, Summer decided to do the same thing to remind herself to be more like Christ. Because she shared the locker with her non-LDS friend, she asked for her approval before putting the picture up in their locker. Her friend told her that she had no problem with the idea and even encouraged her.

But when she hung up the picture, she heard mocking comments from other students. Several laughed at her, and some used profanity while talking about the picture. She heard one boy say to his friend in a disparaging way, "I told you she had a picture of Jesus in her locker." She thought it was strange that a number of those taunting her hung pornography in their lockers, yet she never heard anyone mock them.

After several days of ridicule from classmates, Summer decided to take the picture down. She did not want the Savior ridiculed by the crowds. As she was removing the picture, her locker mate walked up and asked what she was doing. Summer reminded her friend of the daily mockery the picture had generated from the crowds. Her friend said, "Please don't take it down. Every time I am tempted to do something wrong, I think about this picture of Christ, and I am able to resist."

Thinking about the Savior and his mission daily can help all of us deal with the temptations we face. President Gordon B. Hinckley made this profound statement about what the Book of Mormon can do for the prayerful reader: "The test of its truth lies in reading it. It is a book of God. Reasonable people may sincerely question its origin; but those who have read it prayerfully have come to know by a power beyond their natural senses that it is true, that it contains the word of God, that it outlines saving truths of the everlasting gospel, that it 'came forth by the gift and power of God . . . to the convincing of the Jew and Gentile that Jesus is the Christ.'"[1]

As an undergraduate at Brigham Young University, I often attended "The Last Lecture Series," sponsored by a student organization on campus. A highly accomplished individual was invited to speak to the student body, offering counsel they would give others if they only had one last time to speak. These lectures were inspiring, and in some cases life-changing for the speaker as well as the audience. People who know they are going to die usually communicate the things they have learned to value throughout their lifetime. Several writers in the Book of Mormon realized they were going to die and gave their last messages to their loved ones and the world. Let's look at a few of them and see what they had to say.

Final Words of Lehi

2 Nephi 2 (emphasis added)

28 And now, my sons, I would that ye should look to *the great Mediator*, and hearken unto his great commandments; and be faithful unto his words, and choose eternal life, according to the will of his Holy Spirit;

29 And not choose eternal death, according to the will of the flesh and the evil which is therein, which giveth the spirit of the devil

power to captivate, to bring you down to hell, that he may reign over you in his own kingdom.

30 I have spoken these few words unto you all, my sons, in the last days of my probation; and I have chosen the good part, according to the words of the prophet. And I have none other object save it be the everlasting welfare of your souls. Amen.

Final Message of Nephi

2 Nephi 33 (emphasis added)

13 And now, my beloved brethren, all those who are of the house of Israel, and all ye ends of the earth, I speak unto you as the voice of one crying from the dust: Farewell until that great day shall come.

14 And you that will not partake of the goodness of *God*, and respect the words of the Jews, and also my words, and the words which shall proceed forth out of the mouth of *the Lamb of God*, behold, I bid you an everlasting farewell, for these words shall condemn you at the last day.

15 For what I seal on earth, shall be brought against you at the judgment bar; for thus hath *the Lord* commanded me, and I must obey. Amen.

Final Message of Jacob

Jacob 6 (emphasis added)

8 Behold, will ye reject these words? Will ye reject the words of the prophets; and will ye reject all the words which have been spoken concerning *Christ*, after so many have spoken concerning him; and deny the good word of *Christ*, and the power of *God*, and the gift of the Holy Ghost, and quench the Holy Spirit, and make a mock of the great plan of redemption, which hath been laid for you?

9 Know ye not that if ye will do these things, that the power of the redemption and the resurrection, which is in *Christ*, will bring you to stand with shame and awful guilt before the bar of *God*?

10 And according to the power of justice, for justice cannot be denied, ye must go away into that lake of fire and brimstone, whose flames are unquenchable, and whose smoke ascendeth up forever and ever, which lake of fire and brimstone is endless torment.

11 O then, my beloved brethren, repent ye, and enter in at the strait gate, and continue in the way which is narrow, until ye shall obtain eternal life.

12 O be wise; what can I say more?

13 Finally, I bid you farewell, until I shall meet you before the pleasing bar of *God*, which bar striketh the wicked with awful dread and fear. Amen.

Final Message of Enos

Enos 1 (emphasis added)

26 And I saw that I must soon go down to my grave, having been wrought upon by the power of *God* that I must preach and prophesy unto this people, and declare the word according to the truth which is in *Christ*. And I have declared it in all my days, and have rejoiced in it above that of the world.

27 And I soon go to the place of my rest, which is with my *Redeemer;* for I know that in him I shall rest. And I rejoice in the day when my mortal shall put on immortality, and shall stand before him; then shall I see his face with pleasure, and he will say unto me: Come unto me, ye blessed, there is a place prepared for you in the mansions of my Father. Amen.

Final Message of Amaleki

Omni 1 (emphasis added)

25 And it came to pass that I began to be old; and, having no seed, and knowing king Benjamin to be a just man before the Lord, wherefore, I shall deliver up these plates unto him, exhorting all men to come unto *God, the Holy One of Israel*, and believe in prophesying, and in revelations, and in the ministering of angels, and in the gift of speaking with tongues, and in the gift of interpreting languages, and in all things which are good; for there is nothing which is good save it comes from the *Lord:* and that which is evil cometh from the devil.

26 And now, my beloved brethren, I would that ye should come unto *Christ*, who is *the Holy One of Israel*, and partake of his salvation, and the power of his redemption. Yea, come unto him, and offer your whole souls as an offering unto him, and continue in fasting and praying, and endure to the end; and as *the Lord* liveth ye will be saved.

Final Address of King Benjamin

Mosiah 5 (emphasis added)

13 For how knoweth a man the master whom he has not served, and who is a stranger unto him, and is far from the thoughts and intents of his heart?

14 And again, doth a man take an ass which belongeth to his neighbor, and keep him? I say unto you, Nay; he will not even suffer that he shall feed among his flocks, but will drive him away, and cast him out. I say unto you, that even so shall it be among you if ye know not the name by which ye are called.

15 Therefore, I would that ye should be steadfast and immovable, always abounding in good works, that *Christ, the Lord God Omnipotent,* may seal you his, that you may be brought to heaven, that ye may have everlasting salvation and eternal life, through the wisdom, and power, and justice, and mercy of him who created all things, in heaven and in earth, who is *God* above all. Amen.

Final Message of Amulek

Alma 34 (emphasis added)

38 That ye contend no more against the Holy Ghost, but that ye receive it, and take upon you the name of *Christ*; that ye humble yourselves even to the dust, and worship *God*, in whatsoever place ye may be in, in spirit and in truth; and that ye live in thanksgiving daily, for the many mercies and blessings which he doth bestow upon you.

39 Yea, and I also exhort you, my brethren, that ye be watchful unto prayer continually, that ye may not be led away by the temptations of the devil, that he may not overpower you, that ye may not become his subjects at the last day; for behold, he rewardeth you no good thing.

40 And now my beloved brethren, I would exhort you to have patience, and that ye bear with all manner of afflictions; that ye do not revile against those who do cast you out because of your exceeding poverty, lest ye become sinners like unto them;

41 But that ye have patience, and bear with those afflictions, with a firm hope that ye shall one day rest from all your afflictions.

Final Message of Helaman

Helaman 5 (emphasis added)

11 And he hath power given unto him from the Father to redeem them from their sins because of repentance; therefore he hath sent his angels to declare the tidings of the conditions of repentance, which bringeth unto the power of *the Redeemer*, unto the salvation of their souls.

12 And now, my sons, remember, remember that it is upon the rock of our *Redeemer*, who is *Christ, the Son of God*, that ye must build your foundation; that when the devil shall send forth his mighty winds, yea, his shafts in the whirlwind, yea, when all his hail and his mighty storm shall beat upon you, it shall have no power over you to drag you down to the gulf of misery and endless wo, because of the rock upon which ye are built, which is a sure foundation, a foundation whereon if men build they cannot fall.

Final Message of Mormon

Mormon 9 (emphasis added)

35 And these things are written that we may rid our garments of the blood of our brethren, who have dwindled in unbelief.

36 And behold, these things which we have desired concerning our brethren, yea, even their restoration to the knowledge of *Christ*, are according to the prayers of all the saints who have dwelt in the land.

37 And may *the Lord Jesus Christ* grant that their prayers may be answered according to their faith; and may God the Father remember the covenant which he hath made with the house of Israel; and may he bless them forever, through faith on the name of *Jesus Christ*. Amen.

Final Message of Moroni

Moroni 10 (emphasis added)

32 Yea, come unto *Christ*, and be perfected in him, and deny yourselves of all ungodliness; and if ye shall deny yourselves of all ungodliness, and love *God* with all your might, mind and strength, then is his grace sufficient for you, that by his grace ye may be perfect in *Christ*; and if by the grace of *God* ye are perfect in *Christ*, ye can in nowise deny the power of *God*.

33 And again, if ye by the grace of *God* are perfect in *Christ*, and deny not his power, then are ye sanctified in *Christ* by the grace of *God*, through the shedding of the blood of *Christ*, which is in the covenant of the Father unto the remission of your sins, that ye become holy, without spot.

34 And now I bid unto all, farewell. I soon go to rest in the paradise of *God*, until my spirit and body shall again reunite, and I am brought forth triumphant through the air, to meet you before the pleasing bar of the great *Jehovah, the Eternal Judge* of both quick and dead. Amen.

In each of these final messages from Book of Mormon prophets, we find at least one reference to Jesus Christ. Many are poignant, with the feeling that there was a deep relationship between the speaker and the Savior. Some included warnings, and others the anticipation of seeing the Redeemer after passing from mortality. All of these prophets wanted their final words to include personal testimonies, with words of the reality and love of the Son of God.

On January 7, 1996, President Gordon B. Hinckley spoke at a regional conference in Corpus Christi, Texas. In his address, he stated,

> I would like to urge every man and woman . . . and every boy and girl who is old enough to again read the Book of Mormon during this coming year. This was written for the convincing of the Jew and the Gentile that Jesus is the Christ. There is nothing we could do of greater importance than to have fortified in our individual lives an unshakable conviction that Jesus is the Christ, the living Son of the living God. And, my brothers and sisters, that is the purpose of the coming forth of this remarkable and wonderful book. May I suggest that you read it again and take a pencil, a red one if you have one, and put a little check mark every time there is a reference to Jesus Christ in that book. And there will come to you a very real conviction as you do so that this is in very deed another witness for the Lord Jesus Christ.[2]

One of the more meaningful things I've ever done was to follow his counsel and read the Book of Mormon with a red pencil and note every reference to Jesus Christ. I knew the book was subtitled "Another Testament of Jesus Christ," but I was shocked at how many references to Him were included. I have read the Book of Mormon multiple times but never realized how completely it is focused on Christ. There are several thousand references to Him and only about thirty pages in the entire book where some name for Him does not appear. That is remarkable, especially when you include the long war chapters in that total.

Recently, I was reading the first chapter of Alma and decided to identify any original three- to seven-word phrase that included any possible references to Christ. By *original* I mean that the phrase is not found in any other scripture so Joseph Smith could not have plagiarized it. I did not try to determine whether God was referring to God the Father or Jesus Christ because they are one in purpose. This project included any names that could refer to Jesus Christ, such as *God, Lord, the Only Begotten, the Holy One,* and others.

When I got to the end of Alma 37, I stopped. Those thirty-seven chapters covered ninety-six pages of text and included 540 unique phrases referring to deity, or 5.6 per page. Remember, I did not include any three- to seven-word phrases that are in the Bible. I am still shocked that there are so many different ways the Book of Mormon writers referred to Christ in their writing. If the rest of the record keepers used as many different phrases as the first thirty-seven chapters of Alma, there would be approximately 2,973 original phrases referencing Christ in some way.

A Sample of 100 of the 540 Original Phrases that Refer to Christ in Alma 1–37

the Lord had created all men	withstood him with the words of God
taken upon them the name of Christ	they did impart the word of God
the Lord God might preserve his people	the word of God is fulfilled
deliverance of Jesus Christ	the holy order of God
having power and authority from God	the mercy and power of God
they awoke unto God	have ye spiritually been born of God

can lie unto the Lord in that day	blameless before God
white through the blood of Christ	whatsoever is good cometh from God
according to the holy order of God	the manifestation of the Spirit of God
I know that Jesus Christ shall come	the Son of God cometh in his glory
the Holy One hath spoken it	the good shepherd doth call after you
according to the order of God	humble themselves before God
word of God was liberal unto all	humbled yourselves before God
according to the Spirit of God	the true and the living God
the Lord God hath power	have faith on the Lamb of God
be received into the kingdom of God	always returning thanks unto God
and may the Lord bless you	may the peace of God rest upon you
wrestling with God in mighty prayer	thou art a holy prophet of God
high priest over the church of God	the miraculous power of God
having been commanded of God	highly favored people of the Lord
visited by the Spirit of God	by the voice of the Lord
the Son of God shall come in his glory	the glory of the Only Begotten
the power and deliverance of Jesus Christ	written by the finger of God
an angel of the Lord appeared	a chosen man of God
bring down the wrath of God	the existence of a Supreme Being
the true and living God	the very Eternal Father
brought to stand before God	the bar of Christ the Son
not dare to look up to our God	a time to prepare to meet God
God conversed with men	through mine Only Begotten Son

the rest of the Lord	provoke not the Lord our God
after the order of his Son	to look forward to his Son for redemption
through the atonement of the Only Begotten Son	the Only Begotten of the Father
through the blood of the Lamb	the rest of the Lord their God
our faith which is in Christ	power of Christ unto salvation
to worship God before the altar	they did impart the word of God
the Lord did pour out his Spirit	the coming of the Son of God
the promises of the Lord	the word and power of God
having imparted the word of God	being filled with the Spirit of God
was created after the image of God	a prophet of a holy God
the light of the glory of God	believe in the power of God
the death and sufferings of Christ	led by the Spirit of the Lord
through the merits of his Son	since God hath taken away our stains
bright through the blood of the Son	Oh, how merciful is our God
look forward to the coming of Christ	blessed be the name of our God
the power and wisdom of God	the light of Christ unto life
speak with the trump of God	an instrument in the hands of God
give heed to the word of Christ	look to God and live
comfort my soul in Christ	that the word is in Christ unto salvation
redemption cometh through the Son of God	the great plan of the Eternal God
be saved, only in and through Christ	may the Lord bless your soul

The 540 references to Jesus Christ not only give His names, but they also clarify aspects of His character, life, and mission. They describe our relationships with Him. Phrases refer to His church, the priesthood of God, and the people of God. They describe qualities of the followers of Christ: prayerful, thankful, humble, repentant, blameless, and many more. They also refer to the consequences of not being obedient to His commandments. And with tenderness, the phrases tell of His merciful Atonement and love.

Nephi states the intent of his writings in one of the early chapters of the Book of Mormon. He said, "For the fulness of mine intent is that I may *persuade men to come unto the God of Abraham, and the God of Isaac, and the God of Jacob, and be saved*" (1 Nephi 6:4; emphasis added). There can be no doubt that he influenced the writers that followed him, and together they have created a powerful second witness that Jesus is the Christ and our Savior.

Reason to Believe

The Book of Mormon is focused on Jesus Christ from the opening chapters to the closing sentence. Thousands of references to Christ are contained in its pages. Many names used to describe Christ are original to the Book of Mormon. What motive would a fraud have to write a book that is totally focused on bringing people to Jesus Christ? How could anyone write a Christ-centered book that has touched the lives of millions of people from all nations and all walks of life?

When I even think about trying to write a ninety-six page book that includes 540 original three- to seven-word phrases like from Alma 1–37, it makes me cringe. And yet some would have us believe that Joseph Smith conjured up this 588-page book (original 1830 edition) that contained more than five times the number of pages in Alma 1–37 and accompanying phrases and references to Christ. I don't believe he could do it under any circumstances. Therefore, I believe the story he told about its origins is true.

Notes

1. Gordon B. Hinckley, "Four Cornerstones of Faith," *Ensign*, February 2004, 6.
2. "Messages of Inspiration from President Hinckley," *Church News*, Saturday, January 1, 2000.

Chapter 8: The Power of the Word

"I am one of his witnesses, and in a coming day I shall feel the nail marks in his hands and in his feet and shall wet his feet with my tears. But I shall not know any better then than I know now that he is God's Almighty Son, that he is our Savior and Redeemer, and that salvation comes in and through his atoning blood and in no other way."[1]

—Bruce R. McConkie

H ave you ever stopped to consider the power of words? Through mere words, wars have started and ended. Tender feelings have been hurt and soothed. Courage has been instilled, and fear has been planted. Lives have been destroyed, and others changed for the better. Words have the power to change history.

These words penned by Thomas Jefferson have had a lasting impact on mankind: "We hold these truths to be self-evident, that all men are created equal, that they are endowed by their Creator with certain unalienable Rights, that among these are Life, Liberty and the pursuit of Happiness.—That to secure these rights, Governments are instituted among Men, deriving their just powers from the consent of the governed."[2] These inspired words have not only affected America but also the entire world.

Recently, I was doing research on the words spoken in famous speeches and the impact they have had on the course of human history. As I read through some of these, I thought about an observation made by Mormon in the Book of Mormon. In Alma 31:5, he said (emphasis added), "And now, as the preaching of the word had a great tendency to lead the people to do *that which was just*—yea, it had had more powerful effect upon the minds of the people than the sword, or anything else." While Alma was specifically referring to the word of God as contained in scripture, perhaps any time inspiration is involved when words are spoken or written, it is the word of God, regardless of the subject matter.

Included here are excerpts from two speeches that I personally believe were inspired because of their positive impact upon society. "The Gettysburg Address" is included in its entirety. As you read the words of these masterful talks, think how many people have been influenced to do "that which was just" (Alma 31:5) simply because these words were spoken.

Abraham Lincoln: "The Gettysburg Address"

Four score and seven years ago our fathers brought forth on this continent, a new nation, conceived in liberty, and dedicated to the proposition that all men are created equal.

Now we are engaged in a great civil war, testing whether that nation, or any nation so conceived and so dedicated, can long endure. We are met on a great battlefield of that war. We have come to dedicate a portion of that field, as a final resting place for those who here gave their lives that that nation might live. It is altogether fitting and proper that we should do this.

But, in a larger sense, we cannot dedicate, we cannot consecrate, we cannot hallow this ground. The brave men, living and dead, who struggled here, have consecrated it, far above our poor power to add or detract. The world will little note, nor long remember what we say here, but it can never forget what they did here. It is for us the living, rather, to be dedicated here to the unfinished work which they who fought here have thus far so nobly advanced. It is rather for us to be here dedicated to the great task remaining before us—that from these honored dead we take increased devotion to that cause for which they gave the last full measure of devotion—that we here highly resolve that these dead shall not have died in vain—that this nation, under God, shall have a new birth of freedom—and that government of the people, by the people, for the people, shall not perish from the earth.[3]

Martin Luther King Jr.: "I Have a Dream"

Let us not wallow in the valley of despair, I say to you today, my friends.

And so even though we face the difficulties of today and tomorrow, I still have a dream.

It is a dream deeply rooted in the American dream.

I have a dream that one day this nation will rise up and live out the true meaning of its creed: "We hold these truths to be self-evident, that all men are created equal."

I have a dream that one day on the red hills of Georgia, the sons of former slaves and the sons of former slave owners will be able to sit down together at the table of brotherhood.

I have a dream that one day even the state of Mississippi, a state sweltering with the heat of injustice, sweltering with the heat of oppression, will be transformed into an oasis of freedom and justice.

I have a dream that my four little children will one day live in a nation where they will not be judged by the color of their skin but by the content of their character.[4]

These speeches have influenced millions of people throughout the world. The tremendous price of freedom, standing for rights, and the infinite dignity of mankind are universal themes, but these two men have elevated those ideas with the power of their words. Because of their poignant words and the personal power behind them, hearts and minds have burst open to ponder and act.

Most members of the Church have had the opportunity to speak in front of crowds at some point and realize how much thought and effort goes into preparation. That seems to be the case even when most of the talk is spent quoting other people's ideas. Presenting original material would require personal pondering and be much more difficult.

Sometimes as I organize talks, I wonder how much time went into preparing the "classic" talks of the past. This brings us to some of the classic talks included in the Book of Mormon that changed people's hearts when they were spoken and continue to change millions today through reading the written word. Savor the power of their words.

Nephi: "Believe in Christ" (2 Nephi 33:10–15)

10 And now, my beloved brethren, and also Jew, and all ye ends of the earth, hearken unto these words and believe in Christ; and if ye believe not in these words believe in Christ. And if ye shall believe in Christ ye will believe in these words, for they are the words of Christ, and he hath given them unto me; and they teach all men that they should do good.

11 And if they are not the words of Christ, judge ye—for Christ will show unto you, with power and great glory, that they are his words,

at the last day; and you and I shall stand face to face before his bar; and ye shall know that I have been commanded of him to write these things, notwithstanding my weakness.

12 And I pray the Father in the name of Christ that many of us, if not all, may be saved in his kingdom at that great and last day.

13 And now, my beloved brethren, all those who are of the house of Israel, and all ye ends of the earth, I speak unto you as the voice of one crying from the dust: Farewell until that great day shall come.

14 And you that will not partake of the goodness of God, and respect the words of the Jews, and also my words, and the words which shall proceed forth out of the mouth of the Lamb of God, behold, I bid you an everlasting farewell, for these words shall condemn you at the last day.

15 For what I seal on earth, shall be brought against you at the judgment bar; for thus hath the Lord commanded me, and I must obey. Amen.

Jacob: "The Holy One of Israel" (2 Nephi 9:17–23)

17 O the greatness and the justice of our God! For he executeth all his words, and they have gone forth out of his mouth, and his law must be fulfilled.

18 But, behold, the righteous, the saints of the Holy One of Israel, they who have believed in the Holy One of Israel, they who have endured the crosses of the world, and despised the shame of it, they shall inherit the kingdom of God, which was prepared for them from the foundation of the world, and their joy shall be full forever.

19 O the greatness of the mercy of our God, the Holy One of Israel! For he delivereth his saints from that awful monster the devil, and death, and hell, and that lake of fire and brimstone, which is endless torment.

20 O how great the holiness of our God! For he knoweth all things, and there is not anything save he knows it.

21 And he cometh into the world that he may save all men if they will hearken unto his voice; for behold, he suffereth the pains of all men, yea, the pains of every living creature, both men, women, and children, who belong to the family of Adam.

22 And he suffereth this that the resurrection might pass upon all men, that all might stand before him at the great and judgment day.

23 And he commandeth all men that they must repent, and be baptized in his name, having perfect faith in the Holy One of Israel, or they cannot be saved in the kingdom of God.

Lehi: "Free to Choose" (2 Nephi 2:21–27)

21 And the days of the children of men were prolonged, according to the will of God, that they might repent while in the flesh; wherefore, their state became a state of probation, and their time was lengthened, according to the commandments which the Lord God gave unto the children of men. For he gave commandment that all men must repent; for he showed unto all men that they were lost, because of the transgression of their parents.

22 And now, behold, if Adam had not transgressed he would not have fallen, but he would have remained in the garden of Eden. And all things which were created must have remained in the same state in which they were after they were created; and they must have remained forever, and had no end.

23 And they would have had no children; wherefore they would have remained in a state of innocence, having no joy, for they knew no misery; doing no good, for they knew no sin.

24 But behold, all things have been done in the wisdom of him who knoweth all things.

25 Adam fell that men might be; and men are, that they might have joy.

26 And the Messiah cometh in the fulness of time, that he may redeem the children of men from the fall. And because that they are redeemed from the fall they have become free forever, knowing good from evil; to act for themselves and not to be acted upon, save it be by the punishment of the law at the great and last day, according to the commandments which God hath given.

27 Wherefore, men are free according to the flesh; and all things are given them which are expedient unto man. And they are free to choose liberty and eternal life, through the great Mediator of all men, or to choose captivity and death, according to the captivity and power of the devil; for he seeketh that all men might be miserable like unto himself.

King Benjamin: "Thank Your Heavenly King" (Mosiah 2:17–22)

17 And behold, I tell you these things that ye may learn wisdom; that ye may learn that when ye are in the service of your fellow beings ye are only in the service of your God.

18 Behold, ye have called me your king; and if I, whom ye call your king, do labor to serve you, then ought not ye to labor to serve one another?

19 And behold also, if I, whom ye call your king, who has spent his days in your service, and yet has been in the service of God, do merit any thanks from you, O how you ought to thank your heavenly King!

20 I say unto you, my brethren, that if you should render all the thanks and praise which your whole soul has power to possess, to that God who has created you, and has kept and preserved you, and has caused that ye should rejoice, and has granted that ye should live in peace one with another—

21 I say unto you that if ye should serve him who has created you from the beginning, and is preserving you from day to day, by lending you breath, that ye may live and move and do according to your own will, and even supporting you from one moment to another—I say, if ye should serve him with all your whole souls yet ye would be unprofitable servants.

22 And behold, all that he requires of you is to keep his commandments; and he has promised you that if ye would keep his commandments ye should prosper in the land; and he never doth vary from that which he hath said; therefore, if ye do keep his commandments he doth bless you and prosper you.

Abinadi: "Death Is Swallowed Up in Christ " (Mosiah 16:7–15)

7 And if Christ had not risen from the dead, or have broken the bands of death that the grave should have no victory, and that death should have no sting, there could have been no resurrection.

8 But there is a resurrection, therefore the grave hath no victory, and the sting of death is swallowed up in Christ.

9 He is the light and the life of the world; yea, a light that is endless, that can never be darkened; yea, and also a life which is endless, that there can be no more death.

10 Even this mortal shall put on immortality, and this corruption shall put on incorruption, and shall be brought to stand before the bar of God, to be judged of him according to their works whether they be good or whether they be evil—

11 If they be good, to the resurrection of endless life and happiness; and if they be evil, to the resurrection of endless damnation, being delivered up to the devil, who hath subjected them, which is damnation—

12 Having gone according to their own carnal wills and desires; having never called upon the Lord while the arms of mercy were extended towards them; for the arms of mercy were extended towards them, and they would not; they being warned of their iniquities and yet they would not depart from them; and they were commanded to repent and yet they would not repent.

13 And now, ought ye not to tremble and repent of your sins, and remember that only in and through Christ ye can be saved?

14 Therefore, if ye teach the law of Moses, also teach that it is a shadow of those things which are to come—

15 Teach them that redemption cometh through Christ the Lord, who is the very Eternal Father. Amen.

Alma: "His Image in Your Countenance" (Alma 5:14–19)

14 And now behold, I ask of you, my brethren of the church, have ye spiritually been born of God? Have ye received his image in your countenances? Have ye experienced this mighty change in your hearts?

15 Do ye exercise faith in the redemption of him who created you? Do you look forward with an eye of faith, and view this mortal body raised in immortality, and this corruption raised in incorruption, to stand before God to be judged according to the deeds which have been done in the mortal body?

16 I say unto you, can you imagine to yourselves that ye hear the voice of the Lord, saying unto you, in that day: Come unto me ye blessed, for behold, your works have been the works of righteousness upon the face of the earth?

17 Or do ye imagine to yourselves that ye can lie unto the Lord in that day, and say—Lord, our works have been righteous works upon the face of the earth—and that he will save you?

18 Or otherwise, can ye imagine yourselves brought before the tribunal of God with your souls filled with guilt and remorse, having a remembrance of all your guilt, yea, a perfect remembrance of all your wickedness, yea, a remembrance that ye have set at defiance the commandments of God?

19 I say unto you, can ye look up to God at that day with a pure heart and clean hands? I say unto you, can you look up, having the image of God engraven upon your countenances?

King Anti-Nephi-Lehi: "How Merciful Is Our God" (Alma 24:11–15)

11 And now behold, my brethren, since it has been all that we could do (as we were the most lost of all mankind) to repent of all our sins and the many murders which we have committed, and to get God to take them away from our hearts, for it was all we could do to repent sufficiently before God that he would take away our stain—

12 Now, my best beloved brethren, since God hath taken away our stains, and our swords have become bright, then let us stain our swords no more with the blood of our brethren.

13 Behold, I say unto you, Nay, let us retain our swords that they be not stained with the blood of our brethren; for perhaps, if we should stain our swords again they can no more be washed bright through the blood of the Son of our great God, which shall be shed for the atonement of our sins.

14 And the great God has had mercy on us, and made these things known unto us that we might not perish; yea, and he has made these things known unto us beforehand, because he loveth our souls as well as he loveth our children; therefore, in his mercy he doth visit us by his angels, that the plan of salvation might be made known unto us as well as unto future generations.

15 Oh, how merciful is our God! And now behold, since it has been as much as we could do to get our stains taken away from us, and our swords are made bright, let us hide them away that they may be kept bright, as a testimony to our God at the last day, or at the day that we shall be brought to stand before him to be judged, that we have not stained our swords in the blood of our brethren since he imparted his word unto us and has made us clean thereby.

Amulek: "He Shall Atone" (Alma 34:8–14)

8 And now, behold, I will testify unto you of myself that these things are true. Behold, I say unto you, that I do know that Christ shall come among the children of men, to take upon him the transgressions of his people, and that he shall atone for the sins of the world; for the Lord God hath spoken it.

9 For it is expedient that an atonement should be made; for according to the great plan of the Eternal God there must be an atonement made, or else all mankind must unavoidably perish; yea, all are hardened; yea, all are fallen and are lost, and must perish except it be through the atonement which it is expedient should be made.

10 For it is expedient that there should be a great and last sacrifice; yea, not a sacrifice of man, neither of beast, neither of any manner of fowl; for it shall not be a human sacrifice; but it must be an infinite and eternal sacrifice.

11 Now there is not any man that can sacrifice his own blood which will atone for the sins of another. Now, if a man murdereth, behold will our law, which is just, take the life of his brother? I say unto you, Nay.

12 But the law requireth the life of him who hath murdered; therefore there can be nothing which is short of an infinite atonement which will suffice for the sins of the world.

13 Therefore, it is expedient that there should be a great and last sacrifice, and then shall there be, or it is expedient there should be, a stop to the shedding of blood; then shall the law of Moses be fulfilled; yea, it shall be all fulfilled, every jot and tittle, and none shall have passed away.

14 And behold, this is the whole meaning of the law, every whit pointing to that great and last sacrifice; and that great and last sacrifice will be the Son of God, yea, infinite and eternal.

Mormon: "The Way to Judge" (Moroni 7:16–22)

16 For behold, the Spirit of Christ is given to every man, that he may know good from evil; wherefore, I show unto you the way to judge; for every thing which inviteth to do good, and to persuade to believe in Christ, is sent forth by the power and gift of Christ; wherefore ye may know with a perfect knowledge it is of God.

17 But whatsoever thing persuadeth men to do evil, and believe not in Christ, and deny him, and serve not God, then ye may know with a perfect knowledge it is of the devil; for after this manner doth the devil work, for he persuadeth no man to do good, no, not one; neither do his angels; neither do they who subject themselves unto him.

18 And now, my brethren, seeing that ye know the light by which ye may judge, which light is the light of Christ, see that ye do not judge wrongfully; for with that same judgment which ye judge ye shall also be judged.

19 Wherefore, I beseech of you, brethren, that ye should search diligently in the light of Christ that ye may know good from evil; and if ye will lay hold upon every good thing, and condemn it not, ye certainly will be a child of Christ.

20 And now, my brethren, how is it possible that ye can lay hold upon every good thing?

21 And now I come to that faith, of which I said I would speak; and I will tell you the way whereby ye may lay hold on every good thing.

22 For behold, God knowing all things, being from everlasting to everlasting, behold, he sent angels to minister unto the children of men, to make manifest concerning the coming of Christ; and in Christ there should come every good thing.

These powerful speeches by Book of Mormon prophets show the great love they had for the people. They taught and clarified doctrine so that the people might have the necessary knowledge to choose righteously, live the principles of the gospel, and come to Christ. They taught principles of basic good living, such as selecting good political leaders and making riches less important than following the prophets. And these prophets stressed the goodness of a merciful God and the infinite Atonement. Their discourses about repentance, preparing for the day of judgment, and looking to the Savior changed the lives of people then and affect all who read these words and act upon them today.

These words have changed the lives of millions worldwide. People can mock and ridicule these discourses, but it does not alter the tremendous power for good they have had upon those who have contemplated their content. Elder Bruce R. McConkie said, "What does it matter if a few barking dogs snap at the heels of the weary travelers? Or that predators claim those few who fall by the way? The caravan moves on."[5]

Lincoln's "Gettysburg Address" is widely regarded as one of the greatest speeches given in American history. There were a few barking at that speech too, but the American dream moved on. This comment was printed in the *Chicago Times* about his speech: "The cheek of every American must tingle with shame as he reads the silly, flat and dishwatery utterances of the man who has to be pointed out to intelligent foreigners as the President of the United States."[6] This remark says far more about the critic than it does about Lincoln and his speech.

Reason to Believe

Most great speakers are remembered for only one or two of their speeches, rarely ever more than that. If Joseph Smith wrote the Book of Mormon, it means he also wrote every inspiring speech included within its pages. I don't believe for a moment that a boy with no experience in public speaking could have possibly come up with these brilliant masterpieces of doctrine.

I'm convinced that the vast majority of speeches given today are nothing more than a collection of thoughts and quotes from other people with an occasional personal experience thrown in. Imagine giving an hour-long talk on a doctrinal subject where you can't quote anyone else or use any personal experiences! Just try to speak for an hour teaching a doctrinal subject with original material that leaves readers inspired and motivated. Personally, I wouldn't even attempt it. For this reason, I believe the speeches in the Book of Mormon were given by the person identified as the author to Joseph Smith. He did not write them.

Notes

1. Bruce R. McConkie, "The Purifying Power of Gethsemane," *Ensign*, May 1985, 9.
2. "The Declaration of Independence," http://www.archives.gov.
3. "Gettysburg Address," http://www.abrahamlincolnonline.org.

4. "I Have a Dream." Delivered 28 August 1963, at the Lincoln Memorial, Washington, D.C.
5. Bruce R. McConkie, "The Caravan Moves On," *Ensign*, November 1984.
6. Carl Sandburg, *Abraham Lincoln: The Prairie Years and the War Years*, (New York: Harcourt, Brace & World, 1954), 445.

Chapter 9: Jewish Customs, Language, and Traditions

"There is no point at all to the question: Who wrote the Book of Mormon? It would have been quite as impossible for the most learned man alive in 1830 to have written the book as it was for Joseph Smith. And whoever would account for the Book of Mormon by any theory suggested so far—save one—must completely rule out the first forty pages."[1]

—Hugh Nibley

An anachronism is the act of attributing a custom, event, or object to a period to which it does not really belong. Let's imagine for a moment that you are doing family history research on your father's side and find information online about a family in your direct line living in New York in 1829. The family consists of a father, mother, and six boys. Would you be surprised if the father's name was John and the six boys were named William, James, George, Thomas, Henry, and Charles? Probably not, seeing as those names are the top seven most common male names in America that year.

However, if the source listed the father's occupation in 1829 as a computer programmer, then you would know that the records were incorrect.

Popular names change over time and occupations evolve through the years. If you were doing research on your mother's side and found a family in your direct line living in Alabama in 1829, would you be surprised if you found that the name of the father was Jaxon and his six sons were named Aiden, Liam, Mason, Jayden, Ethan, or Caden? You probably would because these names do not fit well within that time period. They are some of the more popular names in recent years. As pointed out in another chapter, if the Book of Mormon is to be credible, the customs, events, names, geography, and objects must fit both the time and the place.

We have no way of knowing exactly what names were the most popular in Israel in 600 BC. We do know many names used in the Bible and names that have been found in other historical documents and artifacts from that time period. The Book of Mormon starts off in Jerusalem, so it should be expected that some of the names would fit with the Bible or records from that era. Names first mentioned in the Book of Mormon are Lehi, Sariah, Laman, Lemuel, Sam, Nephi, Laban, Zoram, Ishmael, Jacob, and Joseph. Do these names fit the time and place? If not, then Joseph Smith would be a fraud. Of course, if they do fit, then critics could argue that he plagiarized them.

According to Paul Y. Hoskisson, there are 337 proper names in the Book of Mormon and 188 are original to the Book of Mormon.[2] The majority of these names would not have been available to Joseph from any 1829 source. However, since that time, there have been multiple discoveries of ancient documents and artifacts that include unusual Book of Mormon names. An exciting new website[3] reveals the latest research on Book of Mormon names. It provides powerful evidence that Joseph Smith could not have made up the names included. Let's look at the first eleven individuals mentioned in the book to see if the names fit ancient Israel in 600 BC.

- *Lehi:* "Then the Philistines went up, and pitched in Judah, and spread themselves in Lehi" (Judges 15:9).
- *Sariah:* "Sariah, written either with an A or an E, is attested as a man's name, and not as a woman's name in the Bible. However, it does appear in the Elephantine papyri as a Hebrew woman's name, not as an Aramaic name but as a Hebrew name for a woman and we note the interchangeability of men's and women's name in Hebrew."[4]
- *Laman:* "Laman is primarily used in Arabic and English, and it is of Arabic origin."[5]
- *Lemuel:* "The words of king Lemuel, the prophecy that his mother taught him" (Proverbs 31:1).

- *Sam:* "The name Sam is attested on a bronze ring mounted seal dated to the seventh century BC"[6]
- *Nephi:* "And Neemias called this thing Naphthar, which is as much as to say, a cleansing: but many men call it Nephi" (2 Maccabees 1:36 [the Apocrypha]).
- *Laban:* "And Rebekah had a brother, and his name was Laban: and Laban ran out unto the man, unto the well" (Genesis 24:29).
- *Zoram:* "While the name Zoram is not mentioned in the Bible or any documents or artifacts discovered in recent years, there are some interesting possibilities about its origins."[7]
- *Ishmael:* "And Hagar bare Abram a son: and Abram called his son's name, which Hagar bare, Ishmael" (Genesis 16:15).
- *Jacob:* "And he set three days' journey betwixt himself and Jacob: and Jacob fed the rest of Laban's flocks" (Genesis 30:36).
- *Joseph:* "And when Joseph's brethren saw that their father was dead, they said, Joseph will peradventure hate us, and will certainly requite us all the evil which we did unto him" (Genesis 50:15).

Researchers have pointed out that "in addition to Alma and Sariah, a number of other Nephite names are attested in ancient Hebrew inscriptions. These include Aha, Ammonihah, Chemish, Hagoth, Himni, Isabel, Jarom, Josh, Luram, Mathoni, Mathonihah, Muloki, and Sam, none of which appear in English Bibles."[8] How could Joseph Smith have possibly guessed that these names would be discovered long after the Book of Mormon was in print?

The Bible certainly backs up the names that are used in the Book of Mormon. In addition, the Bible also backs up language usage—based on cultural practices—found in the Book of Mormon.

For example, there are many different traditions related to marriage language in various cultures and countries around the world. Many are vastly different from the ones associated with wedding traditions in America. Did brides in ancient Israel have elaborate white wedding gowns, bridesmaids in matching dresses, wedding showers, beautiful wedding cakes, bouquets to toss to the unmarried women in attendance, rice thrown, or honeymoons? Probably not. Americans also use certain language when discussing marriage. Would you think it unusual to hear phrases like, "How did he propose to you?" or "Where are you going on your honeymoon?" or "What are your wedding colors?" I heard many trite phrases like these in my years working with college-age LDS students.

Never once, however, have I heard anyone use a phrase like, "Did you hear that John Evans *had taken to wife* the daughter of Bishop Jones?" That would surely be an anachronism, not fitting either time or place. And yet the short phrase *had taken to wife* is found in both the Bible and the Book of Mormon:

"And his house where he dwelt had another court within the porch, which was of the like work. Solomon made also an house for Pharaoh's daughter, whom he *had taken to wife*, like unto this porch" (1 Kings 7:8; emphasis added).

"And it came to pass that those who were the children of Amulon and his brethren, who *had taken to wife* the daughters of the Lamanites" (Mosiah 25:12; emphasis added).

It is worth noting that the phrase *had taken to wife* is only used one time in the entire Bible and one time in the Book of Mormon. Critics would have you believe that Joseph Smith was writing the Book of Mormon and creating thousands of original phrases only to be out of ideas when he was speaking of the wicked priests of King Noah. So he searched through the entire Bible to find the one phrase in 1 Kings that seemed to be just what he needed and included it in his narrative.

There are multiple times when the Book of Mormon serves as a second witness to events mentioned in the Bible. For example, before Moses led the children of Israel out of Egyptian slavery, they witnessed a great miracle during the Passover. Recall that the Lord inflicted ten plagues on the Egyptians to convince Pharaoh to free the Hebrew slaves. It wasn't until the tenth plague, the death of the Egyptian firstborn children, that Pharaoh agreed to let them go. To save their firstborn, the Israelites were instructed to mark the doorposts of their homes with the blood of a lamb so these homes would be passed over. The children in those marked homes lived.

After being freed, the Israelites saw several more miracles, including passing through the Red Sea on dry ground while the pursuing armies of Pharaoh were swallowed up in the sea. They were also miraculously fed with manna and quail.

Despite obvious signs that the Lord was with them, the children of Israel murmured incessantly and rebelled against Moses. One such incident happened in a place called Meribah. While scholars have not identified its modern location, it was definitely in a hot and dry area. It was here that the Lord tested the faith of the Israelites with lack of drinking water. They responded to that test by saying, "Wherefore is this that thou hast brought us up out of Egypt, to kill us and our children and our cattle with thirst?" (Exodus 17:3.)

In prayer, Moses turned to the Lord and asked, "What shall I do unto this people? they be almost ready to stone me" (Exodus 17:4). He received this answer from the Lord: "Behold, I will stand before thee there upon the rock in Horeb; and thou shalt smite the rock, and there shall come water out of it, that the people may drink. And Moses did so in the sight of the elders of Israel. And he called the name of the place Massah, and Meribah" (Exodus 17:6–7). The book of Psalms refers to this incident as the Provocation.

Psalms 95 (emphasis added)

7 For he is our God; and we are the people of his pasture, and the sheep of his hand. To day if ye will *hear his voice,*

8 *Harden not your heart, as in the provocation, and as in the day of temptation in the wilderness.*

Now, look how effortlessly Jacob ties this incident to the work he is doing in trying to persuade his people to come unto Christ. It is almost as if he has read about the experience in the wilderness from the brass plates.

Jacob 1 (emphasis added)

7 Wherefore we labored diligently among our people, that we might persuade them to come unto Christ, and partake of the goodness of God, that they might enter into his rest, lest by any means he should swear in his wrath they should not enter in, *as in the provocation in the days of temptation while the children of Israel were in the wilderness.*

One critic wrote that the Book of Mormon was supposedly about devout Jews but there was little evidence of the people living the Mosaic law. It is interesting to note that the Old Testament only mentions the law of Moses fourteen times while the Book of Mormon mentions it thirty-three times. While the book of Joshua tells how the law of Moses was recorded, the Book of Mormon gives a description of its purpose.

Joshua 8 (emphasis added)

32 And he wrote there upon the stones a copy of the *law of Moses*, which he wrote in the presence of the children of Israel.

Alma 25 (emphasis added)

15 Yea, and they did keep *the law of Moses*; for it was expedient that they should keep *the law of Moses* as yet, for it was not all fulfilled. But notwithstanding *the law of Moses*, they did look forward to the coming of Christ, considering that *the law of Moses* was a type of his coming, and believing that they must keep those outward performances until the time that he should be revealed unto them.

16 Now they did not suppose that salvation came by *the law of Moses*; but *the law of Moses* did serve to strengthen their faith in Christ; and thus they did retain a hope through faith, unto eternal salvation, relying upon the spirit of prophecy, which spake of those things to come.

The following are examples of the people of the Old Testament and the people of the Book of Mormon offering sacrifices and burnt offerings. Notice that both records use the exact same phrases to describe the practice.

Exodus 10 (emphasis added)

25 And Moses said, Thou must give us also *sacrifices and burnt offerings*, that we may sacrifice unto the Lord our God.

Mosiah 2 (emphasis added)

3 And they also took of the firstlings of their flocks, that they might *offer sacrifice and burnt offerings* according to the law of Moses.

In biblical times, altars were built to offer sacrifices and remember a sacred occurrence that happened at a specific location. Altars also symbolized a place of worship where a person could communicate with the Lord and remember His covenants. If I were to refer to an altar that was made of stone, I would never say "an altar of stones." However, that is how an Old Testament writer referred to it. The exact phrase is also used in the Book of Mormon.

Deuteronomy 27 (emphasis added)

5 And there shalt thou build an altar unto the Lord thy God, *an altar of stones*: thou shalt not lift up any iron tool upon them.

1 Nephi 2 (emphasis added)

7 And it came to pass that he built *an altar of stones*, and made an offering unto the Lord, and gave thanks unto the Lord our God.

The Book of Mormon uses some of the exact phrases that appear in the Bible. If both are inspired ancient records, you would expect that to be the case. Surely it would be a legitimate reason to question the validity of a document that claimed to be ancient scripture if that were not the case. Both books also contain instances when the Lord communicated directly with a prophet and declared His identity. The following are examples of the Lord speaking:

Exodus 29 (emphasis added)

46 *And they shall know that I am the Lord their God*, that brought them forth out of the land of Egypt, that I may dwell among them: *I am the Lord their God.*

Mosiah 26 (emphasis added)

26 *And then shall they know that I am the Lord their God*, that I am their Redeemer; but they would not be redeemed.

Both the Bible and the Book of Mormon refer to assorted weapons used during the various time periods that their records cover. One of the most commonly used weapons in ancient times was a sword. Both records describe how people died from swords in ways that likely seem foreign in our day.

Ezekiel 35 (emphasis added)

8 And I will fill his mountains with his slain men: in thy hills, and in thy valleys, and in all thy rivers, shall they fall that are *slain with the sword.*

Alma 3 (emphasis added)

2 Now many women and children had been *slain with the sword*, and also many of their flocks and their herds; and also many of their fields of grain were destroyed, for they were trodden down by the hosts of men.

For years, critics of the Book of Mormon have pointed out that the mention of Nephi having a bow of steel is an anachronism. It is believed that carbonized steel was not in existence then. Obviously, Nephi is not referring to the modern steel we know. If the Book of Mormon has it wrong, then the Bible has the same problem as "bow of steel" is mentioned three different times (2 Samuel 22:35, Job 20:24, and Psalm 18:34) in records that pre-dated Nephi's broken bow by hundreds of years.

2 Samuel 22 (emphasis added)

35 He teacheth my hands to war; so that a *bow of steel* is broken by mine arms.

1 Nephi 16 (emphasis added)

18 And it came to pass that as I, Nephi, went forth to slay food, behold, I did break my *bow*, which was made *of* fine *steel*; and after I did break my bow, behold, my brethren were angry with me because of the loss of my bow, for we did obtain no food.

Americans often say "I promise you" or "I swear to you" if we want someone to believe that we are telling the truth. In the past, children said "I cross my heart, hope to die, stick a needle in my eye" to indicate they were not lying. The president of the United States is required by the Constitution to take an oath to preserve, protect, and defend it. Several presidents have raised their right hand to the square with their left hand on a Bible while taking the oath. All of these show affirmation to the person's honesty or commitment to follow through.

In the ancient Jewish culture, the phrase *as the Lord liveth* was used when making a sacred oath. It is used in the Bible and also in the Book of Mormon. That would be expected if the latter is an actual record of a people who came out of Jerusalem.

2 Kings 4 (emphasis added)

30 And the mother of the child said, *As the Lord liveth*, and as thy soul liveth, I will not leave thee. And he arose, and followed her.

1 Nephi 3 (emphasis added)

15 But behold I said unto them that: *As the Lord liveth*, and as we live, we will not go down unto our father in the wilderness until we have accomplished the thing which the Lord hath commanded us.

Critics have long contended that Joseph Smith's claim of translating records from metal plates was completely implausible. If he wrote the Book of Mormon, why would he claim to have translated it from metal plates when it sounded so absurd? Hugh Nibley said, "It will not be long before men forget that in Joseph Smith's day the prophet was mocked and derided for his description of the plates more than anything else."[9] We now know that writing upon metal plates was a common practice in Mesopotamia and the lands of the Mediterranean. Perhaps if people read the Bible more closely, they would see it was not as implausible as they thought it was.

1 Kings 7 (emphasis added)

30 And every base had four brasen wheels, and *plates of brass*: and the four corners thereof had undersetters: under the laver were undersetters molten, at the side of every addition.

1 Nephi 3 (emphasis added)

3 For behold, Laban hath the record of the Jews and also a genealogy of my forefathers, and they are engraven upon *plates of brass*.

If anyone wanted to plagiarize the phrase *plates of brass* from the Bible, they would have to look really closely because it is only used one time in the entire Old Testament.

The Red Sea is mentioned twenty-six times in the Old Testament, two times in the New Testament, and eleven times in the Book of Mormon. However, there is a phrase in 1 Kings that is only mentioned once, and the exact phrase is also found once in the Book of Mormon. While no one is certain as to who wrote 1 Kings, traditional Jewish scholarship has identified the prophet Jeremiah as the writer or compiler. If so, it is worth noting that he was a contemporary of Lehi.

1 Kings 9 (emphasis added)

26 And king Solomon made a navy of ships in Ezion-geber, which is beside Eloth, on *the shore of the Red sea*, in the land of Edom.

1 Nephi 2 (emphasis added)

5 And he came down by the borders near *the shore of the Red Sea*; and he traveled in the wilderness in the borders which are nearer the Red Sea; and he did travel in the wilderness with his family, which consisted of my mother, Sariah, and my elder brothers, who were Laman, Lemuel, and Sam.

In addition to specific language that is exact and confirmatory, a number of significant events also appear in both the Bible and the Book of Mormon. Prophets and other leaders in the Book of Mormon frequently used events that are found in the Bible to teach doctrine and principles.

One such event was the fiery serpent that Moses raised in the wilderness. It required a simple act of faith for his followers to look at it in order to be healed. Alma used this event, with which the people were probably familiar, to teach that the fiery serpent was a type—or symbol—of the Savior who was yet to come.

Numbers 21 (emphasis added)

8 And the Lord said unto Moses, Make thee a fiery serpent, and set it upon a pole: and it shall come to pass, that every one that is bitten, when he looketh upon it, shall live.

9 And Moses made a serpent of brass, and put it upon a pole, and it came to pass, that if a serpent had bitten any man, when he beheld the serpent of brass, he lived.

Alma 33 (emphasis added)

19 Behold, he was spoken of by Moses; yea, and behold a type was raised up in the wilderness, that whosoever would look upon it might live. And many did look and live.

20 But few understood the meaning of those things, and this because of the hardness of their hearts. But there were many who were so hardened that they would not look, therefore they perished. Now the reason they would not look is because they did not believe that it would heal them.

Joseph's coat of many colors was famous far beyond his family, or the Bible. Even the Nephite prophets and their followers knew of the circumstances surrounding that piece of clothing. Captain Moroni in the Book of Mormon summarized this well-known event and then infused it with doctrinal meaning, personal connections for his followers, and powerful motivation for action.

Genesis 37 (emphasis added)

32 And they sent the coat of many colours, and they brought it to their father; and said, This have we found: know now whether it be thy son's coat or no.

33 And he knew it, and said, It is my son's *coat*; an evil beast hath devoured him; *Joseph* is without doubt *rent* in *pieces*.

34 And Jacob rent his clothes, and put sackcloth upon his loins, and mourned for his son many days.

Alma 46 (emphasis added)

23 Moroni said unto them: Behold, we are a remnant of the seed of Jacob; yea, we are a remnant of the seed of *Joseph*, whose *coat* was *rent* by his brethren into many *pieces*; yea, and now behold, let us remember to keep the commandments of God, or our garments shall be rent by our brethren, and we be cast into prison, or be sold, or be slain.

Book of Mormon prophets knew Jewish language, customs, and history, frequently making it part of their own teachings and writings. Because the people they taught also were aware of many of these notable events, they could understand doctrine and principles more clearly and deeply when the prophets used these examples to teach and testify.

Reason to Believe

The Book of Mormon is known as another testament of Jesus Christ. It is that, but it is also another witness of the Bible in general and supports many of the major stories and teachings contained within. Taken alone, it may not be highly significant that a phrase or event mentioned once in the Bible is also found in the Book of Mormon. However, when they fit time and place and consistently back up Jewish customs, language, and traditions, it becomes extremely significant. It would seem that it would take a highly trained scholar to write a book that so perfectly complements the Bible. Joseph Smith was not, so what he did was translate the words of the Book of Mormon prophets and thereby produced another witness for the Bible.

Notes

1. Hugh Nibley, *Lehi in the Desert; the World of the Jaredites; There Were Jaredites,* John W. Welch, Darrell L. Matthew, Stephen R. Callister, eds., (Salt Lake City, Utah: Deseret Book, 1988), 139.
2. See *Encyclopedia of Mormonism*, Daniel H. Ludlow, ed., (New York: Macmillan, 1992), 186–87.
3. See onoma.lib.byu.
4. Stephen Ricks, "Origin of Book of Mormon Names," 2010 Fair Conference, (Sandy, Utah: August 5, 2010).
5. "Laman," www.babynamespedia.com.
6. John Tvedtnes, John Gee, and Matthew Roper, "Book of Mormon Names Attested in Ancient Hebrew Inscriptions," *Journal of Book of Mormon Studies*, vol. 9, no. 1, 2000, 42–51.
7. See onoma.lib.byu to read the latest research.
8. John Tvedtnes, John Gee, Matthew Roper, "Book of Mormon Names Attested in Ancient Hebrew Inscriptions," 40–51, 78–79.
9. Hugh Nibley, *Lehi in the Desert; the World of the Jaredites; There Were Jaredites,* John W. Welch, Darrell L. Matthew, Stephen R. Callister, eds. (Salt Lake City, Utah: Deseret Book, 1988), 107.

Chapter 10: A Second Witness to the Bible

"[One of the] most devastating argument[s] against the Book of Mormon was that it actually quoted the Bible. The early critics were simply staggered by the incredible stupidity of including large sections of the Bible in a book which they insisted was specifically designed to fool the Bible-reading public. They screamed blasphemy and plagiarism at the top of their lungs, but today any biblical scholar knows that it would be extremely suspicious if a book purporting to be the product of a society of pious emigrants from Jerusalem in ancient times did not quote the Bible. No lengthy religious writing of the Hebrews could conceivably be genuine if it was not full of scriptural quotations."[1]

—Hugh Nibley

One of my favorite historical books is *The History of Joseph Smith by His Mother*. I love the insights Lucy Mack Smith provides about her son. She tells readers that after Moroni appeared to Joseph and told him of the special mission the Lord had for him, life began to change for the entire family. She said,

> From this time forth, Joseph continued to receive instructions from the Lord, and we continued to get the children together every evening for the purpose of listening while he gave us a relation of the same. I presume our family presented an aspect as singular as any that ever lived upon the face of the earth—all seated in a circle, father, mother, sons and daughters, and giving the most profound attention to a boy, eighteen years of age, who had never read the Bible through in his life: he seemed much less inclined to the perusal of books than any of the rest of our children, but far more given to meditation and deep study.[2]

I find it interesting that Joseph Smith was not inclined to reading and that he had never even finished the Bible all the way through. That seems highly significant when you realize how integrated the Book of Mormon and the Bible are. There is no doubt that those actually writing the words found in the Book of Mormon were extremely familiar with the Bible. While critics are quick to point out the direct quotes used from prophets like Isaiah, they usually fail to notice how these verses are used. Like good researchers of our day, the Book of Mormon writers used the Bible verses in their writing that entirely backed up the lesson they wanted to teach their readers. These are not random verses being used, but words that perfectly supplement the points being made.

You would have needed extensive knowledge of the Bible to know where to locate content to fit the message you want to convey. As a Bible collector myself, I have owned multiple Bibles from the time period in which Joseph lived, including several published in the 1820s by the H. & E. Phinney Co. I will point out that these Bibles did not have the study guides available today. If someone wanted to use specific verses to make a point, he or she would need to either know beforehand exactly where to find the verses or try to look through the 1,184 pages within to find one that taught the point required. How is it possible that Joseph Smith became this amazing biblical scholar, while his own mother said he wasn't much of a reader?

Not only do the Book of Mormon writers quote biblical writers directly, but they were also clearly well versed in the overall messages previous prophets taught. I remember one night a few years ago when I was out of town and was staying in a hotel. I had plenty of time and nowhere to be. I opened the Book of Mormon and began to look at the footnotes at the bottom of the pages that linked to the Old Testament. I was amazed at how perfectly the two books matched up. In the twenty verses contained in 1 Nephi 1, for example, there are thirty-nine Old Testament verses correlated to them. These are not direct quotes but verses that teach the same message. Below are the Old Testament verses that coincide with the first chapter of 1 Nephi.

Proverbs 22:1	2 Kings 24:18	2 Chronicles 36:19
Jeremiah 37:1	Jeremiah 44:30	Jeremiah 49:34
Jeremiah 52:3	1 Chronicles 9:3	2 Chronicles 15:9

2 Kings 17:13	2 Chronicles 36:15	Jeremiah 7:25
Jeremiah 26:20	Jeremiah 26:18	Jeremiah 29:13
Exodus 14:24	Isaiah 6:5	Daniel 8:27
Daniel 10:8	Ezekiel 1:1	1 Samuel 3:10
Ezekiel 2:9	Genesis 41:38	2 Kings 24:19
2 Chronicles 36:14	Jeremiah 13:27	2 Kings 23:27
2 Kings 24:2	Jeremiah 13:14	Ezekiel 15:6
2 Kings 20:17	Jeremiah 52:15	Ezekiel 1:1
2 Chronicles 36:16	Jeremiah 25:4	Ezekiel 5:6
Jeremiah 13:11	Jeremiah 11:19	Genesis 32:10

Think what would have been required for Joseph Smith or anyone else to write the Book of Mormon. You would have to know that, for the story to begin in Jerusalem in 600 BC, Jeremiah was a prophet at that time and that Zedekiah was the king. In Jeremiah 34:6, we read, "Then Jeremiah the prophet spake all these words unto Zedekiah king of Judah in Jerusalem." According to most Bible scholars, Jeremiah was born about 650 BC and lived to about 570 BC. That would make him a prophet when the Book of Mormon says Lehi was a prophet in Jerusalem.

Isn't it interesting that Jeremiah is traditionally credited with authoring the books of Jeremiah, 1 Kings, and 2 Kings? Consider the fact that Daniel and Ezekiel were also contemporaries of Jeremiah. Again, look at the verses above that are linked to 1 Nephi and see where the majority of the verses are from.

If Joseph Smith wrote the Book of Mormon, then his first chapter coincides perfectly with thirty-nine different Old Testament verses. Not only that, but the majority of the verses that match were written by prophets who preached in Jerusalem at the same time Lehi and his family lived there. It is unlikely that Joseph Smith was such a biblical scholar, as previously established. As I look at the footnotes at the bottom of each page of our modern editions of the Book of Mormon, I often think of this scripture: "Say unto them, Thus saith the Lord God; Behold, I will take *the stick of Joseph*, which *is* in the hand of Ephraim, and the tribes of Israel his fellows, and will put them with him, even with *the stick of Judah*, and make them one stick, and they shall be one in mine hand" (Ezekiel 37:19). How fitting that this statement was made by Ezekiel, a contemporary of Lehi, and possibly a friend.

It is fascinating to see how the Bible and the Book of Mormon are one in so many ways. Consider this simple example. In school, I was taught never to start a sentence with a conjunction. If we used words like *and, but,* or *or* at the beginning of a sentence, we were told to correct this mistake. In graduate school, the same seemed to apply when writing articles in academic journals or dissertations. Even now, I think it feels awkward to start a sentence with a conjunction.

Obviously, those translating the King James Version of the Bible did not follow the same rule. From the first hundred verses of the Old Testament, which we are told were written by Moses, seventy-nine begin with the word *and.* If the Book of Mormon story begins in Jerusalem, it should follow a similar pattern. Of the first hundred verses of Book of Mormon, seventy-four begin with the word *and.* Do those who believe that Joseph Smith wrote the Book of Mormon really believe that he counted the Old Testament sentences to match the percentages almost exactly? And yet in the seventy-five verses of the Joseph Smith—History in the Pearl of Great Price, only one verse begins with the word *and.*

While remembering to start about seventy-four percent of your sentences with the word *and* may not be overwhelming evidence that the Book of Mormon is a true record, surely the way the teachings of both books match up is convincing evidence. President John Taylor made this interesting point: "The gospel in the Book of Mormon and the gospel in the Bible both agree: The doctrines in both books are one."[3] And while critics cry plagiarism, Hugh Nibley pointed out that biblical teachings must be present in the book to be believable.[4]

While it would be difficult for a writer to find large or small passages of the Bible to fit a narrative, finding phrases to use in actual sentences would be infinitely more difficult. The following are some of the exact phrases found in the Bible that are also found in the Book of Mormon. Depending on how readers choose to look at the examples, it is either evidence of plagiarism or evidence that the Nephites did come out of Jerusalem and recorded a history of their people. Remember, however, that it is believed over ninety percent of the short phrases in the Book of Mormon are original.

Let's consider a few of the many phrases that are used in both books. Remember that if Joseph Smith wrote the Book of Mormon, it also means that he was able to invent thousands and thousands of original short phrases. Critics would have us believe that when he got stumped he would have gone searching through the Bible, looking for just the right phrase to use. Notice that in most cases the phrases in the Bible are not used in exactly the same way that they are in the Book of Mormon.

"the land of his nativity"

Genesis 11:28 (emphasis added): "And Haran died before his father Terah in *the land of his nativity*, in Ur of the Chaldees."

Helaman 7:3 (emphasis added): "And they did reject all his words, insomuch that he could not stay among them, but returned again unto *the land of his nativity*."

"a rod of iron"

Psalm 2:9 (emphasis added): "Thou shalt break them with *a rod of iron*; thou shalt dash them in pieces like a potter's vessel."

1 Nephi 8:19 (emphasis added): "And I beheld *a rod of iron*, and it extended along the bank of the river, and led to the tree by which I stood."

"ornaments of gold"

2 Samuel 1:24 (emphasis added): "Ye daughters of Israel, weep over Saul, who clothed you in scarlet, with other delights, who put on *ornaments of gold* upon your apparel."

Alma 31:28 (emphasis added): "Behold, O my God, their costly apparel, and their ringlets, and their bracelets, and their *ornaments of gold*, and all their precious things which they are ornamented with."

"because that ye have"

Numbers 11:20 (emphasis added): "But even a whole month, until it come out at your nostrils, and it be loathsome unto you: *because that ye have* despised the Lord which is among you, and have wept before him, saying, Why came we forth out of Egypt?"

2 Nephi 29:10 (emphasis added): "Wherefore, *because that ye have* a Bible ye need not suppose that it contains all my words; neither need ye suppose that I have not caused more to be written."

"after that ye were"

Deuteronomy 24:9 (emphasis added): "Remember what the Lord thy God did unto Miriam by the way, *after that ye were* come forth out of Egypt."

3 Nephi 20:27 (emphasis added): "And *after that ye were* blessed then fulfilleth the Father the covenant which he made with Abraham, saying: In thy seed shall all the kindreds of the earth be blessed."

"I and my brethren"

Nehemiah 5:14 (emphasis added): "Moreover from the time that I was appointed to be their governor in the land of Judah, from the twentieth year even unto the two and thirtieth year of Artaxerxes the king, that is, twelve years, *I and my brethren* have not eaten the bread of the governor."

1 Nephi 3:10 (emphasis added): "And it came to pass that when we had gone up to the land of Jerusalem, *I and my brethren* did consult one with another."

"and he called their names"

Genesis 26:18 (emphasis added): "And Isaac digged again the wells of water, which they had digged in the days of Abraham his father; for the Philistines had stopped them after the death of Abraham: *and he called their names* after the names by which his father had called them."

Mosiah 1:2 (emphasis added): "And it came to pass that he had three sons; *and he called their names* Mosiah, and Helorum, and Helaman."

"according to the generations"

1 Chronicles 26:31 (emphasis added): "Among the Hebronites was Jerijah the chief, even among the Hebronites, *according to the generations* of his fathers."

Omni 1:11 (emphasis added): "And behold, the record of this people is engraven upon plates which is had by the kings, *according to the generations*."

"not hearken unto my words"

Deuteronomy 18:19 (emphasis added): "And it shall come to pass, that whosoever will *not hearken unto my words* which he shall speak in my name, I will require it of him."

1 Nephi 2:18 (emphasis added): "But, behold, Laman and Lemuel would *not hearken unto my words*; and being grieved because of the hardness of their hearts I cried unto the Lord for them."

"the kings of the isles"

Jeremiah 25:22 (emphasis added): "And all the kings of Tyrus, and all the kings of Zidon, and *the kings of the isles* which are beyond the sea."

1 Nephi 19:12 (emphasis added): "And all these things must surely come, saith the prophet Zenos. And the rocks of the earth must rend; and because of the groanings of the earth, many of *the kings of the isles*

of the sea shall be wrought upon by the Spirit of God, to exclaim: The God of nature suffers."

"I go the way of all the earth"

1 Kings 2:2 (emphasis added): "*I go the way of all the earth*: be thou strong therefore, and shew thyself a man."

2 Nephi 1:14 (emphasis added): "Awake! and arise from the dust, and hear the words of a trembling parent, whose limbs ye must soon lay down in the cold and silent grave, from whence no traveler can return; a few more days and *I go the way of all the earth*."

"spoken by the mouth of Jeremiah"

2 Chronicles 36:22 (emphasis added): "Now in the first year of Cyrus king of Persia, that the word of the Lord *spoken by the mouth of Jeremiah* might be accomplished, the Lord stirred up the spirit of Cyrus king of Persia, that he made a proclamation throughout all his kingdom, and put it also in writing."

1 Nephi 5:13 (emphasis added): "And also the prophecies of the holy prophets, from the beginning, even down to the commencement of the reign of Zedekiah; and also many prophecies which have been *spoken by the mouth of Jeremiah*."

"dwelling in tents"

Genesis 25:27 (emphasis added): "And the boys grew: and Esau was a cunning hunter, a man of the field; and Jacob was a plain man, *dwelling in tents*."

Enos 1:20 (emphasis added): "And I bear record that the people of Nephi did seek diligently to restore the Lamanites unto the true faith in God. But our labors were vain; their hatred was fixed, and they were led by their evil nature that they became wild, and ferocious, and a blood-thirsty people, full of idolatry and filthiness; feeding upon beasts of prey; *dwelling in tents*."

"I have dreamed a dream"

Genesis 37:9 (emphasis added): "And he dreamed yet another dream, and told it his brethren, and said, Behold, *I have dreamed a dream* more; and, behold, the sun and the moon and the eleven stars made obeisance to me."

1 Nephi 8:2 (emphasis added): "And it came to pass that while my father tarried in the wilderness he spake unto us, saying: Behold, *I have dreamed a dream*; or, in other words, I have seen a vision."

"the lot fell upon"

Jonah 1:7 (emphasis added): "And they said every one to his fellow, Come, and let us *cast lots*, that we may know for whose cause this evil is upon us. So they cast lots, and *the lot fell upon* Jonah."

1 Nephi 3:11 (emphasis added): "And we *cast lots*—who of us should go in unto the house of Laban. And it came to pass that *the lot fell upon* Laman."

"ye are a stiffnecked people"

Exodus 33:5 (emphasis added): "For the Lord had said unto Moses, Say unto the children of Israel, *Ye are a stiffnecked people*: I will come up into the midst of thee in a moment, and consume thee: therefore now put off thy ornaments from thee, that I may know what to do unto thee."

2 Nephi 25:28 (emphasis added): "And now behold, my people, *ye are a stiffnecked people*; wherefore, I have spoken plainly unto you, that ye cannot misunderstand."

"while the children of Israel were in the wilderness"

Numbers 15:32 (emphasis added): "And *while the children of Israel were in the wilderness*, they found a man that gathered sticks upon the sabbath day."

Jacob 1:7 (emphasis added): "Wherefore we labored diligently among our people, that we might persuade them to come unto Christ, and partake of the goodness of God, that they might enter into his rest, lest by any means he should swear in his wrath they should not enter in, as in the provocation in the days of temptation *while the children of Israel were in the wilderness*."

"give ear to my words"

Psalm 5:1 (emphasis added): "*Give ear to my words*, O Lord, consider my meditation."

Alma 36:1 (emphasis added): "My son, *give ear to my words*; for I swear unto you, that inasmuch as ye shall keep the commandments of God ye shall prosper in the land."

"to provoke him to anger"

2 Kings 17:17 (emphasis added): "And they caused their sons and their daughters to pass through the fire, and used divination and enchantments, and sold themselves to do evil in the sight of the Lord, *to provoke him to anger*."

Jacob 1:8 (emphasis added): "Wherefore, we would to God that we could persuade all men not to rebel against God, *to provoke him to anger,* but that all men would believe in Christ, and view his death, and suffer his cross and bear the shame of the world; wherefore, I, Jacob, take it upon me to fulfil the commandment of my brother Nephi."

"by the hand of the Lord"

Exodus 16:3 (emphasis added): "And the children of Israel said unto them, Would to God we had died *by the hand of the Lord* in the land of Egypt, when we sat by the flesh pots."

2 Nephi 1:6 (emphasis added): "Wherefore, I, Lehi, prophesy according to the workings of the Spirit which is in me, that there shall none come into this land save they shall be brought *by the hand of the Lord.*"

"as in the provocation in the day of temptation in the wilderness"

Psalm 95:8 (emphasis added): "Harden not your heart, *as in the provocation,* and as *in the day of temptation in the wilderness.*"

Jacob 1:7 (emphasis added): "Wherefore we labored diligently among our people, that we might persuade them to come unto Christ, and partake of the goodness of God, that they might enter into his rest, lest by any means he should swear in his wrath they should not enter in, *as in the provocation in the days of temptation* while the children of Israel were *in the wilderness.*"

There is no question that the Book of Mormon contains multiple phrases that are also used in the Old Testament. It is hard to believe that a *modern* writer could search through the Bible looking for these phrases—that in most cases are found only one time—and then fit them perfectly into the sentence they were writing. There is no doubt that the writers of the Book of Mormon were familiar with the Old Testament, but these phrases were certainly not found among other books available in Joseph Smith's day.

If the writers were following modern referencing techniques, they would quote their sources. However, that is not how they wrote. Look closely at the two previously quoted verses and the following New Testament verse:

Hebrews 3:8 (emphasis added): "Harden not your hearts, *as in the provocation, in the day of temptation in the wilderness.*"

Here we find Paul almost directly quoting a verse found in Psalm 95:8 but giving his readers no indication that he is actually quoting from the Old Testament. Would a critic say that Paul is a plagiarizer? Of course not.

Several critics have pointed out that in some cases the Book of Mormon quotes the New Testament. They say this would be impossible because the New Testament had not yet been compiled when most of the Book of Mormon was being written. One explanation for this is that the Lord can inspire people to use the same language—a totally logical assumption. Another possibility is that Old Testament manuscripts were later altered and "many plain and most precious" teachings were taken away (see 1 Nephi 13:26).

Consider the following example where Luke, the author of the book of Acts, directly quotes from the writings of Moses. While he is possibly referring to Deuteronomy 18:15, the wording of the two verses is quite different. Here is how Luke quotes Moses:

"a prophet shall the Lord your God raise up"

Acts 3:22 (emphasis added): "For Moses truly said unto the fathers, *A prophet shall the Lord* your God raise up unto you of *your brethren, like unto me; him shall ye hear in all things whatsoever he shall say unto you.*"

And it shall come to pass, that every soul, which *will not hear that prophet, shall be* destroyed *from among the people.*"

Now consider a verse written by Nephi between 588 BC and 570 BC that uses almost the exact language that Luke uses.

1 Nephi 22:20 (emphasis added): "And the Lord will surely prepare a way for his people, unto the fulfilling of the words of *Moses*, which he spake, saying: *A prophet shall the Lord your God raise up unto you, like unto me; him shall ye hear in all things whatsoever he shall say unto you. And it shall come to pass that* all those *who will not hear that prophet shall be* cut off *from among the people.*"

This passage seems to be either clear evidence that it was plagiarized from the New Testament or that Nephi was quoting from the same source material as Luke. We do know that the brass plates contained the five books of Moses (see 1 Nephi 5:11). Apparently, both Nephi and Luke had access to the same material. We also know that both of these writers thought this verse was important enough to include in their records. Now consider a statement made by Jesus Christ over 600 years after Nephi quoted Moses.

3 Nephi 20:23 (emphasis added): "Behold, I am he of whom *Moses* spake, saying: *A prophet shall the Lord your God raise up unto you of your brethren, like unto me; him shall ye hear in all things whatsoever he shall say unto you. And it shall come to pass that every soul* who *will not hear that prophet shall be* cut off *from among the people.*"

These three verses teach valuable lessons. One lesson is that the Book of Mormon serves as a second witness to the Bible's teachings. It also restores precious truths that may have been lost or altered from the records of the Old Testament. Even more, in this case, we learn that the prophet Moses was referring to none other than Jesus Christ.

One other thing we learn is about internal consistency. On page fifty-eight of the original 1830 edition of the Book of Mormon, we find the words found in 1 Nephi 22:20 of our current edition. Then on page 497 of the original edition, we read the same words preceded with: "I am he of whom Moses spake." That means that if Joseph Smith is the author of the Book of Mormon, then he dictated the statement by Moses and then remembered 439 pages later to quote the same passage, only this time having Jesus Christ speak to fulfill the prophecy made by Moses.

Reason to Believe

Searching through the footnotes of the modern editions of the Book of Mormon, you see hundreds and hundreds of examples where the things written by its authors are in perfect harmony with the Bible. I personally have discovered many short phrases that are in both books. In many cases, they are found one time in the Bible and one time in the Book of Mormon.

I cannot bring myself to believe that Joseph Smith could create thousands of original phrases and then get stumped and resort to search through 1,184 pages of biblical text, looking for just the right phrase to use in his book. That might be reasonable to do a few times, but to match the same teachings throughout the entire book is impossible. Of course, all of this was given verbally to Oliver Cowdery without any notes or books in front of them. This amazing correspondence between the Book of Mormon and the Bible strengthens my belief.

Notes

1. "Literary Style in the Book of Mormon Ensured Accurate Translation," in *The Prophetic Book of Mormon*, of the *Collected Works of Hugh Nibley*, vol. 8 (Salt Lake City: Deseret Book, 1989), 214–18.

2. Lucy Mack Smith, *History of Joseph Smith,* ed. Preston Nibley (Salt Lake City: Bookcraft, 1958), 82–83.

3. *Journal of Discourses,* 26 vols. (Liverpool: F. D. Richards & Sons, 1851–1886), 5:240.

4. "Literary Style in the Book of Mormon Ensured Accurate Translation," in *The Prophetic Book of Mormon*, of the *Collected Works of Hugh Nibley*, vol. 8 (Salt Lake City: Deseret Book, 1989), 214–18.

Chapter 11: Ties to Ancient Jerusalem

"I cannot understand how any intelligent man could think that anyone without the help of the Lord could have produced the Book of Mormon, which has been before us now for more than a hundred years and has stood the test during all that period of time, notwithstanding the ridicule that has been brought against it, for one reason and then another. Today that book, which was translated by Joseph Smith as the instrumentality of the Lord, stands out supreme. It is today the greatest missionary that we have for proclaiming this gospel; there is nothing else to compare with it."[1]

—Heber J. Grant

Several years ago, some colleagues and I visited the famous Thomas Gilcrease Institute of American History and Art in Oklahoma. While walking through the rooms, one of my friends asked if I had seen the painting named *Custer's Demand*. When I answered that I had not, he insisted that I come with him to see it. Standing before the oil canvas painting by Charles Schreyvogel (1861–1912), I was immediately impressed.

Later, I found that Charles was born in New York City to German immigrant storekeepers and was a self-taught artist who spent most of his life improvising until he began painting western life and military subjects. These paintings brought almost overnight recognition. *Custer's Demand* was completed in 1903, depicting George Armstrong Custer and three of his officers meeting with four Kiowa Indian leaders. Custer's troops and other Indian braves are in the distance. The meeting is said to have occurred in 1869 when Charles was just eight years old. At the time he began painting, he had to create an accurate scene from an event that occurred thirty-four years earlier.

I do not know much about what good art is and what it is not, but I thought the painting was interesting. As I walked away, my friend asked if I had read the criticism displayed next to the painting by another famous western artist named Frederic Remington (1861–1909). He encouraged me to go back and read it, and I did. Later, I found out that Remington was also born in New York City and educated at Yale University. In 1881 at nineteen, he made his first trip west and witnessed some of the last major confrontations of the U.S. cavalry with Native American tribes. These were scenes he had imagined since his childhood, and they created within him a desire to paint western art. *Harper's Weekly* published his first sketches, and his work inspired many western artists who followed after him.

Remington could be highly critical of other western artists if he thought they were historically inaccurate. When the *New York Herald* ran a full-page positive review of Schreyvogel's *Custer's Demand* in 1903, Remington responded with the comments I read in Tulsa that day. He stated, "While I do not want to interfere with Mr. Schreyvogel's hallucinations, I do object to his half baked stuff being considered seriously as history."[2] He then pointed out a list of twelve things in the painting that he deemed inaccurate for the time frame of the historic meeting. His list included boots, spurs, swords, pistols, saddlebags, gloves, uniforms, scarf, hats, saddle blanket, belts and buckles, all of which he alleged were historically out of place.

Artists need to do extensive research on any subject they paint or they may be discredited. Imagine a teenage artist today trying to paint a scene from a party held in a 1980 home without doing any research. All it would take is one little mistake, such as showing two teenagers in the scene texting on an iPhone, to totally destroy the painting, as far as historical accuracy.

As I left the museum later that day, I could not stop comparing my experience there to the Book of Mormon. Just imagine trying to write a 588-page book that begins in Jerusalem in 600 BC and is printed in 1830. Every page would be like a painting, with Joseph Smith waiting for experts from multiple fields to discover any historical mistakes.

Since its release, plenty of people have stepped forward to point out how he and others wrote the book only to see their theories fade away. Through the years, critics have not even been able to agree how the book came to be. Some of the strongest criticisms have turned into the strongest evidences that this book comes from an ancient record. LDS scholar Hugh Nibley made an excellent point when he said, "The Book of Mormon is tough. It thrives on investigation. You may kick it around like a football, as many have done; and I promise you it will wear you out long before you ever make a dent in it."[3]

Any time a person writes about events that happened in the past, he sets himself up to make mistakes. William Shakespeare is often referred to as the greatest writer of the English language, but even he made mistakes in his works. His famous play *Julius Caesar* is set in Rome in the year 44 BC. BYU scholar Daniel Peterson pointed out a critical error Shakespeare made in this creation:

> "Peace!" exclaims Brutus to Cassius in Shakespeare's tragic play "Julius Caesar" (Act II, Scene ii). "Count the clock." And Cassius, obeying, replies, "The clock hath stricken three." Unfortunately, though, there were no clocks in the Rome of 44 BC when the real Brutus and his fellow plotters stabbed Caesar to death in the Roman Senate. Either through carelessness or ignorance, Shakespeare has written an anachronism, something that doesn't fit the claimed historical period of the story, into his play.[4]

For an author to attempt to write a nonfiction book involving people who populated a country from the past would take an enormous amount of research to be accurate. Any slip-ups involving customs, political systems, holidays, geography, language, or any cultural practices would be quickly exposed by experts. If words or concepts do not fit the time or place, the author loses credibility.

Writing about the past is challenging. This is especially true when writing about another culture. Every country has a history and a set of traditions uniquely its own. Many traditions have continued for so many years that no one seems to know where or when they originated. Others can be easily traced to a specific time, country, or even region. The Jewish people, for example, commemorate their liberation from slavery in ancient Egypt by celebrating the Feast of the Passover. This tradition has continued for over 3,300 years and can be traced to a single event as part of their rich history.

Few books in history have been as closely scrutinized as the Book of Mormon. Specialists from multiple disciplines have meticulously examined its pages and content, searching for reasons to either doubt its authenticity or to believe it is true. Fortunately for researchers, the story begins in Jerusalem, noted for its collections of written records of its history—a treasure that compares to perhaps no other ancient city in the world. Scholars with graduate degrees from prestigious universities comprehend a tremendous amount about the Holy Land and its ancient capital's history. If the Book of Mormon is not an ancient record, it should have easily been exposed in a short period of time. Let's consider a few examples to see how well the Book Mormon (or Joseph Smith) does.

Political Systems

The Book of Mormon story begins in 600 BC in the ancient city of Jerusalem. Right off on page one, a political leader is named. His title is King Zedekiah. To name a government leader during a specific time period is risky if you have not done some research. To put the wrong leader in the wrong era means immediate loss of credibility.

Many things have to fit in order to be believable. What was their political title? Were they referred to as commander, president, prime minister, queen, king, governor, judge, chancellor, tsar, monarch, chief executive, premier, sultan, or another title? What kind of power did they possess? Were they wicked or righteous? Who were their contemporaries?

Looking further back in history, it was Moses who led the children of Israel out of bondage in Egypt, but it was Joshua who led them in their conquest of Canaan. After the death of Joshua, the tribes of Israel were a loose confederation led in times of crisis by a series of judges. The first judge was Othniel, who helped deliver the people from the tyranny of the king of Mesopotamia. The people believed that God chose judges from the tribes of Israel. The rule of the judges lasted for many years. Samuel is sometimes referred to as the last of the judges and the first of the prophets, but Samson is usually called the last judge. This period was followed with the three kings of a united Israel.

Old Testament Judges	_Old Testament Kings_
1. Othniel	1. Saul
2. Ehud	2. David
3. Shamagar	3. Solomon
4. Deborah	
5. Gideon	
down to . . .	
12. Samson	

When Solomon died, there was contention between two of his sons and the kingdom was divided. His son Rehoboam became king over the southern kingdom, which consisted of the tribes of Judah and Benjamin and was called the kingdom of Judah. His son Jeroboam became the king of the northern kingdom, which consisted of the other ten tribes and was called Israel.

Kings of Israel (the Northern Kingdom)

1. Jeroboam: 931–910 BC
2. Nadab
down to . . .
19. Hoshea: 732–721 BC

The kingdom of Israel ended in approximately 722 BC with the fall of Samaria to Assyria. At that point, the northern tribes were scattered and became known as the lost ten tribes of Israel.

The kingdom of Judah began at the time the tribes initially split apart. Judah was ruled by kings throughout its history from Rehoboam until Zedekiah.

Kings of Judah (the Southern Kingdom)

1. Rehoboam: 931–913 BC
2. Abijah
down to . . .
42. Zedekiah: 606–586 BC

The kingdom of Judah ended in approximately 586 BC with the destruction of Jerusalem by the Babylonians.

The Reign of Zedekiah, King of Judah

The writer would also need to know how Israelites refer to the time periods their kings were in power. In America, we usually say something along the lines of "during the presidency of . . ." in reference to that time of our history. Israelites often use the phrase "the reign of . . ." in reference to the time period their kings were in power. If the Book of Mormon is a record of a group of Israelites, they would probably do the same thing, and that is exactly what they do. This example shows that parallel language:

Jeremiah 49:34 (emphasis added): "The word of the Lord that came to Jeremiah the prophet against Elam in the beginning of *the reign of Zedekiah king of Judah.*"

1 Nephi 1:4 (emphasis added): "For it came to pass in the commencement of the first year of *the reign of Zedekiah, king of Judah,* (my father, Lehi, having dwelt at Jerusalem in all his days); and in that same year there came many prophets, prophesying unto the people that they must repent, or the great city Jerusalem must be destroyed."

If Joseph Smith wrote the Book of Mormon, he would have had to know that the forty-second king of Judah (not Israel) was named Zedekiah. He would also have needed to know that he was the king in 600 BC at the time Lehi left Jerusalem.

In the two verses, both the Old Testament and the Book of Mormon use the same seven-word phrase to refer to the time Zedekiah reigned as king. The Book of Mormon used the phrase *the reign of* 116 times to refer to time periods when the people were ruled by kings and chief judges. This, however, only occurs during the first six hundred years of the record. After Christ appeared in the Americas, the phrase is never used again. Why? Because they went to a different decentralized form of government. In 3 Nephi 7:3, we read, "And every tribe did appoint a chief or a leader over them; and thus they became tribes and leaders of tribes."

Jeremiah in Prison

Nephi identifies Jeremiah as one of his father's contemporaries. Both prophets warned that Jerusalem would be destroyed if the people did not repent. Zedekiah threw Jeremiah into prison for doing so. Lehi was told by the Lord to flee.

Jeremiah 37:18 (emphasis added): "Moreover *Jeremiah* said unto king Zedekiah, What have I offended against thee, or against thy servants, or against this people, that ye have put me in *prison*?"

1 Nephi 7:18 (emphasis added): "For behold, the Spirit of the Lord ceaseth soon to strive with them; for behold, they have rejected the prophets, and *Jeremiah* have they cast into *prison*. And they have sought to take away the life of my father, insomuch that they have driven him out of the land."

Fate of Zedekiah and His Sons

The first few chapters of the Book of Mormon reveal little-known details of this part of the Old Testament story. The following is another example involving the fate of Zedekiah and his sons when Jerusalem was destroyed, just as Jeremiah and Lehi had prophesied.

2 Kings 25:7 (emphasis added): "And they *slew the sons of Zedekiah* before his eyes, and *put out the eyes of Zedekiah*, and bound him with fetters of brass, and carried him to *Babylon*."

Omni 1:15 (emphasis added): "Behold, it came to pass that Mosiah discovered that the people of Zarahemla came out from Jerusalem at the time that *Zedekiah*, king of Judah, was *carried* away captive into *Babylon*."

Escape of Mulek

The Book of Mormon record often provides extra insights that the Old Testament does not mention. For example, one of the sons of Zedekiah actually escaped the Babylonian massacre. His name was Mulek. He and a number of others also came to the Americas shortly after the families of Lehi and Ishmael. The two groups later merged together in Zarahemla. Nephi shares this insight:

Helaman 8:21 (emphasis added): "And now will you dispute that Jerusalem was destroyed? Will ye say that *the sons of Zedekiah* were not *slain*, all except it were Mulek? Yea, and do ye not behold that the seed of *Zedekiah* are with us, and they were driven out of the land of Jerusalem?"

Consider the amount of historical research required to get these little-known details straight and then dictate them verbally to Oliver Cowdery with no notes. Translation, not writing, seems more plausible.

References to Religious Leaders—the Elders

There are various unique phrases used by Church members when referring to leaders. If members want to emphasize a particular church teaching but don't know who taught it, you might hear them lump general Church leadership together, such as "The Brethren said" or "The General Authorities taught." Sometimes I have heard the general level of Church leadership reduced to "Salt Lake said that."

In Old Testament times, the elders were representatives of the people in various matters. The book of Ezra, written when the Jews returned from the Babylonian captivity, refers to these elders in a unique way. What are the chances that Joseph Smith would have picked up on this little five-word phrase that was only used three times in the entire Old Testament? The phrase is only used once in the Book of Mormon, but it is interesting that it is used at the beginning of the book while Nephi and his brothers were still in Jerusalem.

Ezra 5:5 (emphasis added): "But the eye of their God was upon *the elders of the Jews*, that they could not cause them to cease, till the matter came to Darius: and then they returned answer by letter concerning this matter."

1 Nephi 4:22 (emphasis added): "And he spake unto me concerning *the elders of the Jews*, he knowing that his master, Laban, had been out by night among them."

Reference to Jerusalem

The writers of the Old Testament and the Book of Mormon also had interesting ways of referring to places they lived. I would never say "the land of Austin" to describe the area where I currently live. However, the Book of Mormon writers use the phrase *the land of Jerusalem* forty different times. The Old Testament writers, on the other hand, never use that phrase even one time. It is totally unique to the Book of Mormon. Old Testament writers do, however, use the phrase *the land of . . .* 548 times. It is always used to refer to places like Egypt, Canaan, Goshen, Judah, and Nimrod, but never to Jerusalem.

It seems obvious that the Nephites saw Jerusalem as not just the walled city but also the area around it. They apparently viewed it in about the same way we speak of Salt Lake City. When most people say "Salt Lake," they are most likely not referring to just the city limits. Usually, they are referring to the entire valley, including West Valley City, Taylorsville, Millcreek, Kearns, Sugar House, Murray, and other suburbs. However, I have never heard anyone say "the land of Salt Lake." That seems to only be a scriptural phrase. The Nephites referred to their capital as the "city of Zarahemla" sixteen times, but they referred to the "land of Zarahemla" 102 times. Why does any of this matter?

If Nephi said his family lived in "the land of Jerusalem," does it have to mean that they lived inside the walls of the city? What if he said they lived "at Jerusalem"? In fact, he does say, "For it came to pass in the commencement of the first year of the reign of Zedekiah, king of Judah, (my father, Lehi, having dwelt *at Jerusalem* in all his days)" (1 Nephi 1:4).

However, it does not appear that the family of Lehi actually lived inside the walled city. When Nephi and his brothers went to their home to retrieve their father's treasures in the hopes of using them to bargain for the plates, Nephi says they "went down to the land of our inheritance" (1 Nephi 3:22).

Why does it matter that Nephi uses phrases like *the land of Jerusalem* and *at Jerusalem* to represent the entire area rather than just the walled city? Because it is important to note that one of the suburb cities of Jerusalem is Bethlehem. The distance between the two cities is around four-and-a-half miles. Would Lehi and his descendants consider this small town as being in *the land of Jerusalem* or *at Jerusalem*? The answer would perfectly explain a scripture that many critics have used to mock Joseph Smith from the beginning.

Here is the scripture in question: "And behold, he shall be born of Mary, *at Jerusalem* which is *the land* of our forefathers, she being a virgin, a precious and chosen vessel, who shall be overshadowed and conceive by the power of the Holy Ghost, and bring forth a son, yea, even the Son of God" (Alma 7:10).

Critics often use this as proof that Joseph Smith wrote the Book of Mormon because this is a critical error. According to these critics, saying that Jesus was born "at Jerusalem" shows ignorance because everyone knows that he was born in Bethlehem. But it seems strange that if he wrote the book that he would get the facts right in so many areas but incorrectly designate where Christ was born.

After years of mockery over the apparent mistake, new material was discovered that strongly suggests Joseph truly was translating from the ancient Nephite records when referring to Jerusalem. In 1993, a fascinating book called *The Dead Sea Scrolls Uncovered* was written by biblical scholars and professors Robert Eisenman and Michael Wise. In it, the authors discuss a document that they temporarily named "Pseudo-Jeremiah" (scroll 4Q385). The beginning of the damaged text reads as follows: "Jeremiah the Prophet before the Lord [. . . w]ho were taken captive from the land of Jerusalem."[5]

So here we have the Dead Sea Scrolls using the phrase *the land of Jerusalem* at the exact same time that Jeremiah and Lehi prophesied in Jerusalem. What are the chances of Joseph Smith getting that phrase right when Old Testament writers never used it even once?

Even more interesting is a passage found in a book entitled *The Holy Land: an Oxford Archaeological Guide From Earliest Times to 1700*, published through the Oxford University Press in 2008 by Jerome Murphy-O'Connor. On page 290 is an excerpt from a letter written by Abdi-Heba, who was a local chieftain of Jerusalem, pleading for help during the Amarna period (mid-1330s BC). The letter reads in part: "But now even a town of the land of Jerusalem, Bit-Lahmi [Bethlehem] by name, a town belonging to the king, has gone over to the people of Keilah. Let my king hearken to Abdu-Heba, thy servant, and let him send archers to recover the royal land for the king: But if there are no archers, the land of the king will pass over to the Apiru people."[6]

How would Joseph Smith have possibly gotten any hint from the Bible or any other book that the phrase *the land of Jerusalem* included Bethlehem in ancient times? He obviously translated it exactly how the prophet Alma recorded it, based on what the Spirit revealed to him. He knew the biblical account said Christ was born "in" Bethlehem. I think it is safe to say that Jesus Christ was born in Bethlehem in "the land of Jerusalem," or "at Jerusalem." What first appeared to be a huge mistake should now be considered more evidence for the authenticity of the Book of Mormon.

The Walls of Jerusalem

When Emma Smith was interviewed by her son Joseph Smith III, she made this interesting statement about her husband:

When he stopped for any purpose at any time he would, when he commenced again, begin where he left off without any hesitation, and one time while he was translating he stopped suddenly, pale as a sheet, and said, "Emma, did Jerusalem have walls around it?" When I answered, "Yes," he replied, "Oh! (I didn't know.) I was afraid I had been deceived." He had such a limited knowledge of history at that time that he did not even know that Jerusalem was surrounded by walls.[7]

I have traveled to every state in the United States and almost every major city. I have never seen a wall around any of our cities. I'm fairly certain there were no walls around any city that Joseph Smith ever lived in or visited either. When my wife and I walked the streets of Jerusalem, we learned that a protective wall had been around the old city since ancient times. These walls have been destroyed and rebuilt multiple times. The current wall is about 2.5 miles long with an average height of almost forty feet and is a little over eight feet thick. It has eight gates and thirty-four watchtowers. The western wall is a remnant of the ancient wall that surrounded the Jewish temple courtyard and is considered a sacred place to those of the Jewish faith. For those who know nothing about walls built around a city, I would think it would be difficult to even talk about them. And yet the Book of Mormon manages to get the proper language right.

Jeremiah 52:14 (emphasis added): "And all the army of the Chaldeans, that were with the captain of the guard, brake down all *the walls of Jerusalem* round about."

1 Nephi 4:4 (emphasis added): "Now when I had spoken these words, they were yet wroth, and did still continue to murmur; nevertheless they did follow me up until we came without *the walls of Jerusalem.*"

These are just a few examples showing that Joseph Smith would have needed to conduct an incredible amount of research to pick up on the little traditions distinctly from the Jerusalem area to have written just the beginning chapters of the Book of Mormon.

Geography

Geography played an important role in how people referred to places. Both terrain and location may be part of the designation. Sometimes the words used to designate geographical designations have raised a number of questions for readers of both the Bible and the Book of Mormon.

Up to Jerusalem and Down

Another fascinating point when reading references to Jerusalem in the Bible are those based on the words *up* and *down*. When someone in the Bible is traveling to Jerusalem from another location, the record consistently says they go "up to Jerusalem." This short phrase occurs six times in the Old Testament and nineteen times in the New Testament. Not surprisingly, the same holds true in the Book of Mormon. Here are examples from each:

2 Kings 12:17 (emphasis added): "Then Hazael king of Syria went up, and fought against Gath, and took it: and Hazael set his face to go *up to Jerusalem.*"

Matthew 20:17 (emphasis added): "And Jesus going *up to Jerusalem* took the twelve disciples apart in the way."

1 Nephi 7:3 (emphasis added): "And it came to pass that I, Nephi, did again, with my brethren, go forth into the wilderness to go *up to Jerusalem.*"

On the other hand, when anyone leaves Jerusalem, the record consistently states they "go down to" Egypt, Capernaum, Antioch, and so on. Again, the Book of Mormon does the same:

Genesis 43:15 (emphasis added): "And the men took that present, and they took double money in their hand, and Benjamin; and rose up, and went *down to Egypt,* and stood before Joseph."

John 2:12 (emphasis added): "After this he went *down to Capernaum,* he, and his mother, and his brethren, and his disciples: and they continued there not many days."

Ether 13:7 (emphasis added): "For as Joseph brought his father *down into the land of Egypt,* even so he died there; wherefore, the Lord brought a remnant of the seed of Joseph out of the land of Jerusalem."

Never once is the phrase *up to Egypt* used in scripture. Neither is the phrase *down to Jerusalem.* The scriptures are always consistent when referring to Jerusalem. After years, someone finally figured out the reason for this: Jerusalem is elevated above surrounding areas. Look closely at the elevation of the cities and lands around Jerusalem and it all makes perfect sense.

Jerusalem, Israel	2,550 feet *above* sea level
Tel Aviv, Israel	104 feet *above* sea level
Cairo, Egypt	75 feet *above* sea level
Dead Sea	1,401 feet *below* sea level
Jericho, Egypt	1,200 feet *below* sea level

Reason to Believe

For Joseph Smith to have written the Book of Mormon, he would have needed to be a biblical scholar just to write the first few chapters, as they related to Jerusalem. If he were poring over the Bible and taking notes on what he read and recording key phrases, doesn't it seem likely his family would see him doing it? If he had books to study on Jewish history, where did he get them? Joseph did not have the ability to write the Book of Mormon himself. No one did.

Notes

1. Heber J. Grant, *Gospel Standards: Selections from the Sermons and Writings of Heber J. Grant,* G. Homer Durham, comp. (Salt Lake City: Deseret Book, third edition, 1942), 15.
2. The *New York Herald*, April 28, 1903.
3. Hugh Nibley, *Of All Things! Classic Quotations from Hugh Nibley*, comp. and ed. Gary Gillum (Salt Lake City: Deseret Book, 1993), 125.
4. Daniel Petersen, *Defending the Faith: 2 Book of Mormon "Errors"* (*Deseret News*, Thursday, May 1, 2014).
5. Robert Eisenman and Michael Wise, *the Dead Sea Scrolls Uncovered* (London: Penguin Books, 1993), 58. See Eretz Yerushalayim, column 1, line 2), Amarna Letter no. 290; trans. W. F. Albright.
6. Jerome Murphy-O'Connor, *The Holy Land: an Oxford Archaeological Guide From Earliest Times to 1700* (Oxford University Press: 2008), 290.
7. Joseph Smith III, "Last Testimony of Sister Emma," *Saints' Advocate* 2 (October 1879), 51.

Chapter 12: Considered a Work of Fiction

"The Book of Mormon is a colossal structure. Considered purely as fiction, it is a performance without parallel. What other volume can approach this wealth of detail and tight-woven complexity, this factual precision combined with simple open lucidity? Any book we choose is feeble by comparison. . . . The Book of Mormon combines these usually incompatible qualities in a structure of flawless consistency. . . . This terse, compact religious history of a thousand years is something utterly beyond the scope of creative writing."[1]

—Hugh W. Nibley

Some years ago, a young man named Zack dropped by my office at the institute building where I worked. He was at freshman orientation for new students at the University of Texas–Austin.

As we talked, I found out that he had been a member of the Church all of life, his parents were active, and he had a sister on a mission. He had an earring in each ear and told me that he hadn't been all that active lately. He also told me that the scriptures had some good stories in them, but he believed they were all fiction and that none of the things recorded had actually happened. I asked him if he believed that about the Bible, and he said he did. Then I asked him what he thought about the Book of Mormon. He told me again that he thought it was a book of nice stories but that none of them were true. I asked him if he believed that Joseph Smith wrote the book? He said that he believed that he wrote it, or that he wrote it with help from others.

What this recent high school graduate told me next surprised me. He said that even if an angel did deliver plates to Joseph, the stories and events written upon them were all fiction and never happened. I said, "You mean that you think it is possible that the Lord could have an angel deliver a religious novel?" He said that's what he felt it was. I had never heard anyone propose that possibility. I was not surprised to hear Zack say that he had never read the Book of Mormon. I told him that I had read it multiple times and believed that the events described throughout its pages were all true. I also told him that I felt confident the Lord did not send an angel to Joseph Smith to bring him a book of nice fairy tales.

As he was leaving, I challenged him to read the Book of Mormon for himself and ask if it were true. Unfortunately, I never saw Zach again after that day.

President Boyd K. Packer said, "Perhaps no other book has been denounced so vigorously by those who have never read it as has the Book of Mormon."[2] Some of the same people who refuse to even read it seem to spend a great deal of time trying to disprove it.

While I had never before heard anyone say that it was possible that an angel came to deliver a work of fiction, I have heard and read comments from multiple people who say the Book of Mormon is a work of fiction. Here are some of these comments that I have heard and recorded over the years:

- "The Book of Mormon is nothing more than a work of fiction. It is a novel, heavily plagiarized from the Bible and other books available at the time."
- "Modern science has consistently proven beyond any doubt that the Book of Mormon is a modern work of fiction."
- "Something all experts agree on is that the Book of Mormon is not a record of an ancient people. They agree that it is a modern creation either produced by Joseph Smith or by him with the help of collaborators."

Let's pretend for a moment that the critics have it right and that Joseph Smith wrote the Book of Mormon. That would, of course, make it a work of fiction or a religious novel written in King James language by him. A novel is a fictitious prose narrative of considerable length and complexity that portrays characters and the human experience and is usually presented in a sequential organization of action and structure.

Listed below are some of the great classic books mentioned by various groups that were published between 1800 and 1840, the same general publishing time frame as the Book of Mormon. Most of the books are fiction, though some are nonfiction. Which one of the following classic books has had the greatest influence on people in general?

- *Phenomenology of Mind* (1807) by G. W. F. Hegel
- *Pride and Prejudice* (1813) by Jane Austen
- *Journals* (1814) by Meriwether Lewis and William Clark
- *The World as Will and Idea* (1818) by Arthur Schopenhauer
- *Frankenstein* (1818) by Mary Shelley
- *Ivanhoe* (1819) by Walter Scott
- *The Legend of Sleepy Hollow* (1820) by Washington Irving
- *The Hunchback of Notre Dame* (1831) by Victor Hugo
- *On War* (1832) by Carl Von Clausewitz
- *Oliver Twist* (1837) by Charles Dickens

As you look at this list of ten books, which ones have influenced your life significantly? I wonder how many lives have been changed for the better because of these books? Imagine trying to recruit over 88,000 young single adults to work long hours every day for eighteen to twenty-four months at their own expense to share the message of *Frankenstein* or *The Legend of Sleepy Hollow* with the world. I am not aware of even one person who has ever done that for any of these ten books, even though they regularly appear on lists talking about the greatest works of fiction ever published.

I personally don't believe any of these books individually or perhaps combined has had the influence for good that the Book of Mormon has had. If it is fiction, then it has no equal in producing passionate followers. The fact that well over 88,000 young men and women are willing to leave behind school, family, friends, scholarships, and jobs to spend countless hours telling people about the book at their own expense speaks about its impact. What fictional epic has had that kind of influence? If Joseph Smith imagined and wrote it, then it should be appearing at the top of every list of most important works of fiction. I would love to see critics present evidence concerning fictional books that have had a greater influence for good on the world compared to that of the Book of Mormon.

Trying to determine the number of books sold for a particular title can be tricky. Many books that have been listed on best-seller lists do not have reliable sales figures. Also, nonfiction religious books like the Bible and the Qur'an do not appear on most best-seller lists because many groups have reproduced these books in various forms over centuries of time. Since many view the Book of Mormon as a fictional work, it should then be recognized as one of the bestselling works of fiction of all times. Right now, it would be viewed as second on the bestselling list of all time with over 150 million copies in print. *The Lord of Rings* was written as a single book and is therefore counted that way, but the total sales number is actually the sales of the combined three books of the trilogy.

Book	Author	Published	Copies in Print
A Tale of Two Cites	Charles Dickens	1859	200,000,000
The Lord of the Rings	J. R. R. Tolkien	1954	150,000,000
The Little Prince	de Saint-Exupery	1943	140,000,000

Critics would say that the Book of Mormon should not be counted on bestselling book lists because members and missionaries give away so many copies, which accounts for the huge numbers in print. Is that not like saying a restaurant with long wait times should not be counted among the most popular places to eat because so many patrons like the food so much, they buy their friends gift cards to the restaurant? If it is a work of fiction, then why is Joseph Smith not given credit for being one of the great authors of all time?

Writing a classic book like those listed above is challenging. One reason is because things change over time and material can become obsolete. Every year around the nation, libraries throw out books that contain obsolete material or information proven false. Why keep a book that tells you how to operate a Commodore 64 computer? It is useless in our day. There are many products, customs, theories, styles, and policies that have become obsolete over time. Sometimes, it is fun to play the "remember when" game with friends. For example, remember when entire families would go to the gates of the airport to say goodbye to a loved one or to welcome them home? Remember when there were cassette players, VCR tapes, ditto paper, gas station attendants, hitchhikers, hotel keys, manual car windows, milkmen and handwritten letters? Since so many things change over time, it is difficult for an author to write a book that will remain relevant.

Even in the Church, we see changes in programs and policies over time. I could ask men my age if they remember going to priesthood meetings on Sunday mornings, going back home, and then returning to church with the entire family for Sunday School. Or if they remember when we took the sacrament at Sunday School and then took it again when we returned to the church for the third time that evening to attend sacrament meeting. Remember when kids went to Primary on Tuesday afternoon after school and women went to Relief Society on Thursday mornings? Remember the Gold and Green Ball, all-church softball, and basketball tournaments? Things change and become obsolete with time, even in the Church. Sometimes things change so drastically that they become laughable in a later time. Consider a few of the many options for a Beehive girl to earn awards in 1916:

- Make two articles of underwear by hand
- Cover 25 miles on snowshoes in any six days
- Care for at least two kerosene lamps daily
- During two weeks, keep the house free from flies or destroy at least twenty-five flies daily
- Have your toilet moved to an isolated place in the garden[3]

Can you imagine those requirements being listed as requirements for the Young Womanhood Award today? And yet these were needed skills, normal for those who lived in that day and age. How would they know how unreasonable they would sound a century later? Because of the tremendous changes that occur over time, it is extremely difficult to write a classic book that has mass appeal and where the message does not become obsolete. Many books are immensely popular and respected at the time they are written but then lose their appeal and become obsolete as time passes. A medical book written in the 1800s would be totally out of date today. A history book describing Phoenix, Arizona, in 1900 would describe a city of several thousand people. One written in 2014 would describe a city of 1,600,000 with the metro population passing 4,300,000. The reason so few books become classics may be because it is so difficult for the content to endure over time.

In some cases, books contain information that is dangerous but it is not exposed for many years. For example, in 1946 Benjamin Spock wrote a book called *Baby and Child Care* that went on to become one of the bestselling books of all time. Spock advocated that infants should not be placed on their back when sleeping because of the danger of choking. This advice was almost universally accepted by medical professionals for almost fifty years and was recommended nationwide. However, empirical evidence began to emerge over time that showed a significant correlation between sudden infant death syndrome (SIDS) and babies who sleep on their abdomens. Many believe that thousands of infants died in the United States alone because they followed his advice.

Other books simply lose both their popularity and influence over time. It may take many years before ideas presented in a book become exposed as dangerous or obsolete. *The Communist Manifesto* by Karl Marx is one such example. Entire countries (Russia, China, Cuba, and North Korea) adopted the theories that Marx proposed about society, economics, and politics. According to some estimates, almost a hundred million people have died at the hands of their Communist governments. In recent years, these theories seem to have lost much of their influence.

The bottom line is that it's rare for a book to remain both popular and influential over long periods of time. It remains to be seen whether the popular books of our day like the Harry Potter series will become classics or simply fade away with time. Few books in history—like *A Tale of Two Cities* by Charles Dickens—have attained enduring respect.

Most books are also age specific or topic specific in their appeal. A book written specifically to young teenage girls usually has little appeal to teenage boys or to any other age group. A romance novel would usually not appeal to those who enjoy science fiction. Surely only the most rare of all books would appeal to and influence all ages, cultures, races, education levels, socioeconomic groups, and genders over long periods of time. How many books can you think of that meet those requirements? Only a handful, at most.

Though the Book of Mormon is a complex work and has influenced millions of people, some critics claim it was not a major accomplishment for Joseph Smith to have written it. Here are a few fairly typical statements from critics who buy into that line of reasoning:

"The Book of Mormon is no more complex than many other works of fiction, such as J. R. R. Tolkien's *The Lord of the Rings.*"

"J. R. R. Tolkien began writing his complicated high fantasy books in his early twenties, which makes Joseph Smith's Book of Mormon not all that noteworthy."

It seems ironic that critics would claim that writing the Book of Mormon would be no big deal, and yet not one person has stepped forward to duplicate the feat in the 185-plus years since its publication. Instead of trying every argument imaginable to prove the book wrong, why not produce a similar book of a different ancient group?

I also find it ironic that critics on the one hand paint Joseph Smith as an ignorant fraud, and yet on the other hand are forced to use J. R. R. Tolkien, the internationally renowned Oxford professor, to argue that it is no big deal. After all, if Tolkien could write *Lord of the Rings,* then why couldn't Joseph Smith write the Book of Mormon? If Tolkien really did began writing his renowned book series at that early age, it certainly took him a long time to finish the first book in the series. *The Hobbit* came out in 1937, which means Tolkien was forty-five years old years old at the time. Somehow, an Oxford English professor writing *The Hobbit* at that age seems a little less impressive a feat to me than a twenty-three-year-old farm boy producing the Book of Mormon in sixty-three working days.

In reality, these critics are actually giving Joseph Smith the ultimate compliment by comparing him to one of the most respected writers in history. Let's compare Joseph Smith and J. R. R. Tolkien and ask which one produced the most impressive books when all things are considered. Most people know about Joseph Smith's background, so there's no need to go into great detail about his life.

However, some may not be as familiar with Tolkien. He was born on January 3, 1892 in Bloemfontein, South Africa, but he was moved to England as a child. He is said to have been a child prodigy who could read by age four and began writing shortly afterward. One of his first jobs was serving as a lexicographer for the original *Oxford English Dictionary*. His job required him to not only define words, but also research their history. Dr. Henry Bradley, senior editor of the dictionary, said this of Tolkien: "His work gives evidence of an unusually thorough mastery of Anglo-Saxon and of the facts and principles of the comparative grammar of the Germanic languages. Indeed, I have no hesitation in saying that I have never known a man of his age who was in these respects his equal."[4]

Tolkien wrote *The Lord of the Rings* after years of teaching at Oxford. He had been exposed to different languages at an early age and continued to study languages throughout his career. According to several sources, he had some knowledge of up to thirty languages, including Latin, German, French, Spanish, Middle English, Old English, Finnish, Old Norse, Medieval Welsh, Greek, and modern Welsh. He became a university professor of the English language at a young age and is known as the father of modern high fantasy. His best friend was C. S. Lewis, and both were members of a group called the Inklings, who respected writers and professors who met regularly and shared a common interest in fiction and fantasy. The point here is that no one was better prepared to write *The Lord of the Rings* than Tolkien.

On the other hand, if anyone was *not* trained to write the Book of Mormon, it was Joseph Smith. He had little education, grew up on a farm, and never saw the inside of a middle school or high school, much less a prestigious college. It should be Tolkien, not Joseph Smith, that critics say "no big deal" about. The following is a brief comparison between the two men and their two best-known books.

	Joseph Smith	J. R. R. Tolkien
Birth	1805	1892
Location	Sharon, Vermont	Bloemfontein, South Africa
Father's Occupation	Farmer	British bank manager
Education	Third grade	University of Oxford
Training	Reading / writing	Languages / literature

Occupation	Farmer	Oxford professor
Book	The Book of Mormon	The Lord of the Rings
Year Published	March 1830	July 1954
Age at Publication	24	62
Languages Translated Into	91+ (portions of 24)	38
Time to Complete	63 days	12+ years
Associates	Farmers	Oxford professors
Persecution of Work	Nonstop	Nonexistent
Age at Death	38	81
Books in Print	150,000,000+	150,000,000+
Book Type	Historical (or fiction)	High fantasy fiction
World's View	Great contempt	Great admiration
Influence of Book	Millions of converts	Millions of admirers

In January 1971, Dennis Gerrolt interviewed Tolkien in a broadcast on the BBC Radio 4 program "Now Read On." Look closely at what Tolkien says when asked about his books:

Gerrolt: "You began in '42 did you, to write it?"

Tolkien: "Oh no, I began as soon as *The Hobbit* was out—in the '30s."

Gerrolt: "It was finally finished just before it was published."

Tolkien: "I wrote the last . . . in about 1949—I remember I actually wept at the denouement. But then of course there was a tremendous lot of revision. I typed the whole of that work out twice and lots of it many times, on a bed in an attic. I couldn't afford of course the typing. There's some mistakes too and also [relights pipe] it amuses me to say, as I suppose I'm in a position where it doesn't matter what people think of me now—there were some frightful mistakes in grammar, which from a Professor of English Language and Lit are rather shocking."[5]

So, Tolkien, a brilliant Oxford English professor who taught in one of the most prestigious universities in the world for years, had to do "a tremendous lot of revision" and made "frightful mistakes in grammar." At the other end of the spectrum, Joseph Smith, an uneducated farm boy from rural New York, verbally dictated the

Book of Mormon in approximately sixty-three working days. Even using a scribe and a non-believing typesetter, the book was produced with only minor grammatical mistakes. While Tolkien is universally admired by the literary world for his great accomplishment, Joseph Smith is for the most part treated with great contempt, even though he pulled off something far more amazing, when all things are really considered. Pitting Joseph Smith against J. R. R. Tolkien seems like having an elementary school kid from a farming community who had never played basketball going one on one against an NBA superstar. The amazing thing about using that comparison is that the kid seems to not only hold his own, but in some circles win the game.

If Joseph Smith translated the Book of Mormon, then he is a great prophet. If he wrote the book, then he should be considered one of the greatest fiction writers of all time. And yet, even those who claim this volume to be a work of fiction give neither Joseph Smith nor the Book of Mormon any credit. How many books can you think of that not only endure through the ages, but also actually grow in influence over time instead of diminishing? I propose that the Book of Mormon does exactly that. Such influence makes it quite possibly the most amazing book ever published.

Many things that were laughed at in 1830 are no longer a joke. The more researchers discover, the stronger the case becomes that Joseph Smith did not write the book. Some critics are working non-stop to attempt to explain away the origin of the book in a believable way. It seems that every theory proposed since 1830 to explain its origins has been debunked in time.

The Book of Mormon seems to be like a giant mansion with so many rooms to explore that you would not be able to see them all in one lifetime. When President Ezra Taft Benson gave a classic talk on the Book of Mormon, he encouraged members to read it for half an hour each day. A short time after that talk was given, I was talking to a young man who was about to leave on his mission. I asked him if he had any goals for this two-year time period. He said that his goal was to read the Book of Mormon every month during his mission. I did not think for a minute that he would do it. When he returned home, I asked if he had accomplished his goal. I was shocked when he told me that he had read it twenty-four times during the two years of service. He said he did not get tired of it and even grew to be passionate about the good it contained. I was not surprised when he became a bishop in his mid-twenties, then a member of the stake presidency after that, and then later a mission president.

What novel ever written can hold a candle to the Book of Mormon in terms of impact on its readers for good? After I read books like *The Lord of the Rings*, I acknowledge that they are masterpieces that deserve admiration. I often wonder how any writer could be so incredibly clever with his or her imagination. However, it does not influence my life, either for good or bad. When I read the Book of Mormon, I am always motivated to be a better person. As I listen to the testimonies on fast Sundays, it is obvious that the book is also having a similar impact on many others.

Reason to Believe

Whether it is a novel or a record of an ancient people, The Book of Mormon is a complex book. After intense scrutiny, it has now withstood the test of time and stands as a witness that it is what it claims to be. This book was far beyond the capacity of an uneducated farm boy who had no reference material to guide him. It is impossible that Joseph Smith could be the author of a book that has such incredible influence on so many millions for good.

When the Book of Mormon was published, little was known about the ancient history of the Middle East. Now, with each passing year, more and more knowledge is being accumulated about the astonishing complexity and accuracy of the book. An increasing number of people agree with this statement made by Hugh Nibley: "There is no point at all to the question: Who wrote the Book of Mormon? It would have been quite as impossible for the most learned man alive in 1830 to have written the book as it was for Joseph Smith."[6]

Notes

1. Hugh W. Nibley, *Since Cumorah* (Salt Lake City: Deseret Book, 1967), 156–57.
2. Boyd K. Packer, "The Things of My Soul," *Ensign*, May 1986, 59.
3. *Handbook for the Beehive Girls of the Y.L.M.I.A.* (Salt Lake City: The Church of Jesus Christ of Latter-day Saints, 1916).

4. *J. R. R. Tolkien: Master of Imaginary Worlds* (Berkeley Heights, NJ: Edward Willett-Enslow Publishers Inc., 2004), 51–52.

5. Dennis Gerrolt, "Now Read On," BBC Radio 4, January, 1971.

6. Hugh Nibley, *Of All Things! Classic Quotations from Hugh Nibley*, comp. and ed. Gary Gillum (Salt Lake City: Deseret Book, 1993), 143.

Chapter 13: Names and Places

"Jacob and Joseph. There is no doubt in my mind that these two boys were named after Jacob, the father of the twelve tribes, and Joseph, his son, who was sold into Egypt."[1]

—S. Kent Brown

B ack in 2008, Canada's nationally distributed newspaper, *The Globe and Mail,* asked an international panel to pick the fifty greatest books of all time. Number one on that list was the *Adventures of Huckleberry Finn* by Mark Twain. Many literary critics have raved about this book since it's printing in 1884. Journalist, editor, and critic H. L. Mencken said, "I believe that *Huckleberry Finn* is one of the great masterpieces of the world."[2] Author and journalist Ernest Hemingway said, "All modern American literature comes from one book by Mark Twain called *Huckleberry Finn.*"[3] Across the years, the novel has been criticized, censored, and banned for racial slurs, obscenity, bad grammar, atheism, and a low moral tone.

To create his novel, Mark Twain obviously invented a character list, developed the plot, and then attempted to make the characters believable. He also needed places where the events in the story could unfold. For the most part, he simply used places that already existed. The following are the characters and places he used, along with a brief statement about each:

Character List

- *Huckleberry Finn:* narrator and main character of the novel
- *Jim:* runaway slave who joins Huck in his flight down the Mississippi River

- *Tom Sawyer:* Huck's civilized friend who enjoys extravagant stories and schemes
- *Pap Finn:* Huck's abusive, drunken father who plots to steal his son's reward money
- *The Duke:* river con man who claims that he is the duke of Bridgewater
- *The King:* river con man who claims to be the disappeared heir to the French throne
- *Widow Douglas:* town widow who tries to help civilize Huck through kindness and religion
- *Miss Watson:* Widow Douglas's sister who tries to help Huck with manners and religion
- *Aunt Polly:* Tom Sawyer's aunt and guardian
- *Jo Harper, Ben Rogers, and Tommy Barnes:* members of Tom's "band of robbers"
- *Judge Thatcher:* kindly town judge who watches over Huck's reward money
- *Mrs. Loftus:* St. Petersburg town woman whom Huck visits disguised as a girl
- *Jake Packard, Bill, and Jim Turner:* gang of murderers on the sinking steamboat
- *The Grangerfords:* distinguished family who watches over Huck
- *Buck Grangerford:* boy who befriends Huck and is killed by the Shepherdsons
- *Emmeline Grangerford:* girl who wrote romantic epigraphs and died at fourteen
- *The Shepherdsons:* distinguished family who constantly feud with the Grangerfords
- *Boggs:* Arkansas town drunkard who is later shot by Colonel Sherburn
- *Colonel Sherburn:* man who shoots Boggs and repels lynch mob
- *Peter Wilks:* deceased townsman whose family takes in the Duke, the King, and Huck
- *William and Harvey Wilks:* Peter Wilks' brothers who live in England
- *Mary Jane, Susan, and Joanna:* Peter Wilks' nieces who are tricked by the Duke and the King

- *Dr. Robinson and Levi Bell:* people who do not believe the Duke and the King are Wilks' brothers
- *Silas Phelps:* Tom Sawyer's uncle
- *Aunt Sally Phelps:* Tom Sawyer's aunt

Places

- *St. Petersburg:* town where Huck lived with Widow Douglass
- *Mississippi River:* river near Huck's home that he traveled down
- *St. Louis:* city where Huck and Jim saw the robbers and took their money
- *Jackson Island:* place where Huck and Jim hid out from a storm and where Pap died
- *Cairo:* a town in Illinois that was Huck's and Jim's original destination
- *Missouri:* the state where the story begins and where Huck is from
- *Illinois:* the state where Cairo is located at the mouth of the Ohio River
- *Arkansas:* the state where several events occur with Huck Finn in the story
- *Parkville:* place where Jim was sold towards the end of the story
- *Pikesville:* place where Huck ran away to and left Jim at the raft

You might be wondering what the names and places in this Mark Twain "masterpiece" have to do with the Book of Mormon. Well, if Joseph Smith wrote the Book of Mormon, as many critics contend, then it is a work of fiction. If that is the case, it means he had to invent a totally believable character list and a list of places where the story played out, just like Mark Twain did. From the modern index of the Book of Mormon, we find names that would have been on his character list and a list of place names. The following is a list of each name and place with a brief explanatory statement. Those persons with actual speaking parts in the Book of Mormon are italicized.

Character List (from the modern index)

- Aaron 1: Jaredite king and descendant of Heth 2
- *Aaron 2*: son of Mosiah 2, Nephite missionary
- Aaron 3: king of Lamanites

- *Abinadi*: Nephite prophet, converts Alma 1
- *Abinadom*: son of Chemish, Nephite historian
- Abish: servant of Lamoni's wife, converted
- Abraham: father of the faithful
- Adam: the first man and progenitor of all
- Aha: son of Zoram 2 and Nephite military officer
- Ahah: son of Seth 2, wicked Jaredite king
- *Akish*: son of Kimnor, wicked Jaredite king
- *Alma 1*: priest of Noah, converted by Abinadi
- *Alma 2*: son of Alma[1], prophet, first chief judge
- *Amaleki 1*: son of Abinadom, Nephite historian
- Amaleki 2: on expedition to find Zeniff's group
- *Amalickiah*: Nephite traitor, Lamanite king,
- *Amaron*: son of Omni, Nephite record keeper
- Amgid: Jaredite king overthrown by Com 2
- *Aminadab*: Nephite dissenter reconverted
- Aminadi: ancestor of Amulek
- Amlici: Nephite dissenter, seeks to be king
- Ammah: Nephite missionary to Lamanites,
- *Ammaron*: Nephite record keeper
- *Ammon 1*: leader of expedition to land of Nephi
- *Ammon 2*: missionary, chief judge in Jershon
- *Ammoron*: Nephite traitor, king of Lamanites
- Amnigaddah: son of Aaron 2, Jaredite king
- Amnor: Nephite spy watch camp of Amlicites
- Amoron: a Nephite who reports to Mormon
- Amos 1: son of Nephi 4, Nephite record keeper
- Amos 2: son of Amos 1, Nephite record keeper
- Amoz: father of Isaiah
- *Amulek*: son of Giddonah, Alma's companion
- Amulon: priest of King Noah
- Antiomno: Lamanite king of land of Middoni
- *Antionah*: a chief ruler in Ammonihah,
- Antionum: Nephite commander at Cumorah
- Antipus: Nephite commander in city of Judea
- Archeantus: Nephite military officer
- *Benjamin*: son of Mosiah 1, Nephite prophet

- *Brother of Jared*: first Jaredite prophet
- Cain: son of Adam and Eve, murderer
- Cezoram: wicked Nephite chief judge
- *Chemish*: son of Omni, Nephite record keeper
- Cohor 1: brother of Noah 2, Jaredite
- Cohor 2: son of Noah 2, Jaredite king
- Cohor 3: Jaredite
- Com 1: son of Coriantum 1, Jaredite king
- Com 2: son of Coriantum 2, Jaredite king
- Corianton: son of Alma 2
- Coriantor: son of Moron, Jaredite
- Coriantum 1: son of Emer, Jaredite king
- Coriantum 2: son of Amnigaddah
- Coriantumr 1: son of Omer, Jaredite
- Coriantumr 2: Jaredite king, last Jaredite
- Coriantumr 3: Nephite apostate, joins Lamanites
- Corihor 1: son of Kib, Jaredite
- Corihor 2: Jaredite
- Corom: son of Levi 2, Jaredite king
- Cumenihah: Nephite commander at Cumorah
- David: king of Israel
- Devil: the enemy of all righteousness
- Elijah: prophet of Israel
- Emer: son of Omer, Jaredite king
- Emron: Nephite soldier
- *Enos*: son of Jacob, Nephite prophet
- Esrom: son of Omer, Jaredite
- Ethem: son of Ahah, Jaredite king
- *Ether*: last Jaredite prophet and record keeper
- Eve: the first mortal woman and wife of Adam
- Ezias: a prophet
- Gadianton: leader of robber bands
- Gazelem: name given to servant of God
- *Gid*: Nephite military officer
- *Giddianhi*: chief of Gadianton robbers
- Giddonah 1: father of Amulek
- *Giddonah 2*: high priest in Gideon

- *Gideon*: Nephite patriot
- Gidgiddonah: Nephite commander at Cumorah
- *Gidgiddoni*: Nephite military commander
- Gilead: Jaredite military commander
- Gilgah: son of Jared, Jaredite
- Gilgal: Nephite commander at Cumorah
- God the Father: supreme Governor of universe
- Hagoth: Nephite shipbuilder
- Hearthom: son of Lib, Jaredite king
- Helam: convert baptized by Alma 1
- *Helaman 1*: son of King Benjamin
- *Helaman 2*: son of Alma 2, prophet
- Helaman 3: son of Helaman 2, chief judge
- Helem: brother of Ammon 2
- Helorum: son of King Benjamin
- Hem: brother of Ammon 2
- Heth 1: son of son of Hearrthom, Jaredite
- Heth 2: son of Com, Jaredite
- Himni: son of Mosiah 2
- Isaac: son of Abraham
- Isabel: harlot in land of Siron
- *Isaiah 1*: Hebrew prophet
- Isaiah 2: one of twelve Nephite disciples
- Ishmael 1: an Ephraimite from Jerusalem
- Ishmael 2: grandfather of Amulek
- *Jacob 1*: father of twelve tribes, becomes Israel
- *Jacob 2*: son of Lehi 1, Nephite prophet
- Jacob 3: apostate Nephite of Zoramite sect
- Jacob 4: apostate Nephite, king of secret band
- Jacom: son of Jared 2, Jaredite
- Jared 1: father of Enoch 2
- *Jared 2*: founder of Jaredites
- *Jared 3*: son of Omer, Jaredite king
- *Jarom*: son of Enos 2, Nephite prophet
- Jeneam: Nephite commander at Cumorah
- Jeremiah 1: Hebrew prophet, time of Lehi 1
- Jeremiah 2: one of twelve Nephite disciples

- Jesse: father of David
- *Jesus Christ*: Savior and Redeemer
- Jonas 1: son of Nephi 3, one of twelve disciples
- Jonas 2: one of twelve Nephite disciples
- *Joseph 1*: son of Jacob 1, carried into Egypt
- Joseph 2: son of Lehi 1
- Josh: Nephite commander at Cumorah
- Kib: son of Orihah, Jaredite king
- Kim: son of Morianton, Jaredite king
- Kimnor: father of Akish, Jaredite
- Kish: son of Corm, Jaredite king
- Kishkumen: cofounder of Gadianton robbers
- *Korihor*: an anti-Christ
- Kumen: one of twelve Nephite disciples
- Kumenonhi: one of twelve Nephite disciples
- *Laban*: custodian of the brass plates
- *Lachoneus 1*: Nephite chief judge and governor
- Lachoneus 2: son of Lachoneus 1, chief judge
- Lamah: Nephite commander at Cumorah
- *Laman 1*: eldest son of Lehi 1
- *Laman 2*: Lamanite king
- Laman 3: son of Laman 3, Lamanite king
- *Laman 4*: Nephite soldier
- *Lamoni*: Lamanite king converted by Ammon 2
- *Lehi 1*: Hebrew prophet to promised land
- Lehi 2: son of Zoram 2, possibly same as Lehi 3
- Lehi 3: Nephite military commander
- *Lehi 4*: son of Helaman 2, Nephite missionary
- Lehonti: Lamanite officer
- *Lemuel*: second son of Lehi 1
- Levi 1: son of Jacob 1
- Levi 2: son of Kim, Jaredite king
- Lib 1: son of Kish, Jaredite king
- Lib 2: Jaredite king
- Limhah: Nephite commander
- Limher: Nephite soldier
- *Limhi*: son of Noah 3, king in Lehi-Nephi

- Luram: Nephite officer
- Mahah: son of Jared 3
- Maher-Shalal-Hash-Baz: son of Isaiah
- *Malachi*: Jewish prophet
- Manasseh: son of Joseph 1, father of a tribe
- Manti: Nephite soldier
- Mathoni: one of twelve Nephite disciples
- Mathonihah: one of twelve Nephite disciples
- Morianton 1: son of Riplakis, Jaredite king
- Morianton 2: Nephite traitor and founder of city
- Mormon 1: father of Mormon 2
- *Mormon 2*: Nephite prophet, general, abridger
- Moron: son of Ethem, Jaredite king
- *Moroni 1*: righteous Nephite military commander
- *Moroni 2*: son of Mormon 2, Nephite prophet
- Moronihah 1: son of Moroni 1, Nephite general
- Moronihah 2: Nephite general at Cumorah
- *Moses*: great Hebrew prophet
- *Mosiah 1*: Nephite prophet and king
- *Mosiah 2*: Nephite prophet and king
- Mulek: son of Jewish king Zedekiah
- Muloki: Nephite missionary
- Nehor: Nephite apostate
- *Nephi 1*: son of Lehi 1, founder of Nephites
- *Nephi 2*: son of Helaman 2, Nephite chief judge,
- Nephi 3: son of Nephi 2, one of the twelve disciples
- Nephi 4: son of Nephi 3, record keeper
- Nephihah: Nephite chief judge
- Neum: Hebrew prophet quoted by Nephi 1
- Nimrah: son of Akish, Jaredite
- Nimrod 1: grandson of Ham
- Nimrod 2: son of Cohor, Jaredite
- Noah 1: patriarch at time of flood
- Noah 2: son of Corhihor, Jaredite king
- *Noah 3*: son of Zeniff, king in land of Nephi
- Omer: son of Shule, Jaredite king
- Omner: son of Mosiah 2, converted by angel

- *Omni*: son of Jarom, Nephite record keeper
- Orihah: first Jaredite king
- Paanchi: son of Pahoran 1, Nephite rebel
- Pachus: king of Nephite dissenters
- Pacumeni: son of Pahoran 1, Nephite governor
- Pagag: son of brother of Jared[2]
- *Pahoran 1*: son of Nephihah, Nephite chief judge
- Pahoran 2: son of Pahoran 1, Nephite chief judge
- Riplakish: son of Shez 1, Jaredite king
- Sam: third son of Lehi 1
- Samuel 1: Hebrew prophet
- *Samuel 2*: Lamanite prophet
- Sarah: wife of Abraham
- *Sariah*: wife of Lehi 1
- Seantum: Nephite member of Gadianton band
- Seezoram: chief judge, Gadianton band
- Seth: son of Shiblon 1, Jaredite
- Shared: Jaredite military leader
- Shem: Nephite commander at Cumorah
- Shemnon: one of the twelve Nephite disciples
- *Sherem*: an anti-Christ
- Shez 1: son of Heth, Jaredite king
- Shez 2: son of Shez 1
- Shiblom 1: son of Com, Jaredite king
- Shiblom 2: Nephite commander at Cumorah
- Shiblon: son of Alma 2, Nephite missionary
- Shiz: Jaredite military leader
- Shule: Jaredite king
- Teancum: Nephite military leader
- Teomner: Nephite military officer
- Timothy: one of twelve Nephite disciples
- Tubaloth: son of Ammoron, Lamanite king
- Zarahemla: descendant of Mulek, leader
- Zedekiah 1: last king of Judah
- Zedekiah 2: one of twelve Nephite disciples
- *Zeezrom*: lawyer, converted by Alma 2 and Amulek, missionary
- Zemnarihah: captain of Gadianton band

- Zenephi: Nephite commander
- Zeniff: first king of Nephites in Lehi-Nephi
- *Zenock*: prophet of Israel
- *Zenos*: prophet of Israel
- *Zerahemnah*: Lamanite commander
- Zeram: Nephite military officer
- Zoram 1: servant of Laban
- Zoram 2: Nephite chief captain
- Zoram 3: Nephite apostate

List of Book of Mormon Places

- Aaron, City of: near Moroni and Nephihah
- Ablom: Jaredite city
- Agosh, Plains of: Jaredite battle area
- Aiath, City of: mentioned by Isaiah
- Akish, Wilderness of: Jaredite battle area
- Alma, Valley of: a day's travel north of Helam
- Ammonihah, City of: near Melek, Noah, Aaron
- Ammonihah, Land of: west of the river Sidon
- Amnihu: hill on east of the River Sidon
- Amulon, Land of: settled by Amulon
- Anathoth: Levite city near old Jerusalem
- Angola: Nephite city
- Ani-Anti: Lamanite village in the land of Nephi
- Antionum, Land of: east of Sidon
- Antiparah: a Nephite city
- Antipas, Mount: gathering place for Lehonti
- Antum, Land of: place of hill Shim and records
- Assyria: country in western Asia
- Babel, Tower: near original home of Jaredites
- Babylon: capital of Babylonia
- Bethabara: John was to baptize Messiah there
- Boaz, City of: Nephite retreat and battle area
- Bountiful, City: in land of Bountiful 2
- Bountiful, Land of 1: area in southern Arabia
- Bountiful, Land of 2: north of Zarahemla
- Calno: possibly town near Babylon

- Chaldea: land southeast corner of Mesopotamia
- Comnor,: hill near Valley of Shur
- Corihor, Land or Valley: Jaredite area
- Cumeni, Ctiy of: Nephite city to southwest
- Cumorah: last battle site and records buried
- David, Land of: Nephite land
- Desolation, City of: Nephite city to the north
- Desolation, Land of: north of Bountiful
- Eden, Garden of: home of Adam and Eve
- Egypt: land of Israel's captivity
- Ephraim, Hill of: hill in Jaredite lands
- Gad, City of: destroyed at the Crucifixion
- Gadiani, City of: destroyed at the Crucifixion
- Gadiomnah, City of: destroyed at Crucifixion
- Gid, City: used as a prison camp
- Gideon, City: east of River Sidon
- Gideon, Land or Valley of: east of river Sidon
- Gilgal, City of: destroyed at the Crucifixion
- Gilgal, Valley of: Jaredite battleground
- Gimgimno, City: destroyed at the Crucifixion
- Helam, Land of: inhabited by people of Alma 1
- Hermounts: wilderness on west and north
- Heshlon, Plains of: Jaredite battleground
- Heth, Land of: Jaredite land
- Ishmael, Land of: portion of land of Nephi
- Jacob, City of: destroyed at the Crucifixion
- Jacobugath: city of followers of Jacob
- Jashon, City and Land of: near land where Ammaron deposits records
- Jershon, Land of: land on east by sea
- Jerusalem 1: chief city of Jews
- Jerusalem 2: Lamanite city in land of Nephi
- Jordan River: river in Palestine
- Jordan, City of: a city of retreat for Nephites
- Josh, City of: destroyed at the Crucifixion
- Joshua, Land of: land in borders by seashore
- Judah: Southern kingdom of Israelites

- Judea, City of: Nephite city
- Kishkumen, City of: destroyed at Crucifixion
- Laman, City of: destroyed at the Crucifixion
- Laman, River: river emptying into Red Sea
- Land of First Inheritance: original landing
- Lebanon: country in the Middle East
- Lehi 1, City or Land: adjoining land of Morianton
- Lehi 2, Land of: apparently the entire land south
- Lehi-Nephi, City or Land of: land of Nephi
- Lemuel, City of: Lamanite city
- Lemuel, Valley of: near of Red Sea
- Manti, City of: chief city in land of Manti
- Manti, Hill of: near city of Zarahemla
- Manti, Land of: southerly land of Nephites
- Melek: Nephite land west of Sidon
- Middoni: Lamanite land
- Midian, Land of: Lamanite land
- Minon: Nephite land west bank of river Sidon
- Mocum, City of: destroyed at the Crucifixion
- Moriancumer: Jaredite land
- Morianton, City or Land: settled by Morianton 2
- Moriantum: Nephite area
- Mormon, Forest of: near waters of Mormon
- Mormon, Place of: region near Lehi-Nephi
- Mormon, Waters of: fountain in land of
- Moron, Land of: north of land of Desolation
- Moroni, City or Land of: southeast of Nephite lands
- Moronihah, City of: iniquitous Nephite city
- Mulek, City of: Nephite city south of Bountiful
- Nahom: place in Arabian desert
- Nazareth: city of Christ's childhood
- Nehor, City of: Jaredite city
- Nephi, City of: chief city in land of Nephi
- Nephi, Land of: land of first inheritance
- Nephihah, City of: possibly two cities by name
- Nephihah, Plains of: near the city of Nephihah
- Nimrod, Valley of: in Mesopotamia

- Noah, City or Land of: near Ammonihah.
- Ogath: place near hill Ramah
- Omner, City of: Nephite city by seashore
- Onidah: place for dissatisfied Lamanites
- Onidah, Hill: in land of Antionum
- Onihah: destroyed at the Crucifixion
- Ramah, Hill: Jaredite name for Hill Cumorah
- Riplah: east of river Sidon, near land of Manti
- Ripliancum, Waters of: aquatic region northwest
- Salem: earlier name for Jerusalem
- Sebus, Waters of: in land of Ishmael
- Shazer: campsite in Arabian Desert
- Shelem, Mount: mountain in old world
- Shem 2, City or Land: north of Antum and Jashon
- Shemlon, Land of: borders land of Lehi-Nephi
- Sherrizah: city conquered by Lamanites
- Shiloah, Waters of: pool near Jerusalem
- Shilom, City or Land: next to land of Lehi-Nephi
- Shim, Hill: in land Antum
- Shimnilom: city in the land of Nephi
- Shurr, Valley of: Coriantumr 2 and army camp
- Sidom, Land of: converts from Ammonihah
- Sidon River: river in Nephite territory
- Sinai, Mount: Moses and the Ten Commandments
- Sinim: possibly land of China
- Siron, Land of: land by borders of Laman
- Teancum, City of: near city of Desolation
- Zarahemla, City of: major capital of Nephites
- Zarahemla, Land of: region around city of
- Zeezrom, City of: Nephite city in southwest
- Zerin, Mount: moved by the brother of Jared 2
- Zion: the city of God

Whereas the character names that Mark Twain created were names that were likely familiar to people who read his book, the names in the Book of Mormon are, for the most part, unique, and readers would not readily recognize them. These names represent complex arrays of relationships and interactions among the people. The number and complexity of character contacts is made even more complicated by the number and names of places where these people lived or visited in the Book of Mormon.

Most of the place names in the Book of Mormon are unfamiliar as well. Names of places in *The Adventures of Huckleberry Finn* are familiar and largely real. Many readers may have even visited the places that served as the settings of the book. Meanwhile, locations of the vast majority of places in the Book of Mormon are totally unknown to its readers. Since the places may have been distant in time as well as location, orchestrating the many events with the many individuals and groups included in the Book of Mormon would have been an enormous undertaking, if Joseph Smith wrote it.

In spite of these lengthy lists, the list of names located at the end of the Book of Mormon does not include many of the people in the book. If Joseph Smith wrote the book, it means he also invented another extremely complicated and almost hidden layer of characters and gave them important speaking parts, just as he did for his main characters. Many who read the Book of Mormon (even multiple times) never even realize these persons exist. I once asked a highly educated Church leader who had read the Book of Mormon multiple times how many different individuals had speaking parts in the book. He said, "At least ten and probably more." Actually, there are approximately 153 individuals and groups who speak, depending on how you count them.

For example, the text may say that "the Lord said . . ." and then much later you find Jesus Christ speaking. In the following list, both names are listed, even though they are most likely the same person. There are also several angels who appear to various individuals over time, but there is no way of knowing if it is the same angel speaking.

These are the background or "hidden" individuals and groups with speaking parts in the Book of Mormon. This, I assume, is because in many cases they are nameless. Nonetheless, they have important dialogue within the text. On the previous list, people who clearly spoke were marked in italics. Names on this list are not included in the previous list of speakers, which came from the modern Book of Mormon index.

List of Background or Hidden Individuals and Groups Who Speak in the Book of Mormon

Angel of the Lord	The Spirit
John the Baptist	Angel from Nephi's vision
Nephi's brethren	The daughters of Ishmael
The sons of Ishmael	Zion
The Father	Unknown prophet
Angel quoted in 2 Nephi 6	Seraph 1
Seraph 2	Unidentified person
Syria, Ephraim of Remaliah	Ahaz
Ephraim or Samaria	The unlearned
The learned	Lord or Master of the Vineyard
The servant	Angel to King Benjamin
People of King Benjamin	The People of King Noah
Prophets who speak good tidings	Priests of King Noah
A priest of King Noah	The people of Alma 1
The people of Limhi	The king of Lamanites
Angel speaking to Alma 2	The people of Mosiah
Zeram, Amnor, Manti, Limher	The people of Ammonihah
Angel who appears to Alma	Angel to Amulek
Angel speaking to many	Angels quoting the Lord
Chief judge of Ammonihah	People of Ammonihah
Wife of King Lamoni	Lamanites under King Lamoni
Father of King Lamoni	Amalekite
Father of Lamoni's servants	King Anti-Nephi-Lehi
Ammon and his brethren	Brethren of Zarahemla
The sons of Mosiah	The voice of the people
Joshua	Zoramites
A poor Zoramite	Zerahemnah
Moroni's soldier	Nephites who make covenant
Servants of Amalickiah	The Lamanite guards
Stripling warriors	Gid

Nephite army spies	Servant of Helam
Multitude at the prison	Gadianton judges
People garden of Nephi	Five men sent
People seat of Cezoram	People burial of Cezoram
People at Nephi's trial	People pleading in war
Angel to Samuel the Lamanite	People rejecting Samuel
People who harden their hearts	Doubters of Christ's coming
People to Gidgiddoni	Army that beats Zemnarihah
People of Zarahemla	People of Moronihah
People in 3 Nephi	People who watch Jesus pray
The disciples	Nine Nephite disciples
Unknown prophet	The Brother of Jared
The daughter of Jared	Cry in Jaredite land
Elders and priest	Servants of the king

I think it is safe to say that the names and places included in the Book of Mormon would have been infinitely more difficult to invent than the ones Mark Twain developed for *The Adventures of Huckleberry Finn*. You would think that, as an author himself, Mark Twain would be stunned by the complexity of the Book of Mormon. Unfortunately, he chose to mock it. Perhaps the reason he was not impressed is because he never really read it. Nonetheless, he expressed his negative opinion about it. He said,

> All men have heard of the Mormon Bible, but few except the "elect" have seen it, or, at least, taken the trouble to read it. I brought away a copy from Salt Lake. The book is a curiosity to me, it is such a pretentious affair, and yet so "slow," so sleepy; such an insipid mess of inspiration. It is chloroform in print. If Joseph Smith composed this book, the act was a miracle—keeping awake while he did it was, at any rate.[4]

I read *The Adventures of Huckleberry Finn* once when I was young but have no desire to ever read it again. Growing up in the South, I came to hate racial slurs and really do not care about the author's intent when he uses the N-word 219 times in that book. As I read the Book of Mormon over and over again, I find new insights every time that I have never before seen. I get more excited to read it again and again. I am amazed at how the people in that book speak directly to me and leave me wanting to be better.

Reason to Believe

If Joseph Smith wrote the Book of Mormon, he obviously did an amazing job of creating characters that have inspired millions since it first came off the printing press. However, I don't believe it was possible for an uneducated twenty-three-year-old farm boy to invent all of the characters, places, and plots, and turn it into a complicated 588-page (first edition) book in sixty-three working days. In fact, I don't believe than *any* mortal could accomplish this feat.

For this reason, I conclude that Joseph Smith, even if he had the help of others, did not write the Book of Mormon. Since we know the book did not fall out of the sky, that only leaves one other option; that, of course, is that he translated it by the gift and power of God from ancient records, just as he stated.

Notes

1. Brown, S., *From Jerusalem to Zarahemla: Literary and Historical Studies of the Book of Mormon* (Provo, Utah: Religious Studies Center, Brigham Young University, 1998), 16.
2. H. L. Mencken, "Review of Albert Bigelow Paine's biography of Mark Twain," *The Smart Set*, February 1913.
3. Ernest Hemingway, *The Green Hills of Africa* (New York: Charles Scribner's Sons, 1934), chapter 1.
4. Mark Twain, *Roughing It* (Hartford, Connecticut: American Publishing Company, 1872), 127.

Chapter 14: Original Phrases

"The Book of Mormon is a literary and a religious masterpiece, and is far beyond even the fondest hopes or abilities of any farm boy. It is a modern revelation from end to end. It is God-given."[1]

—Mark E. Petersen

Critics have charged Joseph Smith with plagiarism since the Book of Mormon was first published. In 1830, for example, a writer for the *Cleveland Herald* made this negative comment: "The only opinion we have of the origin of this Golden Bible, is that Mr. Cowdery and Mr. Smith the reputed author, have taken the old Bible to keep up a train of circumstances, and by altering names and language have produced the string of jargon called the 'Book of Mormon,' with the intention of making money by the sale of their books."[2]

Mark Twain took up a similar line of reasoning: "The book seems to be merely a prosy detail of imaginary history, with the Old Testament for a model; followed by a tedious plagiarism of the New Testament. The author labored to give his words and phrases the quaint, old-fashioned sound and structure of our King James's translation of the Scriptures; and the result is a mongrel—half modern glibness, and half ancient simplicity and gravity."[3]

A few years later, the "brilliant" Harvard-trained author and philosopher John Fiske stated his opinion of the Book of Mormon: "It is all pure fiction, and of a very clumsy sort, such as might easily be devised by an *ignorant man* accustomed to *the language of the Bible*."[4] Unfortunately, Fiske failed to give any examples of an equivalent book being produced by an ignorant man. Nor did this full-time author of twenty-four books give an example of a brilliant man producing one. He, and others like him over the years, threw out outrageous comments with no evidence to demonstrate that what they said was true, but many bought into their views. If I said, "St. Paul's Cathedral in London is a clumsy architectural joke, such as could be built by a common laborer accustomed to looking at St. Peter's Basilica in Rome," I would likely be mocked by experts.

After almost two hundred years, critics are still trying to explain where the Book of Mormon came from. Because it makes no sense that a farm boy could have written it, charges of plagiarism continue today while the sources to prove plagiarism are still searched for. Plagiarism is defined as using and publishing the language, thoughts, ideas, or expressions of another author and passing them off as one's own.

Critics often cite the Isaiah chapters that are quoted in the Book of Mormon as proof of plagiarism. Note that Joseph Smith never claimed to have written the Book of Mormon, so it is hard to see how any of it could be considered plagiarism. If anyone plagiarized, it would have to be someone like Nephi or his brother Jacob. Does Nephi try to pass off the words of Isaiah as his own before he quotes several chapters? Not at all. He specifically noted this as he introduced a section where several chapters of Isaiah are quoted: "And now I write some of the words of Isaiah, that whoso of my people shall see these words may lift up their hearts and rejoice for all men" (2 Nephi 11:8). How much clearer could he be that he is not trying to take credit for what he is about to quote? However, I would expect Nephi to use phrases from Isaiah when he speaks because of his great admiration for him.

Using the same logic that the critics use against the Book of Mormon could just as easily be used to say that the New Testament writers plagiarized from the Old Testament. In fact, there are excerpts from every book in the Old Testament except Ezra, Nehemiah, Esther, Ecclesiastes, and the Song of Solomon in the New Testament. Would critics also say that Jesus plagiarized since He quoted from twenty-four different Old Testament books without referencing chapter and verse? Here is an example from the Old Testament and what Jesus said:

Deuteronomy 6:5 (emphasis added): "And *thou shalt love the Lord thy God with all thine heart, and with all thy soul, and with all thy might.*"

Matthew 22:36–37 (emphasis added): "Master, which is the great commandment in the law?"

"Jesus said unto him, Thou shalt love the Lord thy God with all thy heart, and with all thy soul, and with all thy mind."

Would a critic also say that Jesus Christ took the words of Moses and passed them on as His own without giving credit?

If we were to go through the entire Book of Mormon and take out every short phrase that could have possibly been copied from the Bible or another book printed before 1830, would we merely have a pamphlet left, as Mark Twain suggested? No; in fact, we would still have the vast majority of a large, complex, and inspirational book. So if Joseph Smith didn't translate it, then where did it come from? It appears we don't have a lot of options left because either Joseph Smith wrote it alone (or with help) or he translated it. If he wrote it, then he came up with every phrase that he could not have copied from others.

The following are the results of computer searches made on 360 phrases from a sample of twenty of the 153 speakers who have their words recorded in the Book of Mormon. I took their words from the original two verses where they first speak. The phrases are all between three and seven words long and were more or less chosen randomly. They could have easily been divided differently, but I'm confident the results would be about the same. Please note that if the print is regular (no italics, bold, or underline), the phrase is only used by that speaker. If the phrase is underlined, it means that it is also original to the Book of Mormon, but more than one speaker used the same phrase. If the phrase is in bold, then the same phrase is also found in the Bible.

Key

Hyphen: separates a three- to seven-word phrase used by the speaker
Regular Print: an original phrase used by that speaker only
Underline: an original Book of Mormon phrase used by more than one speaker
Bold: a phrase used by *both* Book of Mormon and Bible speakers

Abinadom: Omni 1

10 Behold, I, Abinadom, - am the son of Chemish. - <u>Behold, it came to pass that</u> - I saw much war and contention - between my people, the Nephites, - <u>and the Lamanites;</u> - and I, with my own sword, - have taken the lives - of many of the Lamanites - in the defence of my brethren.

11 And behold, the record of - this people is engraven upon plates - which is had by the kings, - **according to the generations**; - and I know of no revelation - save that which has been written, - neither prophecy; wherefore, - that which is sufficient is written. - <u>And I make an end.</u>

Alma: Mosiah 18

8 Behold, here are the - <u>waters of Mormon</u> . . . - and now, as ye - are desirous to come - <u>into the fold of God</u>, - and to be called his people, - and are willing to - bear one another's burdens, - that they may be light;

9 Yea, and are willing to - mourn with those that mourn; - yea, and comfort those that - stand in need of comfort, - and to stand as - witnesses of God at all times - **and in all things**, - and in all places that - <u>ye may be in</u>, - <u>even until death</u>, - **that ye may** - be redeemed of God, - and be numbered with - those of the first resurrection, - that ye may have eternal life—

Ammaron: Mormon 1

2 I perceive that thou - art a sober child, - and art quick to observe;

3 Therefore, when ye are about - twenty and four years old - <u>I would that ye should</u> - remember the things that ye have - observed concerning this people; - and when ye are of that age - go to the land Antum, - unto a hill which - shall be called Shim; - and there have I - deposited unto the Lord all the - sacred engravings concerning this people.

Antionah: Alma 12

20 What is this that thou hast said, - that man should rise from the dead - and be changed from this mortal - to an immortal state, - that the soul can never die?

21 What does the scripture mean, - which saith that God placed cherubim - and a flaming sword on the - east of the garden of Eden, - lest our first parents should - enter and partake of the - <u>fruit of the tree of life</u>, - <u>and live forever</u>? - <u>And thus we see that</u> - there was no possible chance - that they should live forever.

Brother of Jared: Ether 2

18 O Lord, I have performed - the work which thou hast commanded me, - and I have made the barges - according as thou hast directed me.

19 And behold, O Lord, - in them there is no light; - whither shall we steer? - And also we shall perish, - for in them we cannot breathe, - <u>save it is the</u> - air which is in them; -therefore we shall perish.

Chief Judge of Ammonihah: Alma 14

14 After what ye have seen, - will ye preach again unto this people, - that they shall be cast into - <u>a lake of fire and brimstone</u>?

15 <u>Behold, ye see that</u> - ye had not power - to save those who - <u>had been cast into the fire</u>; - neither has God saved them - because they were of thy faith . . . - What say ye for yourselves?

Daughter of Jared: Ether 8

9 Whereby hath my father - so much sorrow? - Hath he not read - the record which our fathers - brought across the great deep? - Behold, is there not an account - concerning them of old, - that they by their - secret plans did obtain - kingdoms and great glory?

10 And now, therefore, let - my father send for Akish, - the son of Kimnor; - and behold, I am fair, - and I will dance before him, - and I will please him, - that he will desire me to wife; - wherefore if he shall - desire of thee that ye shall - give unto him me to wife, - <u>then shall ye say</u>: - I will give her if ye - <u>will bring unto me the head</u> - <u>of my father, the king</u>.

Giddianhi: 3 Nephi 3

2 Lachoneus, most noble - and chief governor of the land, - behold, I write - this epistle unto you, - and do give unto you - exceedingly great praise - because of your firmness, -and also the firmness - of your people, - in maintaining that which - ye suppose to be -your right and liberty; - yea, ye do stand well, - as if ye were supported - by the hand of a god, - in the defence of your liberty, - and your property, - and your country, - or that which ye do call so.

3 And it seemeth - a pity unto me, - most noble Lachoneus, - that ye should be so - <u>foolish and vain</u> - as to suppose that - ye can stand

against - so many brave men - who are at my command, - who do now at this time - stand in their arms, - and do await - with great anxiety for the word - Go down upon the - Nephites and destroy them.

Gideon: Mosiah 20

17 I pray thee forbear, - and do not search this people, - and lay not this - thing to their charge.

18 For do ye not remember - the priests of thy father, - whom this people sought to destroy? - And are they not in the wilderness? - And are not they the ones - who have stolen the - <u>daughters of the Lamanites</u>?

Jarom: Jarom 1

1 Now behold, I, Jarom, - write a few words according to - the commandment of my father, Enos, - that our genealogy may be kept.

2 And as these plates are small, - and as these things - are written for the intent - of the benefit of - <u>our brethren the Lamanites</u>, - <u>wherefore, it must needs be</u> - that I write a little; - but I shall not write - the things of my prophesying, - nor of my revelations. - For what could I write more - than my fathers have written? - For have not they revealed - <u>the plan of salvation</u>? - <u>I say unto you, Yea</u>; - and this sufficeth me.

King Anti-Nephi-Lehi: Alma 24

7 **I thank my God**, - my beloved people, - that our great God - has in goodness sent these - <u>our brethren, the Nephites</u>, - unto us to preach unto us, - and to convince us of - the traditions of our wicked fathers.

8 And behold, I thank - my great God - that he has given us - <u>a portion of his Spirit</u> - to soften our hearts, - that we have opened - <u>a correspondence with</u> - these brethren, the Nephites.

King Lamoni: Alma 18

4 Now I know that it - is the Great Spirit; - and he has come down - at this time to -preserve your lives, - that I might not slay you - as I did your brethren. - Now this is the Great Spirit - of whom our fathers have spoken.

8 Where is this man that - <u>has such great power</u>?

King of the Lamanites: Mosiah 20

15 I have broken the oath - because thy people did carry away - the daughters of my people; - therefore, in my anger I did - cause my people to come up - to war against thy people.

24 Let us go forth to - meet my people, without arms; - and I swear unto you - with an oath that my people - shall not slay thy people.

Korihor: Alma 30

13 O ye that are bound down - under a foolish - and a vain hope, - why do ye yoke yourselves - with such foolish things? - Why do ye look for a Christ? - For no man can know of - anything which is to come.

14 Behold, these things - which ye call prophecies, - which ye say are - handed down by holy prophets, - behold, they are foolish traditions - **of your fathers**.

Laman: 1 Nephi 16

37 Behold, let us slay our father, - and also our brother Nephi, - who has taken it upon him - to be our ruler - and our teacher, - who are his elder brethren.

38 Now, he says that - the Lord has talked with him, - and also that angels - have ministered unto him. - But behold, we know - that he lies unto us; - and he tells us these things, - and he worketh many things - by his cunning arts, - that he may deceive our eyes, - thinking, perhaps, that - he may lead us away - into some strange wilderness; - and after he has led us away, - he has thought to - make himself a king - and a ruler over us, - that he may do with us - according to his will and pleasure.

Limhi: Mosiah 7

9 Behold, I am Limhi, - the son of Noah, - who was the son of Zeniff, - who came up out of - the land of Zarahemla - to inherit this land, - which was the land of their fathers, -who was made a king by - **the voice of the people**.

10 And now, I desire to know - the cause whereby ye - were so bold as to come near - the walls of the city, - when I, myself, was with - my guards without the gate?

Mormon: Words of Mormon

1 And now I, Mormon, - being about to deliver up - <u>the record which</u> - I have been making into - the hands of my son Moroni, - behold I have witnessed - almost all the destruction - <u>of my people, the Nephites</u>.

2 And it is many hundred years - <u>after the coming of Christ</u> - that I deliver these records - <u>into the hands of my son;</u> - <u>and it supposeth me</u> - that he will witness the - entire destruction of my people. - But may God grant that - he may survive them, - that he may write - somewhat concerning them, - and somewhat concerning Christ, - that perhaps some day - it may profit them.

Moroni: Alma 44

1 Behold, Zerahemnah, that we - do not desire to be - men of blood. - Ye know that ye are - **in our hands**, - yet we do not - desire to slay you.

2 Behold, we have not - <u>come out to battle</u> - against you that we might - shed your blood for power; - neither do we desire - to bring any one - to the yoke of bondage. - But this is the - very cause for which ye - have come against us; - yea, and ye are angry - with us because of our religion.

Omni: Omni 1

1 <u>Behold, it came to pass</u> - that I, Omni, being commanded - by my father, Jarom, - <u>that I should write</u> - somewhat upon these plates, - to preserve our genealogy—

2 Wherefore, in my days, - <u>I would that ye should know</u> - that I fought much with the sword - to preserve my people, the Nephites, - <u>from falling into the hands</u> - of their enemies, the Lamanites. - <u>But behold, I of myself</u> - am a wicked man, - and I have not kept - <u>the statutes and the commandments</u> - of the Lord as I ought - **to have done**.

Sherem: Jacob 7

6 Brother Jacob, I have - <u>sought much opportunity that</u> - I might speak unto you; - **for I have heard** - and also know that - thou goest about much, - preaching that which ye call the gospel, - or the doctrine of Christ.

7 And ye have led away - much of this people - that they pervert - the right way of God, - and keep not the law of Moses - which is the right way; - and convert the law of Moses -into the worship of a being - which ye say shall come - many hundred years hence. - And now behold, I, Sherem, - declare unto you that this is blasphemy; - for no man knoweth

It is obvious that original phrases are predominant in these examples. Throughout the Book of Mormon, the pattern remains constant. The actual numbers are amazing. A summary of the data from these verses is provided below:

- 360 total three- to seven-word phrases in the verses quoted
- 350 total unique phrases in the Book of Mormon (regular print)
- 10 total phrases also in the Bible (bold print)

Reason to Believe

There are 268,163 words in the Book of Mormon, not counting chapter headings and verse numbers. By taking out all of the verses and phrases that could have been copied from the Bible, I estimate that there would still be over 45,000 original phrases that Joseph Smith would have had to create to write the Book of Mormon. These phrases are not in the Bible or other likely sources. Though linguists explain that people are capable of creating new combinations of words in their lives, many phrases in the Book of Mormon are not typical of conversational language. Thinking that Joseph Smith came up with thousands and thousands of totally unique phrases in the Book of Mormon is about as easy for me to believe as saying there was an explosion at the library and the Book of Mormon came down from the sky. For this reason, I believe it is what it claims to be.

Notes

1. Mark E. Petersen, "It Was a Miracle!" *Ensign*, November 1977, 11.
2. "The Golden Bible," *Ashtabula (Ohio) Journal,* 4 December 1830, quoting the *Cleveland Herald.*
3. Mark Twain, *Roughing It* (Hartford, Connecticut: American Publishing, 1901), 133.
4. John Fiske, *The Historical Writings of John Fiske* (Boston, Massachusetts: Houghton Mifflin Company, 1902), 4.

Chapter 15: Original Phrases Used More than Once

"Q. Had he [Joseph Smith] not a book or manuscript from which he read, or dictated to you?

"A. He had neither manuscript or book to read from.

"Q. Could he not have had, and you not know it?

"A. If he had anything of the kind he could not have concealed it from me."[1]

—Emma Smith

I magine trying to dictate a really complicated 588-page document without any notes whatsoever in front of you. Everything would have to have been thought out beforehand, memorized, and dictated to scribes, or have been made up spontaneously. Joseph Smith not having pre-written notes during the translation process appears to be an established fact. Of course, even if he had notes, where in the world did they come from? I cannot comprehend dictating hour after hour the great doctrinal speeches, stories of war and wickedness, counsel to family members, experiences with apostates and dictators, and other proclamations with no notes.

However, this is not just any story, seeing as the Book of Mormon is also filled with thousands of original phrases that would have needed to be created. Most of these unique phrases are only used one time in the entire Book of Mormon. Other phrases are used more than one time either by the same writer or by two or more other writers. Think about how difficult it would be to have exact phrases used more than one time by a different writer in a totally different context. Let's look at a small sampling of phrases that are only used by one or two writers, that are not found anywhere else in the Book of Mormon or in the Old or New Testaments.

The following is a sample of eight phrases used more than once by the same Book of Mormon character, but not used by anyone else.

Nephi: "of worth unto the children of men"

1 Nephi 6:6 (emphasis added): "Wherefore, I shall give commandment unto my seed, that they shall not occupy these plates with things which are not *of worth unto the children of men.*"

2 Nephi 25:8 (emphasis added): "Wherefore, they are *of worth unto the children of men*, and he that supposeth that they are not, unto them will I speak particularly, and confine the words unto mine own people."

Jacob: "the pleasing word of God"

Jacob 2:8 (emphasis added): "And it supposeth me that they have come up hither to hear *the pleasing word of God*, yea, the word which healeth the wounded soul."

Jacob 3:2 (emphasis added): "O all ye that are pure in heart, lift up your heads and receive *the pleasing word of God*, and feast upon his love; for ye may, if your minds are firm, forever."

Mormon: "the destruction of my people, the Nephites"

Words of Mormon 1:1 (emphasis added): "And now I, Mormon, being about to deliver up the record which I have been making into the hands of my son Moroni, behold I have witnessed almost all *the destruction of my people, the Nephites.*"

Mormon 6:1 (emphasis added): "And now I finish my record concerning *the destruction of my people, the Nephites*. And it came to pass that we did march forth before the Lamanites."

King Benjamin: "I would that ye should remember to"

Mosiah 1:7 (emphasis added): "And now, my sons, *I would that ye should remember to* search them diligently, that ye may profit thereby; and I would that ye should keep the commandments of God, that ye may prosper in the land according to the promises which the Lord made unto our fathers."

Mosiah 5:12 (emphasis added): "I say unto you, *I would that ye should remember to* retain the name written always in your hearts, that ye are not found on the left hand of God, but that ye hear and know the voice by which ye shall be called, and also, the name by which he shall call you."

Alma: "if I had not been born of God I should not have known these things"

Alma 36:5 (emphasis added): "Now, behold, I say unto you, *if I had not been born of God I should not have known these things*; but God has, by the mouth of his holy angel, made these things known unto me, not of any worthiness of myself."

Alma 38:6 (emphasis added): "Now, my son, I would not that ye should think that I know these things of myself, but it is the Spirit of God which is in me which maketh these things known unto me; for *if I had not been born of God I should not have known these things*."

Mormon: "in the borders by the seashore"

Alma 22:28 (emphasis added): "Now, the more idle part of the Lamanites lived in the wilderness, and dwelt in tents; and they were spread through the wilderness on the west, in the land of Nephi; yea, and also on the west of the land of Zarahemla, *in the borders by the seashore*."

Alma 51:22 (emphasis added): "Behold, it came to pass that while Moroni was thus breaking down the wars and contentions among his own people, and subjecting them to peace and civilization, and making regulations to prepare for war against the Lamanites, behold, the Lamanites had come into the land of Moroni, which was *in the borders by the seashore*."[2]

Jacob: "great condescensions unto the children of men"

2 Nephi 9:53 (emphasis added): "And behold how great the covenants of the Lord, and how *great* his *condescensions unto the children of men*; and because of his greatness, and his grace and mercy."

Jacob 4:7 (emphasis added): "Nevertheless, the Lord God showeth us our weakness that we may know that it is by his grace, and his *great condescensions unto the children of men*, that we have power to do these things."

Jacob: "O, my beloved brethren"

2 Nephi 9:39 (emphasis added): "*O, my beloved brethren*, remember the awfulness in transgressing against that Holy God, and also the awfulness of yielding to the enticings of that cunning one. Remember, to be carnally-minded is death, and to be spiritually-minded is life eternal."

2 Nephi 9:45 (emphasis added): "*O, my beloved brethren,* turn away from your sins; shake off the chains of him that would bind you fast; come unto that God who is the rock of your salvation."

The following is a sample of eight of the hundreds of phrases that are used by two different Book of Mormon writers but are not used by anyone else.

"wild, and ferocious, and a blood-thirsty people"

Enos: Enos 1 (emphasis added)

20 And I bear record that the people of Nephi did seek diligently to restore the Lamanites unto the true faith in God. But our labors were vain; their hatred was fixed, and they were led by their evil nature that they became *wild, and ferocious, and a blood-thirsty people,* full of idolatry and filthiness."

Zeniff: Mosiah 10 (emphasis added)

12 They were a *wild, and ferocious, and a blood-thirsty people,* believing in the tradition of their fathers, which is this—Believing that they were driven out of the land of Jerusalem because of the iniquities of their fathers, and that they were wronged in the wilderness by their brethren, and they were also wronged while crossing the sea.

"the great plan of redemption"

Jacob: Jacob 6 (emphasis added)

8 Behold, will ye reject these words? Will ye reject the words of the prophets; and will ye reject all the words which have been spoken concerning Christ, after so many have spoken concerning him; and deny the good word of Christ, and the power of God, and the gift of the Holy Ghost, and quench the Holy Spirit, and make a mock of *the great plan of redemption,* which hath been laid for you?

Amulek: Alma 34 (emphasis added)

31 Yea, I would that ye would come forth and harden not your hearts any longer; for behold, now is the time and the day of your salvation; and therefore, if ye will repent and harden not your hearts, immediately shall *the great plan of redemption* be brought about unto you.

"behold the marvelous light of God"
Alma: Mosiah 27 (emphasis added)

29 My soul hath been redeemed from the gall of bitterness and bonds of iniquity. I was in the darkest abyss; but now I *behold the marvelous light of God*. My soul was racked with eternal torment; but I am snatched, and my soul is pained no more.

Ammon: Alma 26 (emphasis added)

3 Behold, I answer for you; for our brethren, the Lamanites, were in darkness, yea, even in the darkest abyss, but behold, how many of them are brought to *behold the marvelous light of God!*

"through the atoning blood of Christ"
An angel: Mosiah 3 (emphasis added)

18 For behold he judgeth, and his judgment is just; and the infant perisheth not that dieth in his infancy; but men drink damnation to their own souls except they humble themselves and become as little children, and believe that salvation was, and is, and is to come, in and *through the atoning blood of Christ*, the Lord Omnipotent.

Helaman: Helaman 5 (emphasis added)

9 O remember, remember, my sons, the words which king Benjamin spake unto his people; yea, remember that there is no other way nor means whereby man can be saved, only *through the atoning blood of Jesus Christ*, who shall come; yea, remember that he cometh to redeem the world.

"the high priesthood of the holy order of God"
Mormon: Alma 4 (emphasis added)

20 And thus in the commencement of the ninth year of the reign of the judges over the people of Nephi, Alma delivered up the judgment-seat to Nephihah, and confined himself wholly to *the high priesthood of the holy order of God*, to the testimony of the word, according to the spirit of revelation and prophecy.

Alma: Alma 13 (emphasis added)

6 And thus being called by this holy calling, and ordained unto *the high priesthood of the holy order of God*, to teach his commandments unto the children of men, that they also might enter into his rest.

"were smitten with famine and sore afflictions"
Mormon: Mosiah 1 (emphasis added)

17 Therefore, as they were unfaithful they did not prosper nor progress in their journey, but were driven back, and incurred the

displeasure of God upon them; and therefore they *were smitten with famine and sore afflictions,* to stir them up in remembrance of their duty.

Zeniff: Mosiah 9 (emphasis added)

3 And yet, I being over-zealous to inherit the land of our fathers, collected as many as were desirous to go up to possess the land, and started again on our journey into the wilderness to go up to the land; but we *were smitten with famine and sore afflictions;* for we were slow to *remember* the Lord our God.

"saw God sitting upon his throne, surrounded with numberless concourses of angels"
Nephi: 1 Nephi 1 (emphasis added)

8 And being thus overcome with the Spirit, he was carried away in a vision, even that he saw the heavens open, and he thought he [Lehi] *saw God sitting upon his throne, surrounded with numberless concourses of angels in the attitude of singing and praising their God.*

Alma: Alma 36 (emphasis added)

22 Yea, methought I *saw,* even as our father Lehi saw, *God sitting upon his throne, surrounded with numberless concourses of angels, in the attitude of singing and praising their God;* yea, and my soul did long to be there.

These original phrases, written by one or more writers in the Book of Mormon, have significance to the prophets who said them and to their listeners and readers. Some phrases were of warning, others of hope. Many directly related to the love and mercy of God and the gift of the Atonement. Others alluded to the plan of salvation and the nature of God. Words of counsel were encapsulated in simple phrases. The great diversity of content in these phrases is impressive.

Reason to Believe

The Book of Mormon contains thousands of original phrases that were only used by one person. However, there are multiple cases where one author used the same phrase more than one time while others were only used two times in the entire book but by different writers. In this case, it would appear that one writer had read the writings of another writer and were inspired to use the exact same phrase. Not only is the number of these original phrases astounding, but so is the great variety of content that is included. If Joseph Smith were the author of the book, how could he have repeated earlier used phrases in totally different contexts and often in a totally different time period—all without manuscripts, books, or notes? It does not seem plausible that he could keep these phrases in his mind and dictate them with no hesitation throughout the process.

Notes

1. Joseph Smith III, "Last Testimony of Sister Emma," *Saints' Herald* 26 (October 1, 1879), 289–90.
2. The word *seashore* is not found in the Old or New Testaments, or the writings of Joseph Smith.

Chapter 16 : Internal Consistency

"The book [of Mormon] is like a vast mansion with gardens, towers, courtyards, and wings. There are rooms yet to be entered, with flaming fireplaces waiting to warm us. The rooms glimpsed so far contain further furnishings and rich detail yet to be savored."[1]

—Elder Neal A. Maxwell

One of the most difficult things about writing a long, complex manuscript is avoiding seemingly inevitable mistakes and inconsistencies. In any lengthy, detailed, realistic work, there are almost always holes or errors, even when the manuscripts have been edited multiple times. Astute readers always seem to pick up even minor inconsistencies. For example, in *The Lord of the Rings,* both Tom Bombadil and Treebeard are referred to as the eldest being in Middle Earth. There are several other mistakes and inconsistencies in Tolkien's masterpiece.

In J. K. Rowling's immensely popular Harry Potter series, readers have found numerous mistakes and inconsistencies. For example, in *Harry Potter and the Goblet of Fire*, Harry's fourteenth birthday is listed as July 31, 1994. In the beginning of the book, he writes a letter to Sirius and mentions that his cousin Dudley got angry and threw his PlayStation out of the window. The problem is that PlayStations were not released in Europe until September 29, 1995. J. K. Rowling said, "As obsessive fans will tell you, I do slip up! Several classrooms move floors mysteriously between books and these are the least serious continuity errors! Most of the fansites will point you in the direction of my mistakes."[2]

One of the most amazing things about the Book of Mormon is its internal consistency. Just imagine the difficulty in writing (or translating) such a long, complex book without the aid of modern technology and educated editors. The chances for major holes and errors would be extreme. And yet after 185 years of careful scrutiny, the Book of Mormon has turned out to be extremely consistent from start to finish. Let's consider a few examples of this consistency.

When Christ Is First Mentioned

The name *Christ* means "the anointed" in Greek or "the Messiah" in Hebrew. Christ's name is first mentioned in Matthew 1:1 in the Bible. In the Book of Mormon, the name Christ is first used by Jacob, Lehi's fifth son. Between the years 559 BC and 545 BC, an angel appeared to Jacob and revealed to him what His name would be.

2 Nephi 10

3 Wherefore, as I said unto you, it must needs be expedient that Christ—for in the last night the angel spake unto me that this should be his name—should come among the Jews, among those who are the more wicked part of the world; and they shall crucify him—for thus it behooveth our God, and there is none other nation on earth that would crucify their God.

It is interesting that it was not Lehi or Nephi who first learned that the Messiah would be called Christ. Lehi died somewhere between 588 BC and 570 BC before the angel appeared to Jacob. Lehi never once called Him Christ. Nephi never used the name Christ until after Jacob learned His name from the angel.

Number of Times the Name Christ Is Mentioned in the Book of Mormon

1 Nephi	0
2 Nephi	49
Jacob	25
Enos	3
Omni	1
Words of Mormon	4
Mosiah	28
Alma	74
Helaman	12
3 Nephi	34
4 Nephi	14

Mormon	31
Ether	13
Moroni	64

Nephite Forms of Government

Before Lehi and his family left Jerusalem, they lived under the reign of King Zedekiah. Monarchy was the form of government they were accustomed to. When the group came to the promised land and needed to form a government, both the Nephites and Lamanites naturally wanted to have a king. That is exactly what happened. Though Nephi did not seek that position or even want it, he apparently served as the first king of the Nephites. The reign of the kings began with Nephi, and that form of government lasted for almost five hundred years.

The Reign of the Kings: 2 Nephi 6 (emphasis added)

2 Behold, my beloved brethren, I, Jacob, having been called of God, and ordained after the manner of his holy order, and having been consecrated by my brother Nephi, unto whom ye look as a *king* or a protector, and on whom ye depend for safety, behold ye know that I have spoken unto you exceedingly many things.

Mosiah 29 (emphasis added)

47 And thus ended the *reign of the kings* over the people of Nephi; and thus ended the days of Alma, who was the founder of their church.

The second form of government began when all of the sons of Mosiah refused to be king of the Nephite nation in 92 BC. At that point, Mosiah proposed that a new form of government be instituted. Judges were chosen by the voice of the people, with a chief judge at the head. The first chief judge was Alma the Younger, who was named so in 91 BC. The first time the phrase *reign of the judges* is mentioned is in this verse:

The Reign of the Judges: Mosiah 29 (emphasis added)

44 And thus commenced the *reign of the judges* throughout all the land of Zarahemla, among all the people who were called the Nephites; and Alma was the first and chief judge.

After this verse, the phrase is then mentioned sixty-one times in the Book of Alma and thirty-six times in the Book of Helaman. But then it suddenly stops, and the last time the phrase *reign of the judges* is mentioned is in the following verse:

Helaman 16 (emphasis added)

24 And thus ended the ninetieth year of *the reign of the judges* over the people of Nephi.

Right before the great destruction that occurred when Christ was crucified, the reign of the judges totally collapsed, and the people divided into tribes of kindred and friends. Every tribe then appointed a chief or leader of their tribe.

Chief or Leader of Tribes: 3 Nephi 7 (emphasis added)

3 And every *tribe* did appoint a chief or a leader over them; and thus they became tribes and leaders of *tribes*.

The Book of Mormon is totally consistent when referring to each of the three forms of government used in the various time periods. And yet Joseph Smith lived in America, where none of these forms of government were in place.

Three Ways to Reconcile Time

Just as there are three forms of government among the Nephites, there are also three ways to reconcile time. The book is totally consistent in this area as well.

From the time that Lehi left Jerusalem: Mosiah 6 (emphasis added)

4 And Mosiah began to reign in his father's stead. And he began to reign in the thirtieth year of his age, making in the whole, about *four hundred and seventy-six years from the time that Lehi left Jerusalem.*

The reign of the judges: Helaman 11 (emphasis added)

35 And thus ended *the eighty and first year of the reign of the judges.*

Since the sign was given of Christ's birth: Moroni 10 (emphasis added)

1 Now I, Moroni, write somewhat as seemeth me good; and I write unto my brethren, the Lamanites; and I would that they should know that more than four hundred and twenty years have passed away *since the sign was given of the coming of Christ.*

The following verses mention all three ways to count time:

3 Nephi 2 (emphasis added)

5 And also an hundred years had passed away *since the days of Mosiah*, who was king over the people of the Nephites.

6 And six hundred and nine years had passed away *since Lehi left Jerusalem.*

7 And nine years had passed away *from the time when the sign was given*, which was spoken of by the prophets, that Christ should come into the world.

8 Now the Nephites began to reckon their time from this period when the sign was given, or from the coming of Christ; therefore, nine years had passed away.

These ways of identifying time periods clearly set apart distinct eras in Book of Mormon history. These designations show that chronology and historical accuracy was important to the Nephites.

The Great Spirit

Since it was Nephite record keepers who chronicled the material used in the Book of Mormon, there are few direct quotes from the Lamanites. Mormon did insert quotes from King Lamoni and his father when he spoke to Ammon and his brother Aaron. From their words, we learn that this father and son both believed in a god. We also ascertain that both refer to their deity as the Great Spirit.

Lamoni: Alma 18 (emphasis added)

26 And then Ammon said: Believest thou that there is a *Great Spirit*?
27 And he said, Yea.

28 And Ammon said: This is God. And Ammon said unto him again: Believest thou that this *Great Spirit*, who is God, created all things which are in heaven and in the earth?

29 And he said: Yea, I believe that he created all things which are in the earth; but I do not know the heavens.

Lamoni's father: Alma 22 (emphasis added)

9 And the king said: Is God that *Great Spirit* that brought our fathers out of the land of Jerusalem?

10 And Aaron said unto him: Yea, he is that *Great Spirit*, and he created all things both in heaven and in earth. Believest thou this?

11 And he said: Yea, I believe that the *Great Spirit* created all things, and I desire that ye should tell me concerning all these things, and I will believe thy words.

A few years ago, my wife and I visited the Little Bighorn National Monument in Montana. While there, I read a statement on a plaque made by Crazy Horse, the Native American war leader who fought at the battle. Having just read the Book of Mormon account of Ammon and Aaron, I found his statement interesting. He said,

> We did not ask you white men to come here. The Great Spirit gave us this country as a home. You had yours. We did not interfere with you. The Great Spirit gave us plenty of land to live on, and buffalo, deer, antelope and other game; but you have come here; you are taking my land from me; you are killing off our game, so it is hard for us to live. Now you tell us to work for a living, but the Great Spirit did not make us to work, but to live by hunting. You white men can work if you want to. We do not interfere with you, and again you say, why do you not become civilized? We do not want your civilization! We would live as our fathers did, and their fathers before them.

In the Book of Mormon, the Lamanites often hunted wild game for food while the Nephites raised flocks and crops, just as in Crazy Horse's day. The tradition of referring to God as the Great Spirit also continued into modern times.

I often wondered why Ammon and Aaron corrected Lamoni and his father when they referred to God as the Great Spirit. God has many titles. Why would it matter if the Lamanites added another?

A few years ago, I was talking to a seminary teacher and asked her why she thought they were corrected. She replied that it was because their referring to God as the Great Spirit was false doctrine. She said, "God the Father has a body of flesh and bones. He is not a spirit."

Immediately after visiting the Little Bighorn battle site, my wife and I went to a family reunion held in Billings, Montana. One of my wife's relatives invited a Native American musical group to entertain our family gathering with drums and chants. At one point, someone asked the leader of the group how they got together. He said, "We believe that the Great Spirit brought us together."

It is significant that the only people in the entire Book of Mormon to refer to God by that title are the Lamanites. It is also interesting that many Native Americans still refer to Heavenly Father that way.

Foolish Traditions

We learn from Lehi's dream that one of the adversary's tools is to laugh, point fingers, and mock those who are trying to live righteously. There are several times in the Book of Mormon where mocking is used by the wicked against the righteous. The phrase *foolish traditions* is not used in the Bible, but it is used six different times in the Book of Mormon. Each time, the phrase is used by apostates and is always directed towards members of the Church. Here are four examples:

People of Ammonihah: Alma 8 (emphasis added)

11 Nevertheless, they hardened their hearts, saying unto him: Behold, we know that thou art Alma; and we know that thou art high priest over the church which thou hast established in many parts of the land, according to your tradition; and we are not of thy church, and we do not believe in such *foolish traditions*.

An Amalekite: Alma 21 (emphasis added)

8 And the man said unto him: We do not believe that thou knowest any such thing. We do not believe in these *foolish traditions*. We do not believe that thou knowest of things to come, neither do we believe that thy fathers and also that our fathers did know concerning the things which they spake, of that which is to come.

Korihor: Alma 30 (emphasis added)

14 Behold, these things which ye call prophecies, which ye say are handed down by holy prophets, behold, they are *foolish traditions* of your fathers.

Zoramites: Alma 31 (emphasis added)

17 But thou art the same yesterday, today, and forever; and thou hast elected us that we shall be saved, whilst all around us are elected to be cast by thy wrath down to hell; for the which holiness, O God, we thank thee; and we also thank thee that thou hast elected us, that we may not be led away after the *foolish traditions* of our brethren, which doth bind them down to a belief of Christ, which doth lead their hearts to wander far from thee, our God.

Korihor, an anti-Christ, said, "O ye that are bound down under a *foolish and a vain hope*, why do ye *yoke yourselves* with such *foolish things*?" (Alma 30:13; emphasis added). In our day, some of those who have never believed or no longer believe direct the same kind of mockery toward members trying their best to live good lives. Writing about one of our exceptional scholars, a nonbeliever asked, "How can an educated person possibly believe such foolish things?" Another called one of our outstanding Harvard-trained businessmen "a massively gullible fool."

Show Me a Sign

It appears certain that the Lord is not pleased when nonbelievers seek signs to convince them of truth. When certain scribes and Pharisees asked Christ to show them a sign, He told them, "An evil and adulterous generation seeketh after a sign" (Matthew 12:39). In the Book of Mormon, two men ask to see a sign. In both cases, they are evil anti-Christs who fit the description of sign seekers described in the New Testament.

Sherem: Jacob 7 (emphasis added)

13 And it came to pass that he said unto me: *Show me a sign* by this power of the Holy Ghost, in the which ye know so much.

Korihor: Alma 30 (emphasis added)

43 And now Korihor said unto Alma: If thou wilt *show me a sign*, that I may be convinced that there is a God, yea, show unto me that he hath power, and then will I be convinced of the truth of thy words.

In the Bible, we read that "signs shall follow them that believe" (Mark 16:17). In the Book of Mormon, we read the exact same phrase, that "signs shall follow them that believe" (Mormon 9:24). Here again, the Book of Mormon teachings are not only internally consistent but also back up the Bible and the teachings of the Savior.

The Foolish Imaginations of His Heart

Laman and Lemuel did not have a testimony of the gospel, so they mocked both their brother Nephi and their father, Lehi, for believing.

Laman and Lemuel: 1 Nephi 17 (emphasis added)

20 And thou art like unto our father, led away by *the foolish imaginations of his heart*; yea, he hath led us out of the land of Jerusalem, and we have wandered in the wilderness for these many years; and our women have toiled, being big with child; and they have borne children in the wilderness and suffered all things, save it were death; and it would have been better that they had died before they came out of Jerusalem than to have suffered these afflictions.

Nephi: 1 Nephi 2 (emphasis added)

11 Now this he spake because of the stiffneckedness of Laman and Lemuel; for behold they did murmur in many things against their father, because he was a visionary man, and had led them out

of the land of Jerusalem, to leave the land of their inheritance, and their gold, and their silver, and their precious things, to perish in the wilderness. And this they said he had done because of *the foolish imaginations of his heart.*

The phrase *the foolish imaginations of his heart* is not found in the Bible and only twice in the Book of Mormon. Laman and Lemuel were the originators of the phrase, and then years later Nephi directly quoted what they said. This is another example of Book of Mormon consistency.

A Bible! A Bible!

Over the years, I have associated with hundreds of young single adults while teaching at BYU and in the institute program. I have asked many if they had ever heard anyone say that they have a Bible and don't need another one. Almost every one of our missionaries have heard something along those lines.

2 Nephi 29:3 (emphasis added)

3 And because my words shall hiss forth—many of the Gentiles shall say: A Bible! A Bible! We have got a Bible, and there cannot be any more Bible.

That verse was obviously included in the Book of Mormon text before the book was published. If Joseph Smith wrote the book himself, how would he know that many individuals worldwide would react to the Book of Mormon just as the verse said they would?

Reason to Believe

There are hundreds of examples that show the internal consistency of the Book of Mormon. Both believers and nonbelievers have pored over the pages of the book for 185 years. Many have read it over and over again. If serious holes or errors existed, someone would have picked up on them by now. Many have tried to point out things in the past that they thought were mistakes only to have them verified as correct or appropriate later. Glaring mistakes have been found in some of the most well-researched and well-renowned books of our day, but none on the level of the Book of Mormon. It is amazingly consistent. That internal consistency is another reason for me to believe it is true.

Notes

1. Neal A. Maxwell, *Not My Will, but Thine* (Salt Lake City: Bookcraft, 1988), 33.
2. J. K. Rowling, http://www.harrypotterspage.com.

Chapter 17: Martin Harris, the Witness

"Do I believe it! Do you see the sun shining! Just as surely as the sun is shining on us and gives us light, and the moon and stars give us light by night, just as surely as the breath of life sustains us, so surely do I know that Joseph Smith was a true prophet of God, chosen of God to open the last dispensation of the fulness of times; so surely do I know that the Book of Mormon was divinely translated. I saw the plates; I saw the Angel; I heard the voice of God. I know that the Book of Mormon is true and that Joseph Smith was a true prophet of God. I might as well doubt my own existence as to doubt the divine authenticity of the book of Mormon or the divine calling of Joseph Smith."[1]

—Martin Harris

Martin Harris played a pivotal role in bringing forth the Book of Mormon. He was born May 18, 1783, in Eastown, New York, but little is known of his early years. LDS historian Ronald W. Walker said, "If his later personality and activity are guides, the boy partook of the sturdy values of his neighborhood which included work, honesty, rudimentary education, and godly fear."[2] When he was twenty-five, Martin married his first cousin Lucy Harris on March 27, 1808, in Palmyra, New York. They were parents to at least five children. Four years after his marriage, Martin served with the New York militia in the War of 1812 against Great Britain. He began his military service as a private, was assigned to be a teamster, and ended as a first sergeant.

By 1827, Martin and his family were living a comfortable life on the 320 acres of land that they owned in Palmyra. He was considered a prosperous farmer for the time and place he lived in. Martin's neighbors described him as hard-working and industrious, and he was seen as an excellent provider and father.

Martin Harris first met Joseph Smith when the Smith family moved to Palmyra in 1816. Members of the Smith family worked several times for Martin on various projects. This was the beginning of an association that would last many years. When Joseph Smith first viewed the gold plates on September 22, 1823, he confided in Martin some of the details of his visits from Moroni and the existence of the plates.

On September 22, 1827, Joseph took possession of the plates exactly four years after first seeing them. Sometime that fall, Lucy Mack Smith paid a visit to Martin and his wife, Lucy, and told them that Joseph had taken possession of the plates and intended to translate them and have them published. She was seeking financial assistance to help with the printing since the Smiths were not in a position to pay for it. At that point, Martin had doubts about the story and the plates.

At first, Martin's wife, Lucy, was intrigued by the possibility that Joseph was telling the truth and appeared interested in helping him. Lucy met with him and said, "Joseph, I will tell you what I will do, if I can get a witness that you speak the truth, I will believe all you say about the matter and I shall want to do something about the translation—I mean to help you any way."[3]

The next morning, she related an amazing dream that she had the night before. According to Lucy Mack Smith, "She [Lucy Harris] said that a personage appeared to her who told her that as she had disputed the servant of the Lord, and said his word was not to be believed, and had also asked him many improper questions, she had done that which was not right in the sight of God. After which he said to her, 'Behold, here are the plates, look upon them and believe.'"[4] Lucy then described the record in detail and seemed convinced that it was true and even offered to give Joseph Smith money to assist in its printing. With time, however, her excitement faded, and seeing the plates in a dream was not enough to make a lasting impression. She seemed to become almost obsessed with seeing the plates for herself. When that was not allowed, she became one of the Prophet's persecutors and went to great lengths to pressure Martin into having nothing to do with the Smiths.

Because some hostile neighbors were attempting to steal the plates, Joseph and Emma decided to move to Harmony, Pennsylvania, for the translation process. Martin gave them fifty dollars in silver to help with their trip. By this time, his wife did not believe Joseph's story and became convinced he was trying to defraud them. Martin's increased involvement put a serious strain on their marriage. In Harmony, Joseph almost immediately began the translation process with Emma acting as his scribe.

A short time later, Martin paid a visit, desiring to help any way he could. It was at this point that Martin suggested that he make a trip to New York City to show scholars some of the characters from the plates and a sample translation to get their opinions. Joseph agreed, and Martin visited with scholars Charles Anthon and Samuel L. Mitchill. Martin came away from that trip convinced that Joseph Smith was inspired by God and the record was ancient. At one point during this visit, Professor Anthon told Martin that he could not read a sealed book. Many believe that this fulfilled a prophesy made in Isaiah 29:11, which states, "And the vision of all is become unto you as the words of a book that is sealed, which men deliver to one that is learned, saying, Read this, I pray thee: and he saith, I cannot; for it is sealed."

Martin was now ready to help Joseph in any way he needed. The help that Joseph needed was a scribe, and during the spring and early summer Martin filled that role. From April to June of 1828, the work of translation resulted in a 116-page manuscript that we know now was the book of Lehi. By this time, Lucy Harris was turning more and more hostile. Her husband was not home with his family, not taking care of their farm, supporting Joseph financially, and losing the respect of his neighbors, who thought he was involved in a fraudulent scheme. She was also obviously upset at the prospects of Martin taking a huge financial risk by having a book published.

Lucy Harris desperately wanted to see some kind of evidence that Joseph was translating an ancient record. She had asked to see the plates repeatedly as a witness but was denied. When the book of Lehi was completed, Martin asked to take the manuscript and show it to his family. You can only imagine the pressure he felt to prove that Joseph was not taking advantage of him. This request put Joseph in an awkward position. Martin was a personal friend to the Smith family and was one of the first to believe Joseph. He was more than twenty-one years older than Joseph and had been a well-respected man in the community, but he was now being mocked because of this belief. And he had been willing to volunteer time and money for the project.

Considering all that, it is no wonder that Joseph was willing to ask the Lord for permission. Joseph describes the events this way:

> Some time after Mr. [Martin] Harris had begun to write for me, he began to importune me to give him liberty to carry the writings home and show them; and desired of me that I would inquire of the Lord, through the Urim and Thummim, if he might not do so. I did inquire, and the answer was that he must not. However, he was not satisfied with this answer, and desired that I should inquire again. I did so, and the answer was as before. Still he could not be contented, but insisted that I should inquire once more. After much solicitation I again inquired of the Lord, and permission was granted him to have the writings on certain conditions; which were, that he show them only to his brother, Preserved Harris, his own wife, his father and his mother, and a Mrs. Cobb, a sister to his wife. In accordance with this last answer, I required of him that he should bind himself in a covenant to me in a most solemn manner that he would not do otherwise than had been directed. He did so. He bound himself as I required of him, took the writings, and went his way.[5]

After Martin departed with the manuscript, Emma delivered a baby boy who died shortly thereafter. In Palmyra, Martin showed the manuscript to his wife and others, and then it suddenly disappeared. He searched frantically for it, but it was nowhere to be found. Some believe that his wife, Lucy, took it while he was sleeping and burned it. Regardless of what happened, Martin dreaded facing Joseph with the news that he had lost the manuscript. Almost three weeks passed, and Joseph heard nothing from Martin, contrary to their agreement. Emma suggested that he return to New York to see what had happened to the manuscript, so he went.

Lucy Mack Smith tells what happened the morning after Joseph's arrival back home:

When Joseph had taken a little nourishment, . . . he requested us to send immediately for Mr. Harris. This we did without delay. . . . We commenced preparing breakfast for the family; and we supposed that Mr. Harris would be there, as soon as it was ready, to eat with us, for he generally came in such haste when he was sent for. At eight o'clock we set the victuals on the table, as we were expecting him every moment. We waited till nine, and he came not—till ten, and he was not there—till eleven, still he did not make his appearance. But at half past twelve we saw him walking with a slow and measured tred towards the house, his eyes fixed thoughtfully upon the ground. On coming to the gate, he stopped, instead of passing through, and got upon the fence, and sat there some time with his hat drawn over his eyes. At length he entered the house. Soon after which we sat down to the table, Mr. Harris with the rest. He took up his knife and fork as if he were going to use them, but immediately dropped them. Hyrum, observing this, said "Martin, why do you not eat; are you sick?" Upon which Mr. Harris pressed his hands upon his temples, and cried out in a tone of deep anguish, "Oh, I have lost my soul! I have lost my soul!"

Joseph who had not expressed his fears till now, sprang from the table, exclaiming, "Martin, have you lost that manuscript? Have you broken your oath, and brought down condemnation upon my head as well as your own?"

"Yes; it is gone," replied Martin, "and I know not where."

"Oh, my God!" said Joseph, clinching his hands. "All is lost! all is lost! What shall I do? I have sinned—it is I who tempted the wrath of God. I should have been satisfied with the first answer which I received from the Lord; for he told me that it was not safe to let the writing go out of my possession." He wept and groaned, and walked the floor continually.

At length he told Martin to go back and search again.

"No," said Martin, "it is all in vain; for I have ripped open beds and pillows; and I know it is not there."

"Then must I," said Joseph, "return with such a tale as this? I dare not do it. And how shall I appear before the Lord? Of what rebuke am I not worthy from the angel of the Most High?"

I besought him not to mourn so, for perhaps the Lord would forgive him, after a short season of humiliation and repentance. But what could I do to comfort him, when he saw all the family in the same situation of mind as himself; for sobs and groans, and the most bitter lamentations filled the house. However, Joseph was more distressed than the rest, as he better understood the consequences of disobedience. And he continued pacing back and forth, meantime weeping and grieving, until about sunset, when, by persuasion, he took a little nourishment.

> The next morning, he set out for home. We parted with heavy
> hearts, for it now appeared that all which we had so fondly anticipated,
> and which had been the source of so much secret gratification, had in a
> moment fled, and fled forever.[6]

If Joseph were making all of this up, why would he write the lost
manuscript into the story? How could anyone believe after reading
his mother's detailed description of Martin and Joseph's behavior that
something important was not lost? Joseph also had the Urim and
Thummim and the gift to translate taken away from him. However,
from this experience Joseph learned to be obedient to God and never
give in to the pressures of men.

After deep repentance, he describes what happened next: "After
my return home, I was walking out a little distance, when, behold, the
former heavenly messenger appeared and handed to me the Urim and
Thummim again—for it had been taken from me in consequence of
my having wearied the Lord in asking for the privilege of letting Martin
Harris take the writings, which he lost by transgression—and I inquired
of the Lord through it, and obtained [D&C 3]."[7] This revelation was
dictated to his wife, Emma, and some believe is the first revelation
Joseph received that was written down. The following are some of the
significant verses of that revelation:

D&C 3

9 Behold, thou art Joseph, and thou wast chosen to do the work
of the Lord, but because of transgression, if thou art not aware thou
wilt fall.

10 But remember, God is merciful; therefore, repent of that
which thou hast done which is contrary to the commandment
which I gave you, and thou art still chosen, and art again called to
the work;

11 Except thou do this, thou shalt be delivered up and become
as other men, and have no more gift.

12 And when thou deliveredst up that which God had given
thee sight and power to translate, thou deliveredst up that which
was sacred into the hands of a wicked man,

13 Who has set at naught the counsels of God, and has broken
the most sacred promises which were made before God, and has
depended upon his own judgment and boasted in his own wisdom.

14 And this is the reason that thou hast lost thy privileges for a season.

I remember in years past being surprised to read that Martin Harris was called a wicked man in the revelation. I guess I always thought wicked had only one definition: evil. However, another definition of *wicked* is "causing or likely to cause harm, distress, or trouble." I guess by that definition the word *wicked* fits this situation well. This revelation gives four reasons why the Lord would refer to him that way. Martin Harris disregarded God's direction, broke his promise, depended on his own judgment, and felt overly confident in his own knowledge. Joseph was also rebuked in this revelation, but fortunately for both men, "God is merciful."

After the loss of the book of Lehi manuscript in the summer of 1828, the translation came to a standstill. Despite the humiliation Martin felt at losing the manuscript and being rebuked by the Lord, he did not lose the faith. Because he desired an additional witness of the plates, he returned to Harmony in March 1829. He also requested a revelation be sought in his behalf. That desire was granted and is now found in Doctrine and Covenants 5.

D&C 5

11 And in addition to your testimony, the testimony of three of my servants, whom I shall call and ordain, unto whom I will show these things, and they shall go forth with my words that are given through you.

12 Yea, they shall know of a surety that these things are true, for from heaven will I declare it unto them.

13 I will give them power that they may behold and view these things as they are.

While Martin was not allowed to act as Joseph's scribe again in the translation process, he was given hope that he would see the plates at a future time. On April 5, 1829, shortly after the revelation was received, Oliver Cowdery came to Harmony, Pennsylvania, to meet Joseph Smith. He had boarded with the Smith family and heard about Joseph Smith's work and became deeply interested. On April 7, 1829, the translation began again with Oliver as the primary scribe. The two men finished the work of translation in June 1829.

The fulfillment of the promise of three additional witnesses was granted on June 28, 1829. Joseph Smith, along with Martin Harris, David Whitmer, and Oliver Cowdery, retired to the woods near the Whitmer home. They knelt down, and Joseph Smith offered a vocal prayer desiring that his companions be allowed to see the plates. The other three followed in succession, but their prayers were not answered. The same procedure was tried a second time but with no results. After the second failure, Martin proposed he withdraw himself from the group, suggesting that he was the reason for the failure to receive an answer. A short time after Martin left, an angel appeared and showed the plates to the three remaining individuals, who testified to them that the translation was correct and that they were to become witnesses to its truthfulness.

Joseph Smith describes what happened next:

> I now left David and Oliver, and went in pursuit of Martin Harris, whom I found at a considerable distance, fervently engaged in prayer. He soon told me, however, that he had not yet prevailed with the Lord, and earnestly requested me to join him in prayer, that he also might realize the same blessings which we had just received. We accordingly joined in prayer, and ultimately obtained our desires, for before we had yet finished, the same vision was opened to our view, at least it was again opened to me, and I once more beheld and heard the same things; whilst at the same moment, Martin Harris cried out, apparently in an ecstasy of joy, "'Tis enough; 'tis enough; mine eyes have beheld; mine eyes have beheld;" and jumping up, he shouted, "Hosanna," blessing God, and otherwise rejoiced exceedingly.[8]

Joseph Smith was overjoyed that he no longer stood alone in his testimony of the gold plates. With the translation of the plates completed and witnesses in place, it was time to have the manuscript published as a book. The Prophet approached twenty-three-year-old newspaper publisher and print shop owner Egbert Bratt Grandin about the possibility of publishing the Book of Mormon. At first, he refused because he believed the work to be fraudulent and because of the significant financial risk involved. Grandin, however, changed his mind and finally agreed to print 5,000 copies, provided that a $3,000 security deposit was put down. There was no way the Smith family could come up with that kind of money. At that point, Martin, who had caused so much heartache the year before, showed his devotion and true character. He stepped forward and mortgaged his valuable farm to cover the cost of the printing. The $3,000 security in our day would be around $75,000.[9] It was a huge financial risk for him, and, by most accounts, his wife was furious with him. According to LDS historians James Allen and Glen Leonard, the Book of Mormon "was not a commercial success, however, and a year later Martin Harris, true to his word, sold his mortgaged farm and paid the $3,000."[10] Martin deserves the respect of every believer for his generosity in funding the book that has now blessed the lives of millions of people. Unfortunately, that gesture cost him his reputation, his wealth, and, according to some, his marriage.

Martin Harris was present at the organization of the Church on April 6, 1830, and was baptized that day by Oliver Cowdery. The next year, the following article was published in the local newspaper:

> Several families, numbering about fifty souls, took up their line of march from this town last week for the "promised land," among whom was Martin Harris, one of the original believers in the "Book of Mormon." Mr. Harris was among the early settlers of this town, and has ever borne the character of an honorable and upright man, and an obliging and benevolent neighbor. He had secured to himself by honest industry a respectable fortune—and he has left a large circle of acquaintances and friends to pity his delusion.[11]

In Ohio, another newspaper reported on the arrival of Martin and his group of New York believers.

> *Martin Harris*, another chief of Mormon imposters, arrived here last Saturday from the bible *quarry* in New-York. He immediately planted himself in the bar-room of the hotel, where he soon commenced reading and explaining the Mormon hoax, and all the dark passages from Genesis to Revelations. He told all about the gold plates, Angels, Spirits, and Jo Smith.—He had seen and handled them all, *by the power of God!*[12]

In February 1834, a revelation was received, calling fifty-year-old Martin to serve on the first high council in the Church (see D&C 102:3). A few months later, he left Kirtland with Zion's Camp to help relieve the suffering of the persecuted Saints living there. Needless to say, the 805 miles one way between Kirtland, Ohio, and Independence, Missouri, was a difficult endeavor for all those who volunteered to go.

On February 14, 1835, Martin, along with Oliver Cowdery and David Whitmer, helped select the first Quorum of the Twelve Apostles in this dispensation. It is interesting that none of the Three Witnesses were part of the Twelve.

On August 27, 1835, another significant event happened in the life of Martin Harris. On this day, he received his patriarchal blessing from Joseph Smith Sr., who was serving as the first Presiding Patriarch. In it, Martin was told, "Thy mind shall be enlarged, and thy testimony shall yet convince its thousands and its tens of thousands; yea, it shall shine like the sun, and though the wicked seek to overthrow it, it shall be in vain, for the Lord God shall bear it off victorious. The holy angels will watch over thee and bear thee up in their hands. Thou shalt have a tongue and wisdom that all the enemies of truth can not withstand nor gainsay."[13]

In 1836, Martin attended the Kirtland Temple dedication and partook of the spiritual feast that followed. However, in 1837, events surrounding the failure of the Church's Kirtland Safety Society led to widespread apostasy. A group of dissenters led by Warren Parrish attempted to reorganize the Church, and Martin became part of that group. Joseph Smith and Sidney Rigdon had moved to Far West, Missouri, and were not present during this time. Martin was released from the High Council in September 1837 and three months later was excommunicated from the Church.

Martin Harris remained in Kirtland when the majority of the Saints moved to Missouri and Illinois. He was rebaptized by a visiting missionary in 1842 but did not then join the main body of the Saints. In the fall of 1846, Martin went to England to bear testimony of the Book of Mormon. In 1860, he obviously still considered himself a member of the Church because the census taker that year listed his occupation as "Mormon preacher." At one point, he told one of his visitors, "I never did leave the Church; the Church left me."[14]

In 1859, David B. Dille of Ogden, Utah, stopped in Kirtland to visit Martin on his way to Britain. While there, he asked Martin what he thought of the Book of Mormon and if it was a divine record.

Mr. Harris replied: "I was the right hand man of Joseph Smith, and I know that he was a prophet of God. I know the Book of Mormon is true—and you know that I know that it is true. I know that the plates have been translated by the gift and power of God, for His voice declared it unto us; therefore I know of a surety that the work is true; for did I not at one time hold the plates on my knee an hour and a half, while in conversation with Joseph, when we went to bury them in the woods, that the enemy might not obtain them? Yes, I did. And as many of the plates as Joseph Smith translated, I handled with my hands, plate after plate."[15]

For many years, Martin had been invited to come to the Salt Lake Valley. When he finally expressed interest in doing so, Edward Stevenson, William H. Homer, President Brigham Young, and others donated money to help pay his way to come. Accompanied by Edward Stevenson, the eighty-seven-year-old Martin arrived in Salt Lake City by train on August 30, 1870. The following Sunday, the two men were asked to speak in the Salt Lake Tabernacle. Afterward, Martin received many opportunities to speak and had hundreds of visitors wanting to hear his testimony. One listener who heard him speak quoted him as saying, "It is not a mere belief, but is a matter of knowledge. I saw the plates and the inscriptions thereon. I saw the angel, and he showed them unto me."[16]

He stayed with his grandniece Irinda McEwen and her husband while in Salt Lake. She said, "Anyone who heard Martin Harris describe the scenes and bear his testimony to the truthfulness of the Book of Mormon could not help but be deeply impressed with his sincerity and his absolute conviction of the truth of what he was saying."[17]

Many were thrilled when Martin expressed a desire to be baptized again. His friend Edward Stevenson baptized him in the Endowment House on September 17, 1870. Those in attendance included his sister Naomi Harris Bent and Elders George A. Smith, John Taylor, Wilford Woodruff, Orson Pratt, and Joseph F. Smith, and many others. He was confirmed a member of the Church by Orson Pratt. Martin also fulfilled his desire to be baptized by proxy for his father, Nathan Harris, and for his brother Solomon Harris that same day. On October 21, 1870, he returned to the Endowment House where he received his own endowment.

While in Salt Lake, Martin was able to ride in a carriage with friends to a mountain peak where they had a view of the valley below. Looking at the Tabernacle and the Salt Lake Temple under construction, he made this comment: "Who would have thought that the Book of Mormon would have done all of this?"[18]

After about six weeks, Martin accepted an invitation from his son Martin Harris Jr. to live with him and his family in Cache County, Utah. During the last years of his life, he was frequently visited and interviewed. The following are a few of the statements he made about the Book of Mormon:

"The Book of Mormon is no fake. I know what I know. I have seen what I have seen and I have heard what I have heard. I have seen the gold plates from which the Book of Mormon is written. An angel appeared to me and others and testified to the truthfulness of the record, and had I been willing to have perjured myself and sworn falsely to the testimony I now bear I could have been a rich man, but I could not have testified other than I have done and am now doing for these things are true."[19]

"No man heard me in any way deny the truth of the Book of Mormon [or] the administration of the angel that showed me the plates."[20]

"I do say that the angel did show to me the plates containing the Book of Mormon. Further, the translation that I carried to Prof. Anthon was copied from these same plates; also, that the Professor did testify to it being a correct translation. I do firmly believe and do know that Joseph Smith was a prophet of God, for without I know he [Joseph Smith] could not [have] had that gift; neither could he have translated the same."[21]

William Harrison Homer, a friend, reported the testimony that he heard from Martin Harris when he was near death:

"I stood by the bedside holding the patient's right hand and my mother at the foot of the bed, Martin Harris had been unconscious for a number of days. When we first entered the room the old gentleman appeared to be sleeping. He soon woke up and asked for a drink of water. I put my arm under the old gentleman, raised him, and my mother held the glass to his lips. He drank freely, then he looked up at me and recognized me. He said, "I know you. You are my friend." He said, "Yes, I did see the plates on which the Book of Mormon was written; I did see the angel; I did hear the voice of God; and I do know that Joseph Smith is a Prophet of God, holding the keys of the Holy Priesthood." This was the end. Martin Harris, divinely-chosen witness of the work of God, relaxed, gave up my hand. He lay back on his pillow and just as the sun went down behind the Clarkston mountains, the soul of Martin Harris passed on.[22]

Martin Harris declared in definitive language that he had seen the angel, had seen and held the plates, and knew that Joseph Smith was a prophet of God. His unchanging witness and fervent testimony spanned many years.

He passed away on July 10, 1875, at the age of ninety-two. He was buried in the cemetery in Clarkston, Utah, with a copy of the Book of Mormon in his right hand and a copy of the Doctrine and Covenants in his left.

Reason to Believe

If Joseph Smith deceived Martin Harris in any way, he had around forty-five years between signing his name as one of the Three Witnesses until he passed away to think it over and come to his senses. However, he never denied that he had seen an angel and handled the plates. What could his motives possibly have been for continuing to bear his testimony of the Book of Mormon? Was it for money? He lost his farm because of his testimony. Was it for respect? He lost the respect of friends and neighbors alike, and it destroyed his marriage. Was it for hope of leadership positions in a new church? He was excommunicated. Martin had his comfortable life shattered because of his involvement with Joseph Smith. If the Book of Mormon were not true, Martin was in the perfect position to expose it. The fact that he still bore his testimony of its truthfulness on his deathbed leads me to believe he was being truthful.

Notes

1. William Harrison Homer, "The Passing of Martin Harris," *Improvement Era*, March 1926, 470.
2. Ronald W. Walker, "Martin Harris: Mormonism's Early Convert," *Dialogue: A Journal of Mormon Thought* (Winter, 1986) 19 (4), 31.

3. Lucy Mack Smith, *History of Joseph Smith*, ed. Preston Nibley (Salt Lake City: Bookcraft, 1958), 116–17.

4. Ibid., 117.

5. Joseph Smith, *History of the Church of Jesus Christ of Latter-day Saints*, ed. B. H. Roberts, 2nd ed. rev., 7 vols. (Salt Lake City: The Church of Jesus Christ of Latter-day Saints, 1932–1951), 1:21.

6. Lucy Mack Smith, *History of Joseph Smith,* ed. Preston Nibley Salt Lake City: Bookcraft, 1958), 124–29.

7. *History of the Church,* 1:21–22.

8. Ibid., 1:54–55.

9. http://www.davemanuel.com/inflation-calculator.php.

10. James Allen and Glen Leonard, *Story of the Latter-day Saints* (Salt Lake City: Deseret Book, 1992), 53.

11. "Mormon Emigration," *Wayne Sentinel,* 27 May 1831, 3.

12. *Painesville Telegraph*, Painesville, Ohio 2, no. 39, 15 March 1831.

13. Oliver Cowdery, clerk and recorder. Given on August 27, 1835, and recorded in this book October 7, 1835, (*Patriarchal Blessing Book* 1:16–17).

14. As quoted in William H. Homer Jr., "'Publish It Upon the Mountains': The Story of Martin Harris," *Improvement Era,* July 1955, 505.

15. "Testimonies of Oliver Cowdery and Martin Harris," *The Latter-day Saints' Millennial Star* August 20, 1859, 21:545.

16. Richard L. Anderson, *Investigating the Book of Mormon Witnesses* (Salt Lake City: Deseret Book, 1989), 116.

17. Franklin Harris, "Minutes of Harris Family Reunion," 3 August, 1928, Geneva Resort, Utah County, Utah, USU Special Collections.

18. Stevenson, "The Three Witnesses to the Book of Mormon, No. III," 390; see *Journal History of the Church,* 1 June 1877, 1–2.

19. Recorded by Martin Harris on his deathbed. Cited by George Godfrey, "Testimony of Martin Harris," from an unpublished manuscript copy in the possession of his descendants, quoted in Eldin Ricks, *The Case of the Book of Mormon Witnesses,* (Salt Lake City: Deseret News Press, 1971), 65–66.

20. Letter from Martin Harris Sr. to Hanna B. Emerson, January 1871, Smithfield, Utah Territory, *Saints' Herald* 22 (15 October 1875), 630.
21. *Saints' Herald* 22 (15 October, 1875), 630.
22. William Harrison Homer, "The Passing of Martin Harris," 472.

Chapter 18: Oliver Cowdery, the Witness

"Jacob, I want you to remember what I say to you. I am a dying man, and what would it profit me to tell you a lie? I know . . . that this Book of Mormon was translated by the gift and power of God. My eyes saw, my ears heard, and my understanding was touched, and I know that whereof I testified is true. It was no dream, no vain imagination of the mind—it was real."[1]

—Oliver Cowdery to Jacob Gates in 1849

Oliver Cowdery was born October 3, 1806, in Wells, Vermont. Oliver was the youngest of eight children born to William and Rebecca Cowdery. His ancestors appear to have had strong traditions of patriotism, education, and religion. Early on, heartbreak struck the family on September 9, 1809, when Rebecca died of consumption (tuberculosis) at the age of forty-three, one month before Oliver turned three years old. Some have suggested that Oliver lived for a time with his aunt Huldah Glass (his mother's oldest sister) and her husband, Rufus, but that has not been verified. It is known that the two families were close and lived one mile apart, and both had eight children. On March 18, 1810, Oliver's father, William, married a widow named Keziah Pearch Austin, who had a daughter from her previous marriage. She and William then had three daughters together, making a total of twelve children in the blended family.

In 1813, grief came again to the Cowdery family when both Oliver's Aunt Huldah and Uncle Rufus died within two weeks of each other from an epidemic that swept the area. Little is known about this period of Oliver's life. Records indicate that he left Vermont around 1825 and went to live in New York, where several siblings had moved previously. Lucy, who was one of his younger half-sisters, said, "Oliver's occupation was clerking in a store until 1829, when he taught the district school in the town of Manchester."[2]

Oliver was twenty-two years old when he started teaching school and apparently had some training to be qualified as a teacher. He was hired by the Manchester school trustees, including Hyrum Smith, in early 1829. In that time period, it was the custom in some rural areas for schoolteachers to live with students' families. Since Oliver taught the children of Joseph Smith Sr. and Lucy Mack Smith, he resided with their family soon after being hired. During this time, he heard many rumors about Joseph Smith Jr. and became curious to learn more about Joseph's work. Lucy Smith said that Oliver "began to hear from all quarters concerning the plates, and as soon began to importune Mr. Smith upon the subject, but for a considerable length of time did not succeed in eliciting any information."[3] Because many of their neighbors had mocked the Smiths in the past, Joseph was reluctant to share information with Oliver.

Once Oliver gained the trust of the Smith family, Joseph Sr. told Oliver about his son receiving the plates and his call to translate them. At that time, the Prophet and Emma had moved to Harmony, Pennsylvania, in hopes of finding the peace needed to translate the records. Lucy Mack Smith said,

> Shortly after receiving this information, he [Oliver] told Mr. Smith that he was highly delighted with what he had heard, that he had been in a deep study upon the subject all day, and that it was impressed upon his mind, that he should yet have the privilege of writing for Joseph. Furthermore, that he had determined to pay him a visit at the close of the school. . . . On coming in on the following day, he said, "The subject upon which we were yesterday conversing seems working in my very bones, and I cannot, for a moment, get it out of my mind; finally, I have resolved on what I will do. Samuel [Smith], I understand, is going down to Pennsylvania to spend the spring with Joseph; I shall make my arrangements to be ready to accompany him thither, . . . for I have made it a subject of prayer, and I firmly believe that it is the will of the Lord that I should go. If there is a work for me to do in this thing, I am determined to attend to it."[4]

Oliver's interest in assisting in the work came at a perfect time. Previously, Martin Harris had assisted as scribe, but after the loss of the 116-page manuscript of the book of Lehi, he was no longer involved in the process. Joseph Smith recorded an experience that Oliver Cowdery had before coming to Harmony to assist in the translation. He said the Lord "appeared unto a young man by the name of Oliver Cowdery and showed unto him the plates in a vision, and also the truth of the work, and what the Lord was about to do through me, his unworthy servant. Therefore, he was desirous to come and write for me, and translate."[5]

During this time, Joseph was using Emma as his scribe. Because much of her time was taken with the care of the house, this slowed down the translation process considerably. Joseph was frustrated with the lack of progress being made. Lucy Mack Smith said, "On account of these embarrassments, Joseph called upon the Lord, three days prior to the arrival of Samuel and Oliver, to send him a scribe, according to the promise of the angel; and he was informed that the same should be forthcoming in a few days. Accordingly, when Mr. Cowdery told him the business that he had come upon, Joseph was not at all surprised."[6] When Samuel Smith and Oliver Cowdery arrived in Harmony, Pennsylvania, on April 5, 1829, Joseph was expecting them.

Surely both Joseph and Oliver realized that their meeting was the result of divine intervention and not coincidental. Oliver was an answer to prayer. The Prophet said, "Two days after the arrival of Mr. Cowdery (being the 7th of April) I commenced to translate the Book of Mormon, and he began to write for me, which having continued for some time, I inquired of the Lord through the Urim and Thummim, and obtained the following [D&C 6:18, 20]: 'Stand by my servant Joseph. . . . Behold, thou art Oliver, and I have spoken unto thee because of thy desires.' "[7]

Doctrine and Covenants 6, given specifically to Oliver, began with this prophetic line: "A great and marvelous work is about to come forth unto the children of men" (D&C 6:1). Later in the revelation, the Lord said to Oliver, "Behold, thou knowest that thou hast inquired of me and I did enlighten thy mind; and now I tell thee these things that thou mayest know that thou hast been enlightened by the Spirit of truth"

(D&C 6:15). Joseph describes an experience that occurred shortly after Oliver's arrival in Harmony.

> After we had received this revelation [D&C 6], Oliver Cowdery stated to me that after he had gone to my father's to board, and after the family had communicated to him concerning my having obtained the plates, that one night after he had retired to bed he called upon the Lord to know if these things were so, and the Lord manifested to him that they were true, but he had kept the circumstance entirely secret, and had mentioned it to no one; so that after this revelation was given, he knew that the work was true, because no being living knew of the thing alluded to in the revelation, but God and himself.[8]

A few years after the Book of Mormon was printed, Oliver described what it was like to be involved in the translation. In a letter to W. W. Phelps dated September 7, 1834, he said, "These were days never to be forgotten—to sit under the sound of a voice dictated by the inspiration of heaven, awakened the utmost gratitude of this bosom! Day after day I continued, uninterrupted, to write from his mouth, as he translated with the Urim and Thummim, or, as the Nephites would have said, 'Interpreters,' the history or record called 'The Book of Mormon.'"[9]

During the translation process, Joseph and Oliver came to the events surrounding Christ's visit to America after His Resurrection. At that point, the topic of baptism came up and they decided to pray about it. That prayer led to the appearance of John the Baptist on May 15, 1829, to restore the Aaronic Priesthood to the earth. After receiving priesthood authority, Joseph and Oliver baptized each other in the Susquehanna River. Oliver then described what it was like when they were visited by John the Baptist.

> I shall not attempt to paint to you the feelings of this heart, nor the majestic beauty and glory which surrounded us on this occasion; but you will believe me when I say, that earth, nor men, with the eloquence of time, cannot begin to clothe language in as interesting and sublime a manner as this holy personage. No; nor has this earth power to give the joy, to bestow the peace, or comprehend the wisdom which was contained in each sentence as they were delivered by the power of the Holy Spirit! Man may deceive his fellow-men, deception may

follow deception, and the children of the wicked one may have power to seduce the foolish and untaught, till naught but fiction feeds the many, and the fruit of falsehood carries in its current the giddy to the grave; but one touch with the finger of his love, yes, one ray of glory from the upper world, or one word from the mouth of the Savior, from the bosom of eternity, strikes it all into insignificance, and blots it forever from the mind. The assurance that we were in the presence of an angel, the certainty that we heard the voice of Jesus, and the truth unsullied as it flowed from a pure personage, dictated by the will of God, is to me past description, and I shall ever look upon this expression of the Savior's goodness with wonder and thanksgiving while I am permitted to tarry; and in those mansions where perfection dwells and sin never comes, I hope to adore in that day which shall never cease.[10]

Shortly after the Aaronic Priesthood was restored, Peter, James, and John appeared and restored the Melchizedek Priesthood to Joseph and Oliver. In a letter to Elder Samuel W. Richards, Oliver said,

While darkness covered the earth and gross darkness the people; long after the authority to administer in holy things had been taken away, the Lord opened the heavens and sent forth his word for the salvation of Israel. In fulfillment of the sacred scriptures, the everlasting gospel was proclaimed by the mighty angel (Moroni) who, clothed with the authority of his mission, gave glory to God in the highest. This gospel is the "stone taken from the mountain without hands." John the Baptist, holding the keys of the Aaronic Priesthood; Peter, James and John, holding the keys of the Melchizedek Priesthood, have also ministered for those who shall be heirs of salvation, and with these administrations ordained men to the same priesthood. These priesthoods, with their authority, are now, and must continue to be, in the body of the Church of Jesus Christ of Latter-day Saints. Blessed is the elder who has received the same, and thrice blessed and holy is he who shall endure to the end.

Accept assurances, dear brother, of the unfeigned prayer of him who, in connection with Joseph the Seer, was blessed with the above ministration and who earnestly and devoutly hopes to meet you in the celestial glory.[11]

At the end of May 1829, Oliver and Joseph moved to the home of David Whitmer in New York to complete the translation. After the move to the Whitmer farm, the Three Witnesses (Oliver Cowdery,

David Whitmer, and Martin Harris) were shown the plates by the angel Moroni. Oliver joined the other two in testifying that Moroni showed them the gold plates and that the voice of God declared that they were translated correctly.

Once the original manuscript was finished, Oliver and two other scribes made a copy called the printer's manuscript. Joseph obviously did not want to take the chance of losing another manuscript like with the book of Lehi. Working with the Grandin print shop in Palymra, New York, that fall and winter Oliver supervised the printing of the Book of Mormon. The first printing called for 5,000 copies, a large number for the day. The books were made available on March 26, 1830. Samuel Smith was called on a short mission and took some of the newly printed books with him. The dramatic impact of the Book of Mormon began immediately and has continued over time.

The Prophet Joseph Smith wrote, "Whilst the Book of Mormon was in the hands of the printer, we . . . made known to our brethren that we had received a commandment to organize the church; and accordingly we met together for that purpose, at the house of Mr. Peter Whitmer, Sen., (being six in number,) on Tuesday, the sixth day of April, AD, one thousand eight hundred and thirty."[12]

During this meeting, Joseph proposed that he and Oliver Cowdery be the presiding elders of the Church and asked for a vote. This was in accordance with the Lord's will (see D&C 20:2–3) and made Oliver next in authority to the Prophet. This also satisfied a New York statute requiring two presiding authorities at the incorporation proceedings. Oliver spoke in a meeting the next Sunday. That talk has been called "the first public discourse that was delivered by any of our number."[13]

In September 1830, Joseph Smith received a revelation directed to Oliver Cowdery, which said, "And now, behold, I say unto you that you shall go unto the Lamanites and preach my gospel unto them" (D&C 28:8). Peter Whitmer Jr., Parley P. Pratt, and Ziba Peterson were called to go with him to take the gospel to the Native Americans. In October, Oliver led what is known as the first major missionary expedition of the Church. This mission to western Missouri in the winter of 1830–1831 was important for several reasons. The missionaries stopped in Kirtland, Ohio, and had so much success that it doubled the Church membership there and led to the first gathering place for members. It showed the commitment of the Church to take the gospel to the Lamanites. And it eventually brought Joseph Smith to Jackson County, Missouri, where he identified the place of the New Jerusalem.

When the missionaries stopped in Ohio, they got some local press coverage for the Church. The Painesville press reported,

> *The Golden Bible.*—Some two or three years since, an account was given in the papers, of a book purporting to contain new revelations from Heaven, having been dug out of the ground, in Manchester in Ontario Co. N.Y. The book, it seems, has made its appearance in this vicinity.—It contains about 600 octave pages, which is said to be translated from Egyptian Hieroglyphics, on metal plates, by one Smith, who was enabled to read the characters by instruction from Angels. About two weeks since some persons came along here with the book, one of whom pretends to have seen Angels, and assisted in translating the plates. He . . . holds forth that the ordinances of the gospel, have not been regularly administered since the days of the Apostles, till the said Smith and himself commenced the work—and many other marvelous things too numerous to mention. The name of the person here, who pretends to have a divine mission, and to have seen and conversed with Angels, is *Cowdray.*[14]

Continuing from Kirtland, they headed west. Parley P. Pratt wrote that "for three hundred miles through vast prairies and through trackless wilds of snow—no beaten road; houses few and far between; and the bleak northwest wind always blowing in our faces with a keenness which would almost take the skin off the face. . . . After much fatigue and some suffering we all arrived in Independence, in the county of Jackson, on the extreme western frontiers of Missouri, and of the United States."[15]

From Independence, the missionaries traveled a little ways to Indian lands to teach the Delaware Indians. When meeting with the tribe, Oliver Cowdery gave a stirring message about the Book of Mormon. Chief Anderson was so impressed that he asked the missionaries to remain during the winter and teach them more. Great success appeared to be certain. Parley P. Pratt, however, tells what happened next.

> We found several among them who could read, and to them we gave copies of the Book, explaining to them that it was the Book of their forefathers. Some began to rejoice exceedingly, and took great pains

to tell the news to others, in their own language. The excitement now reached the frontier settlements in Missouri, and stirred up the jealousy and envy of the Indian agents and sectarian missionaries to that degree that we were soon ordered out of the Indian country as disturbers of the peace; and even threatened with the military in case of non-compliance. We accordingly departed from the Indian country. . . . Thus ended our first Indian Mission, in which we had preached the gospel in its fulness, and distributed the record of their forefathers among three tribes, viz: the Catteraugus Indians, near Buffalo, N. Y., the Wyandots of Ohio, and the Delawares west of Missouri. We trust that at some future day, when the servants of God go forth in power to the remnant of Joseph, some precious seed will be found growing in their hearts, which was sown by us in that early day.[16]

From his earliest involvement, Oliver was engaged in writing for the Church. Not only was he the main scribe for the Book of Mormon translation but he also served as an editor or a contributor for many of the Church's first publications. His insightful, thought-provoking articles and letters helped document many of the important events of early Church history. At one point, Oliver was called to work with William W. Phelps, a convert who had established a print shop down in Independence, Missouri, and published the *Evening and Morning Star*. Unfortunately, on July 20, 1833, while working to publish the Book of Commandments, a mob ransacked the Phelps' home and destroyed many papers, along with his printing press.

On December 18, 1832, Oliver Cowdery married Elizabeth Ann Whitmer in Jackson County, Missouri. She was the seventeen-year-old daughter of Peter Whitmer Sr. and his wife, Mary, and the sister of Christian, David, John, Jacob, and Peter. The completion of the Book of Mormon translation happened in her parent's home. Her brothers were among the eleven witnesses of the Book of Mormon, along with her brother-in-law Hiram Page. It was here that her mother, Mary, also testified that she had been visited by an angel and had seen the gold plates as a reward for her sacrifices during the translation.

Oliver Cowdery contributed greatly to the Restoration and was rewarded with another spiritual feast at the dedication of the Kirtland Temple. On April 3, 1836, after the afternoon sacrament service, Joseph and Oliver retired to the pulpit, dropped the veils, and bowed in silent prayer. After they stood up, a vision opened to both of them, now recorded in Doctrine and Covenants 110.

But even with these intense spiritual experiences, Oliver began to be estranged from Joseph by early 1838. He openly disagreed with the Prophet on many topics and appeared to be in competition for leadership. Oliver seemed to have forgotten a warning he received in an April 1830 revelation when the Lord said to him, "Behold, I speak unto you, Oliver, a few words. Behold, thou art blessed, and art under no condemnation. But beware of pride, lest thou shouldst enter into temptation" (D&C 23:1).

One of the saddest entries in Church history is this event:

Wednesday, April 11, [1838]—Elder Seymour Brunson preferred the following charges against Oliver Cowdery, to the High Council at Far West: To the Bishop and Council of the Church of Jesus Christ of Latter-day Saints, I prefer the following charges against President Oliver Cowdery.

First—For persecuting the brethren by urging on vexatious law suits against them, and thus distressing the innocent.

Second—For seeking to destroy the character of President Joseph Smith, Jun., by falsely insinuating that he was guilty of adultery.

Third—For treating the Church with contempt by not attending meetings.

Fourth—For virtually denying the faith by declaring that he would not be governed by any ecclesiastical authority or revelations whatever, in his temporal affairs.

Fifth—For selling his lands in Jackson county, contrary to the revelations.

Sixth—For writing and sending an insulting letter to President Thomas B. Marsh, while the latter was on the High Council, attending to the duties of his office as President of the Council, and by insulting the High Council with the contents of said letter.

Seventh—For leaving his calling to which God had appointed him by revelation, for the sake of filthy lucre, and turning to the practice of law.

Eighth—For disgracing the Church by being connected in the bogus business, as common report says.

Ninth—For dishonestly retaining notes after they had been paid; and finally, for leaving and forsaking the cause of God, and returning to the beggarly elements of the world, and neglecting his high and holy calling, according to his profession.[17]

On April 12, 1838, a church court was held, and Oliver Cowdery was excommunicated after he failed to appear but instead sent a letter resigning from the Church. His brother-in-law and fellow Book of

Mormon witness David Whitmer was also excommunicated. This was a sad day in LDS history. President Joseph Fielding Smith later commented,

> Had Oliver Cowdery remained true, had he been faithful to his testimony and his calling as the "Second Elder" and Assistant President of the Church, I am just as satisfied as I am that I am here that Oliver Cowdery would have gone to Carthage with the Prophet Joseph Smith and laid down his life instead of Hyrum Smith. That would have been his right. Maybe it sounds a little strange to speak of martyrdom as being a right, but it was a right. Oliver Cowdery lost it and Hyrum Smith received it. According to the law of witnesses—and this is a divine law—it had to be.[18]

From 1838 to 1848, Oliver remained outside the Church. He practiced law during much of that time in Tiffin, Ohio, where he also became a political and civic leader. He also joined the Methodist church while living there and served as a secretary. In 1847, Oliver moved to Elkhorn, Wisconsin, and practiced law with one of his brothers. He became co-editor of the *Walworth County Democrat* newspaper.

Evidence suggests that he was deeply hurt at being excommunicated and felt that his character had been slandered. On the other hand, it appears as early as 1842 he was having thoughts of returning to the Church. Critics love to point out that all Three Witnesses to the Book of Mormon found themselves out of the Church during this time period, as if that proved Joseph Smith was not a prophet and the Book of Mormon is not true. Then surely that would have been the time for Oliver to expose the fraud if that were the case. No one other than Joseph Smith knew more about the events related to the coming forth of the Book of Mormon than Oliver. What possible motive could he have to remain true to his printed testimony? During the ten years Oliver was out of the Church, he never once yielded to the significant pressure to deny his testimony of the Book of Mormon.

An interesting experience occurred during the time when Oliver Cowdery was serving as an elected county attorney. A murder trial was held, and Oliver had just finished addressing the jury in his opening statement. When he finished, the attorney for the prisoner challenged Oliver to tell the jury something about his connection with Joseph

Smith. The attorney then insinuated that Oliver was involved in helping to defraud the American people to make money by selling the Mormon Bible and by claiming an angel had appeared to them.

At that point, interest shifted away from the murder case and onto Oliver and how he would respond. Apparently, the people of the town did not know that they had elected a county prosecutor who had been associated with Mormonism. If there was a time that most would feel pressured to deny involvement, it would be at that moment. When the defendant's attorney finished, Oliver stood and calmly responded,

> If your honor please, and gentlemen of the jury, the attorney on the opposite side has challenged me to state my connection with Joseph Smith and the Book of Mormon: and as I cannot now avoid the responsibility, I must admit to you that I am the very Oliver Cowdery whose name is attached to the testimony, with others, as to the appearance of the angel Moroni; and let me tell you that it is not because of my good deeds that I am here, away from the body of the Mormon church, but because I have broken the covenants I once made, and I was cut off from the Church, but, gentlemen of the jury, I have never denied my testimony, which is attached to the Book of Mormon, and I declare to you here that these eyes saw the angel, and these ears of mine heard the voice of the angel, and he told us his name was Moroni; that the book was true, and contained the fulness of the gospel, and we were also told that if we ever denied what we had heard and seen that there would be no forgiveness for us, neither in this world nor in the world to come.[19]

Joseph Smith was killed on June 27, 1844, in Carthage, Illinois. At that time, Oliver was still out of the Church and practicing law. William Lang, his law partner at that time, shared this:

> [Joseph] Smith was killed while C [Oliver Cowdery] lived here. I well remember the effect upon his countenance when he read the news in my presence. He immediately took the paper over to his house to read to his wife. On his return to the office we had a long conversation on the subject, and I was surprised to hear him speak with so much kindness of a man that had so wronged him as Smith had. It elevated him greatly in my already high esteem, and proved to me more than ever the nobility of his nature.[20]

Then in April 1847, Oliver left Tiffin, Ohio, moving to southern Wisconsin, which was still a territory then. He was seeking what he hoped would be better career opportunities in the soon-to-be state. He settled in Elkhorn and was soon practicing law with his brother Lyman. Oliver was apparently thinking seriously about returning to the Church at this time. In November 1847, Brigham Young, on behalf of the Twelve, wrote a letter to Oliver, delivered by Phineas Young around Christmas, inviting him to be rebaptized. He accepted that invitation and made the decision to meet with Church officials in Kanesville (Council Bluffs), Iowa. However, it was late in the season, so he and his wife decided instead to visit Richmond, Missouri. He then returned to Wisconsin in 1848 to take care of some obligations. His letters during this time period speak of his desire to move west with the Saints, but also of his deteriorating health because of a respiratory condition, which included coughing up blood.

By October 1848, the Cowdery family was ready for the journey to Iowa. Oliver's brother-in-law came to southern Wisconsin to help them make the trip. They arrived on Saturday, October 21, during a special conference being held in a grove. Elder Orson Hyde, the presiding authority, was speaking to nearly 2,000 people when the Cowderys entered the meeting. Elder Hyde stopped speaking and came off the stand and embraced Oliver and took him by the arm to the platform. After a brief introduction, he invited Oliver to speak.

Imagine the reaction of those in attendance when they heard these words:

> Friends and Brethren:
> My name is Cowdery—Oliver Cowdery. In the history of the Church, I stood identified with her, and was one in her councils. Not because I was better than other men was I called to fill the purposes of God. He called me to a high and holy calling. I wrote, with my own pen, the entire Book of Mormon (save a few pages), as it fell from the lips of the Prophet Joseph Smith, as he translated it by the gift and power of God, by the means of the Urim and Thummim, or, as it is called by that book, "holy interpreters."
> I beheld with my eyes and handled with my hands, the gold plates from which it was translated. I also saw with my eyes and handled with my hands "The Holy Interpreters." That book is true, Sidney Rigdon did not write it; Mr. Spalding did not write it; I wrote it myself, as it

fell from the lips of the Prophet. It contains the everlasting gospel, to preach to every nation, kindred, tongue, and people. It contains the principles of salvation, and if you, my hearers, will walk by its light, and obey its precepts, you will be saved with an everlasting salvation in the Kingdom of God.

I was present with Joseph Smith when an holy angel from heaven came down and conferred upon us, or restored, the Aaronic Priesthood, and said to us, at the same time, that it should remain on earth while the earth stands. I was also present with Joseph when the Higher, or Melchizedek Priesthood was conferred on each other by the will and commandment of God. This priesthood as was then declared, was also to remain upon the earth until the last remnant of time.

Brethren, for a number of years, I have been separated from you. I now desire to come back. I wish to come humbly and be one in your midst. I seek no station. I only wish to be identified with you. I am out of the Church, but I wish to become a member. I wish to come in at the door; I know the door. I have not come here to seek precedence. I come humbly and throw myself upon the decision of the body, knowing as I do, that its decisions are right.[21]

In his statement requesting rebaptism, Oliver Cowdery stated, "I have not come to seek place, nor to interfere with the business and calling of those men who have borne the burden since the death of Joseph. I throw myself at your feet, and wish to be one of your number, and be a mere member of the Church, and my mere asking to be baptized is an end to all pretensions to authority."[22]

Oliver was rebaptized on November 12, 1848, by Orson Hyde of the Quorum of the Twelve in Indian Creek at Kanesville, Iowa. After the ordinance, Oliver planned to go west in the spring or summer, but health problems prevented him from doing so. Oliver and his wife, Elizabeth Ann, returned to Richmond, Missouri, to visit her relatives until they could make the final move. However, by March 1850, Oliver was dying from tuberculosis. He passed away on March 3, 1850, at age forty-three, being the same age his mother was when she died from the same disease. Oliver used his last hours in mortality to testify of the truthfulness of the Book of Mormon. His half-sister Lucy was at his bedside when he died. She said,

Oliver Cowdery just before breathing his last, asked his attendants to raise him up in bed that he might talk to the family and his friends, who were present. He then told them to live according to the teachings contained in the Book of Mormon, and promised them, if they would do this, that they would meet him in heaven. He then said, "Lay me down and let me fall asleep." A few moments later he died without a struggle.[23]

Reason to Believe

Oliver Cowdery had intimate knowledge of the entire translation process of the Book of Mormon. If Joseph Smith had been involved in fraud, Oliver of all people would have known it. He was also with Joseph when John the Baptist appeared and restored the Aaronic Priesthood. Shortly after that, he and Joseph were together when Peter, James, and John appeared and restored the Melchizedek Priesthood. Later, along with David Whitmer and Martin Harris, he was shown the gold plates, as well as the Urim and Thummim, breastplate, Liahona, and the sword of Laban by the angel Moroni. Still later, he was with the Prophet Joseph at the dedication of the Kirtland Temple. During that event, he saw Jesus Christ, who appeared and accepted His house. Along with Joseph, he also saw Moses, Elias, and Elijah, all of whom returned to restore essential priesthood keys.

Altogether, Oliver saw and heard from at least nine beings from the unseen world. For him to testify throughout his life that all of it was true, if it were a lie, would be extremely hard to believe. What would his motive be to lie about these things? Oliver's wife, Elizabeth, knew him when he was assisting Joseph with the translation at her father's home. She said, "From the hour when the glorious vision of the Holy Messenger revealed to mortal eyes the hidden prophecies which God had promised his faithful followers should come forth in due time, until the moment when he passed away from earth, he always without one doubt or shudder of turning affirmed the divinity and truth of the Book of Mormon."[24]

What would possibly keep this teacher and lawyer from exposing a fraud if there was one to expose? His testimony withstood the test of persecution, the deaths of five of his six children, loss of status, and excommunication. How could anyone write so eloquently about events if they didn't happen? I don't believe anyone could. Oliver's steadfast testimony is another reason I believe that the Book of Mormon is true.

Notes

1. Jacob F. Gates, "Testimony of Jacob Gates," *Improvement Era* 15, March 1912, 92.

2. Lucy Cowdery Young to Andrew Jenson, March 7, 1887, Church Archives.

3. Lucy Smith, *History of Joseph Smith,* ed. Preston Nibley (Salt Lake City: Bookcraft, 1958), 138.

4. Ibid., 139.

5. *The Personal Writings of Joseph Smith*, comp. and ed. Dean C. Jessee (Salt Lake City: Deseret Book, 1984), 8. Spelling and punctuation modernized.

6. Lucy Smith, *History of Joseph Smith* ed. Preston Nibley (Salt Lake City: Bookcraft, 1958), 141.

7. Joseph Smith, *History of The Church of Jesus Christ of Latter-day Saints*, ed. B. H. Roberts, 2nd ed. rev., 7 vols. (Salt Lake City: The Church of Jesus Christ of Latter-day Saints, 1932–1951), 1:32–33.

8. *History of the Church,* 1:35

9. *Latter Day Saints' Messenger and Advocate*, vol. I. no. 1. Kirtland, Ohio, October 1834, 14.

10. Ibid., 16.

11. "Oliver Cowdery's Last Letter," the *Deseret News,* March 22, 1884.

12. Edward H. Anderson, *A Brief History of Joseph Smith, the Prophet* (Salt Lake City: Deseret Sunday School Union, 1910), 44.

13. *History of the Church,* 1:81

14. "The Golden Bible," *Painesville, Ohio, Telegraph,* 16 November 1830.

15. Parley P. Pratt, *Autobiography of Parley P. Pratt* (Salt Lake City: Deseret Book, 1985), 40.

16. Ibid., 54–61.

17. *History of the Church,* 3:16.

18. Joseph Fielding Smith, *Doctrines of Salvation* (Salt Lake City: Bookcraft, 1954), 1:221–22.

19. B. H. Roberts, *Comprehensive History of the Church of Jesus Christ of Latter-day Saints* (Salt Lake City: Deseret News Press, 1930), vol.1, 142.

20. William Lang to Thomas Gregg, 5 November 1881, cit. Charles A. Shook, *The True Origin of The Book of Mormon* (Cincinnati: Standard Publishing, 1914), 56–57.

21. Stanley R. Gunn, *Oliver Cowdery* (Salt Lake City: Bookcraft, 1962), 203–4.

22. "Report to Presidents Brigham Young, Heber C. Kimball, Willard Richards and the Authorities of the Church," April 5, 1849.

23. Andrew Jenson, "Oliver Cowdery," *Latter-day Saint Biographical Encyclopedia* (Salt Lake City: Andrew Jenson History Company, 1901–1936) 1:246.

24. Milton V. Backman, *Eyewitness Accounts of the Restoration* (Salt Lake City: Deseret Book, 1986), 163.

Chapter 19: David Whitmer, the Witness

"Honest, conscientious, and upright in all his dealings, just in his estimate of men, and open, manly, and frank in his treatment of all, he made lasting friends who loved him to the end."[1]

—Richmond Democrat

Several years ago, my family and I took a trip to Independence, Missouri. We visited the headquarters of the RLDS (Community of Christ) Church. At that time, several historical artifacts were being displayed in their auditorium. One of the items fascinated me. I stood looking at it for a long time. It was a short letter written by David Whitmer, addressed to Robert Nelson, and dated July 15, 1887. It was sent from Richmond, Missouri, where David lived at the time. The letter reads:

Dear Sir,

I did see the Angel as it is recorded in my testimony in the Book of Mormon. The Book is true. The gathering to Jackson Co. Missouri, I think they were too hasty. I will send you my pamphlet as soon as it is printed.

Very Respt [Respectfully] Yours,

David Whitmer

As I read that letter, several things went through my mind. I was enthralled by the fact that I was looking at an actual letter from a man whose testimony, along with those of Oliver Cowdery and Martin Harris, is included in almost every copy of the Book of Mormon since its first printing in 1830. When this letter was written, David was no longer a member of the Church. That makes his testimony of the Book of Mormon even more meaningful. He even underlined his belief that the book was true. And realizing the date on the letter was a little over six months before his death made this declaration of what he had seen and heard even more impressive. I asked myself why he would testify that he had seen an angel and that the Book of Mormon was true after all this time if all that had not happened. I walked away that day with a stronger testimony because of a short letter written by David Whitmer.

David Whitmer was born on January 7, 1805, at a trading post near Harrisburg, Pennsylvania, to Peter and Mary Musselman Whitmer. His father was also born in Pennsylvania and his mother was born in Germany, according to the 1850 census. In late 1809, Peter and Mary moved their family from Pennsylvania to a hundred-acre farm in the Fayette township of New York. It was on this farm that the Church would be organized twenty-one years later. We get some insight about Peter Whitmer Sr. from a reporter who visited David in 1885. He said Peter was "a hard-working, God-fearing man . . . [who] brought his children up with rigid sectarian discipline."[2] The family was well respected in the area.

Peter and Mary had seven children who lived to adulthood. The children were, in order, Christian, Jacob, John, David, Catherine, Peter Jr., and Elizabeth Ann. Each member of the Whitmer family was highly associated with the Restoration of the gospel. David was one of the Three Witnesses of the Book of Mormon, along with his brother-in-law Oliver Cowdery, who married his sister Elizabeth Ann. The other four Whitmer boys, Christian, Jacob, John, and Peter Jr., were listed with their brother-in-law Hiram Page as some of the Eight Witnesses of the Book of Mormon. In 1828, David, John, Peter Jr., and Elizabeth Ann were still living at home, while Christian, Jacob, and Catherine were married but lived near their parents.

David wrote how the Whitmer family became involved with the Book of Mormon:

> I first heard of what is now termed Mormonism, in the year 1828. I made a business trip to Palmyra, N. Y., and while there stopped with one Oliver Cowdery. A great many people in the neighborhood were talking about the finding of certain golden plates by one Joseph

Smith, jun., a young man of the neighborhood. Cowdery and I, as well as many others, talked about the matter, but at that time I paid but little attention to it, supposing it to be only the idle gossip of the neighborhood. Mr. Cowdery said he was acquainted with the Smith family, and he believed there must be some truth in the story of the plates, and that he intended to investigate the matter.[3]

That spring, Oliver Cowdery and Samuel Smith made the trip from Manchester, New York, to Harmony, Pennsylvania, to see the Prophet Joseph. David shared this:

After several months, Cowdery told me he was going to Harmony, Penn., whither Joseph Smith had gone with the plates, on account of the persecutions of his neighbors, and see him about the matter. He did go, and on his way he stopped at my father's house and told me that as soon as he found out anything, either truth or untruth, he would let me know. After he got there he became acquainted with Joseph Smith, and shortly after wrote to me, telling me that he was convinced that Smith had the records, and that he (Smith) had told him that it was the will of heaven that he (Cowdery) should be his scribe to assist in the translation of the plates. He went on and Joseph translated from the plates, and he wrote it down. Shortly after this Mr. Cowdery wrote me another letter, in which he gave me a few lines of what they had translated, and he assured me that he knew of a certainty that he had a record of a people that inhabited this continent, and that the plates they were translating from gave a complete history of these people.[4]

The entire Whitmer family stayed informed about the happenings in Harmony. David related, "When Cowdery wrote me these things and told me that he had revealed knowledge concerning the truth of them, I showed these letters to my parents, and brothers and sisters."[5]

Later, as persecution began to increase in Harmony, it became more difficult to finish the translation. Soon afterward, a third letter written by Oliver requested the translation of the Book of Mormon be completed at the Whitmer home in Fayette, New York. David held a family council to determine whether he should make the trip to bring Joseph, Emma, and Oliver to their home. Peter Whitmer pointed out how much work needed to be done on the farm. They decided that he would not go unless he received a witness from God concerning the matter. David prayed to the Lord and asked for help in doing his farm duties faster than he had ever done before. This would be the evidence he needed to know it was God's will that he should assist Joseph Smith.

That divine assistance came in a remarkable way:

> A late May planting was essential for successful fall crops; therefore, David Whitmer had to plow and prepare the soil before he could take his two-horse wagon to pick up Joseph Smith and Oliver Cowdery. At the end of a day of plowing he found he had accomplished in one day what normally would have taken two days to do. David's father was likewise impressed by this apparent miracle. Peter Whitmer, Sr., said, "There must be an overruling hand in this, and I think you would better go down to Pennsylvania as soon as your plaster of paris is sown." (Plaster of paris was used to reduce the acidity of the soil.) The next day David went to the fields to sow the plaster, but to his surprise he found the work had been done. His sister, who lived near the field, said that her children had called her to watch three strangers the day before spread the plaster with remarkable skill. She assumed they were men David had hired.[6]

The miraculous nature of his first meeting with Joseph and Oliver came soon after:

> I was a little over two and a half days going, and traveled over 40 miles the first day, and met them on the third day. . . . Oliver told me, they knew just when I started, where I put up at night and even the name on the sign board of the hotel where I stayed each night, for he had asked Joseph to look in the Seer stone, that he did so and told him all these particulars of my journey. Oliver asked me when I first met them, when I left home, where I stayed on the road, and the names of the persons at Hotels. I could not tell the names; but as we returned I pointed out the several houses where I had stopped, when he took out his book and found them to correspond even to the names on the sign boards, all of which he had written before we met. As had been told to him by the Prophet, and which agreed in every particular.[7]

The Prophet wrote his perspective about the events that surrounded his relocation to the Whitmer home. He recorded,

In the beginning of the month of June, his [Peter Whitmer Sr.'s] son, David Whitmer, came to the place where we were residing, and brought with him a two-horse wagon, for the purpose of having us accompany him to his father's place, and there remain until we should finish the work. . . . Upon our arrival, we found Mr. Whitmer's family very anxious concerning the work, and very friendly toward ourselves. They continued so, boarded and lodged us according to arrangements; and John Whitmer, in particular, assisted us very much in writing during the remainder of the work.[8]

The arrival of Oliver, Joseph, and later Emma at the Whitmer home placed a heavy burden on Mary Whitmer. Her son David said that his mother was going to milk the cows one day when she was met by an old man who said to her,

"You have been very faithful and diligent in your labors, but you are tired because of the increase of your toil; it is proper therefore that you should receive a witness that your faith may be strengthened." Thereupon he showed her the plates. My father and mother had a large family of their own, the addition to it therefore of Joseph, his wife Emma and Oliver very greatly increased the toil and anxiety of my mother. And although she had never complained she had sometimes felt that her labor was too much, or at least she was perhaps beginning to feel so. This circumstance, however, completely removed all such feelings and nerved her up for her increased responsibilities.[9]

Mary's grandson John C. Whitmer said he heard his grandmother testify multiple times that she had seen the plates: "From that moment my grandmother was enabled to perform her household duties with comparative ease, and she felt no more inclination to murmur because her lot was hard. I knew my grandmother to be a good, noble and truthful woman, and I have not the least doubt of her statement in regard to seeing the plates being strictly true. She was a strong believer in the Book of Mormon until the day of her death."[10]

There have been various statements made about the methods used to translate the Book of Mormon. Most scholars believe that the Prophet Joseph used both the Urim and Thummin and a seer stone he possessed. Oliver Cowdery describes the first method by saying, "I wrote, with my own pen, the entire Book of Mormon (save a few pages), as it fell from the lips of the Prophet Joseph Smith, as he translated it by the gift and power of God, by the means of the Urim and Thummim, or, as it is called by that book, 'holy interpreters.'"[11]

David Whitmer gave this description of how the translation came to be when the seer stone was used.

> I will now give you a description of the manner in which the Book of Mormon was translated. Joseph Smith would put the seer stone into a hat, and put his face in the hat, drawing it closely around his face to exclude the light; and in the darkness the spiritual light would shine. A piece of something resembling parchment would appear, and on that appeared the writing. One character at a time would appear, and under it was the interpretation in English. Brother Joseph would read off the English to Oliver Cowdery, who was his principal scribe, and when it was written down and repeated to Brother Joseph to see if it was correct, then it would disappear, and another character with the interpretation would appear. Thus the Book of Mormon was translated by the gift and power of God, and not by any power of man.[12]

During the translation process at the Whitmer home in June 1829, many other important events occurred. For example, several revelations were received by Joseph that are now included in the Doctrine and Covenants. One of those was given specifically to David Whitmer after his request to learn his individual duty. In that revelation, he was promised, "And, if you keep my commandments and endure to the end you shall have eternal life, which gift is the greatest of all the gifts of God" (D&C 14:7).

David was baptized by Joseph in Seneca Lake and soon learned he would be one of three special witnesses allowed to view the plates. He related, "In June, 1829, the Lord called Oliver Cowdery, Martin Harris, and myself as the three witnesses, to behold the vision of the Angel, as recorded in the fore part of the Book of Mormon, and to bear testimony to the world that the Book of Mormon is true."[13] The angel was dressed in white and appeared first to Oliver and David and turned the leaves of the plates one by one. Later on, Martin Harris was allowed the same experience. The next day, Joseph Smith was allowed to show the plates to the Eight Witnesses, many of them being members of the Whitmer family.

In 1878, Parley P. Pratt asked David Whitmer to describe seeing the plates with Joseph and Oliver. At that point, David had been away from the Church for several decades. He said,

> It was in June, 1829—the latter part of the month, and the Eight Witnesses saw them, I think, the next day or the day after (i.e. one or two days after). Joseph showed them the plates himself, but the angel showed us (the Three Witnesses) the plates, as I suppose to fulfill the words of the book itself. Martin Harris was not with us at this time; he obtained a view of them afterwards (the same day). Joseph, Oliver and myself were together when I saw them. We not only saw the plates of the Book of Mormon, but also the brass plates, the plates of the Book of Ether, the plates containing the records of the wickedness and secret combinations of the people of the world down to the time of their being engraved, and many other plates. The fact is, it was just as though Joseph, Oliver and I were sitting just here on a log, when we were overshadowed by a light. It was not like the light of the sun nor like that of a fire, but more glorious and beautiful. It extended away round us, I cannot tell how far, but in the midst of this light about as far off as he sits (pointing to John C. Whitmer, sitting a few feet from him), there appeared, as it were, a table with many records or plates upon it, besides the plates of the Book of Mormon, also the sword of Laban, the directors—i. e., the ball which Lehi had, and the interpreters. I saw them just as plain as I see this bed (striking the bed beside him with his hand), and I heard the voice of the Lord, as distinctly as I ever heard anything in my life, declaring that the records of the plates of the Book of Mormon were translated by the gift and power of God.[14]

In April 1830, soon after the Book of Mormon was published, the Prophet received Section 20 of the Doctrine and Covenants, now known as a revelation on Church organization and government. The first verse reads, "The rise of the Church of Christ in these last days, being one thousand eight hundred and thirty years since the coming of our Lord and Savior Jesus Christ in the flesh, it being regularly organized and established agreeable to the laws of our country, by the will and commandments of God, in the fourth month, and on the sixth day of the month which is called April" (D&C 20:1). On that day, one of the most important events in human history occurred. It was time to formally organize the true Church of Jesus Christ on the earth again.

The meeting was held in the home of Peter Whitmer Sr. in Fayette, Seneca County, New York. Joseph Smith was only twenty-four years old at the time, but the Lord had been preparing him for ten years to lead His Church. Six men were chosen to become incorporators of the Church to meet the requirements of the laws of the land. The original members were Joseph Smith, Oliver Cowdery, Hyrum Smith, Samuel H. Smith, David Whitmer, and Peter Whitmer. All of these original members had been previously baptized. A few others, including Joseph's parents, were invited to attend the meeting.

The Prophet Joseph tells what happened during the meeting:

Having opened the meeting by solemn prayer to Our Heavenly Father, we proceeded, according to previous commandment, to call on our brethren to know whether they accepted us as their teachers in the things of the Kingdom of God, and whether they were satisfied that we should proceed and be organized as a Church according to said commandment which we had received. To these several propositions they consented by a unanimous vote. I then laid my hands upon Oliver Cowdery, and ordained him an Elder of the "Church of Jesus Christ of Latter-day Saints"; after which, he ordained me also to the office of an Elder of said Church. We then took bread, blessed it, and brake it with them; also wine, blessed it, and drank it with them. We then laid our hands on each individual member of the Church present, that they might receive the gift of the Holy Ghost, and be confirmed members of the Church of Christ. The Holy Ghost was poured out upon us to a very great degree—some prophesied, whilst we all praised the Lord, and rejoiced exceedingly.[15]

At some point during that same day, a number of people were also baptized. The Prophet Joseph said, "Several persons who had attended the above meeting, became convinced of the truth and came forward shortly after, and were received into the Church; among the rest, my own father and mother were baptized, to my great joy and consolation."[16] His mother wrote this of that experience: "Joseph stood upon the shore, and taking his father by the hand, he exclaimed, with tears of joy, 'Praise to my God! that I have lived to see my own father baptized into the true Church of Jesus Christ!'"[17] All who were baptized had hands laid on their heads to receive the gift of the Holy Ghost.

If I could attend any meeting in the history of the world, the meeting held on April 6, 1830, at the Whitmer home would be near the top of my list. What a special privilege it was for David Whitmer to be at that meeting and to be among the six original members of the Church in this dispensation.

However, history has shown that being involved in spiritual feasts does not guarantee future obedience. Just months after David was allowed to be involved in some of the most spiritual and dramatic events in history, he was chastised. In a revelation given in September 1830, the Lord said, "Your mind has been on the things of the earth more than on the things of me, your Maker, and the ministry whereunto you have been called; and you have not given heed unto my Spirit, and to those who were set over you, but have been persuaded by those whom I have not commanded" (D&C 30:2).

Like most elders in early Church history, David went on several missions and was influential in numerous baptisms. One of those converts was William E. McLellin, a local schoolteacher who later became one of the Twelve Apostles. William first attended a sparsely attended meeting in July 1831, in Paris, Illinois, where Elders Samuel H. Smith and Reynolds Cahoon told those in attendance about the miraculous coming forth of the Book of Mormon.

In a letter to his relatives, William told what happened next:

> They left Paris very early the next morning and pursued their journey westward. But in a few days two others came into the neighborhood proclaiming that these were the last days, and that God had sent forth the Book of Mormon to show the times of the fulfillment of the ancient prophecies when the Savior shall come to destroy iniquity off the face of the earth, and reign with his saints in Millennial rest. One of these was a witness to the book and had seen an angel which declared its truth (his name was David Whitmer). They were in the neighborhood about a week. I talked much with them by way of enquiry and argument. They believed Joseph Smith to be an inspired prophet.[18]

William was so interested that he closed his school and rode his horse about 450 miles to Independence, Missouri. Once he arrived there, he examined the Book of Mormon and joined the Church.

David moved to Kirtland, Ohio, where Oliver Cowdery ordained him a high priest on October 5, 1831. The Prophet Joseph received a revelation on July 20, 1831, that would dramatically affect David and the entire Whitmer family. It is now found in Doctrine and Covenants 57:1, and it reads, "Hearken, O ye elders of my church, saith the Lord your God, who have assembled yourselves together, according to my commandments, in this land, which is the land of Missouri, which is the land which I have appointed and consecrated for the gathering of the saints." That led to the Saints assembling in both Kirtland and Jackson County, Missouri. By October 1832, David and his wife had moved to Missouri, where his family was severely persecuted by mobs.

At one point, David and other Church leaders were taken by a mob and ordered to say goodbye to their families because they would never see them again. The prisoners were brought to the public square in Independence, stripped of their clothing, then tarred and feathered. John P. Green told what happened next:

> The commanding officer then called twelve of his men, and ordering them to cock their guns and present them at the prisoners' breasts, and to be ready to fire when he gave the word,—he addressed the prisoners, threatening them with instant death, unless they denied the book of Mormon and confessed it to be a fraud; at the same time adding, that if they did so, they might enjoy the privileges of citizens. David Whitmer, hereupon, lifted up his hands and bore witness that the Book of Mormon was the Word of God. The mob then let them go.[19]

By October 1834, David had moved back to Kirtland, Ohio, and in February 1835, he, along with Oliver Cowdery and Martin Harris, selected the men who made up the first Quorum of Twelve Apostles in this dispensation (D&C 18:37). He was also chosen to receive his endowment in the partially completed Kirtland Temple June 13, 1834. Later on, he attended the Kirtland Temple dedication and witnessed the outpouring of the spirit associated with that event.

Despite the many contributions David made to the establishment of the gospel, he began to falter in 1837. It was a time of financial strain in the nation, and it greatly affected the Saints in Kirtland. To help the local economy, Joseph Smith and other Church leaders established the

Kirtland Safety Society. When this financial institution failed, many members lost their savings and became bitter toward these leaders. Some of the strongest members of the Church were so upset about what happened that they lost their testimonies. Some even wanted to replace Joseph Smith with David Whitmer as the prophet. David expressed sympathy toward the apostates in Kirtland and returned to Missouri by July 1837. Joseph and Sidney Rigdon also moved to Missouri. That led to a leadership struggle and the dissolving of the Church presidency in Missouri.

David was excommunicated by the High Council at Far West, Missouri, on April 13, 1838, on multiple charges. Ultimately, all of the Whitmers ended up leaving the Church in 1838, as did their sons-in-law Oliver Cowdery and Hiram Page. Each Whitmer family member was intimately acquainted with events surrounding the coming forth of the Book of Mormon. If there was ever a time to expose a fraud, it was right then. And yet not one of them ever denied their testimony of its truthfulness. David moved with his family to Richmond, Missouri, where he became a respected citizen and ended up operating a successful livery stable. He served on the city council and even served as the mayor of Richmond for a short time.

As the last of the eleven witnesses to die, David was the most interviewed of all the witnesses. After his excommunication and move to Richmond, he lived for more than fifty years. He said this about the visitors he received over the years:

> I have been visited by thousands of people, believers and unbelievers, men and ladies of all degrees, sometimes as many as 15 in one day, and have never failed in my testimony. And they will know some day that my testimony is true.
>
> I had a mob of from four to five hundred surrounding me at one time, demanding that I should deny my published statement in the Book of Mormon; but the testimony I bore the mob made them tremble before me. I heard the voice of the Angel just as stated in said Book, and the engravings on the plates were shown to us, and we were commanded to bear record of them; and if they are not true, then there is not truth, and if there is no truth there is no God; if there is no God then there is no existence. But there is a God, and I know it.[20]

David Whitmer's testimony was consistent and detailed in repeated declarations:

It was in the latter part of June, 1829. Joseph, Oliver Cowdery, and myself were together, and the angel showed them to us. We not only saw the plates of the book of Mormon, but he also showed us the brass plates of the book of Ether and many others. They were shown to us in this way. Joseph and Oliver and I were sitting on a log when we were overshadowed by a light more glorious than that of the sun. In the midst of this light, but a few feet from us appeared a table upon which were many golden plates, also the sword of Laban and the directors. I saw them as plain as I see you now, and distinctly heard the voice of the Lord declaiming that the records of the plates of the Book of Mormon were translated by the gift and the power of God.[21]

David Whitmer defended his testimony and that of Oliver Cowdery. He was emphatic about setting the record straight. He said,

It is recorded in the American Cyclopedia and the Encyclopedia Britannica, that I, David Whitmer, have denied my testimony as one of the three witnesses to the divinity of the Book of Mormon: and that the two other witnesses, Oliver Cowdery and Martin Harris, denied their testimony to that Book. I will say once more to all mankind, that I have never at any time denied that testimony or any part thereof. I also testify to the world, that neither Oliver Cowdery nor Martin Harris ever at any time denied their testimony. They both died affirming the truth of the divine authenticity of the Book of Mormon.

I was present at the death bed of Oliver Cowdery, and his last words were, "Brother David, be true to your testimony to the Book of Mormon." He died here in Richmond, Mo., on March 3d, 1850. Many witnesses yet live in Richmond, who will testify to the truth of these facts, as well as to the good character of Oliver Cowdery. The very powers of darkness have combined against the Book of Mormon, to prove that it is not the word of God, and this should go to prove to men of spiritual understanding, that the Book is true.[22]

David Whitmer died January 25, 1888, at Richmond, Missouri. Following his death, the *Richmond Conservator* wrote:

On Sunday evening before his death he called the family and his attending physician, Dr. George W. Buchanan, to his bedside and said, "Doctor do you consider that I am in my right mind?" to which the Doctor replied, "Yes, you are in your right mind, I have just had a conversation with you." He then addressed himself to all present and said: "I want to give my dying testimony. You must be faithful in Christ. I want to say to you all that the Bible and the record of the Nephites, (The Book of Mormon) are true, so you can say that you have heard me bear my testimony on my death bed." . . . On Monday morning he again called those present to his bedside, and told them that he had seen another vision which reconfirmed the divinity of the "Book of Mormon," and said that he had seen Christ in the fullness of his glory and majesty, sitting upon his great white throne in heaven waiting to receive his children.[23]

Another local newspaper ran a long article about David when he died. Among the things stated were these:

Skeptics may laugh and scoff if they will, but no man can listen to Mr. Whitmer as he talks of his interview with the Angel of the Lord, without being most forcibly convinced that he has heard an honest man tell what he honestly believes to be true. . . . David Whitmer lived in Richmond about half a century, and we can say that no man ever lived here who had among our people more friends and fewer enemies. Honest, conscientious and upright in all his dealings, just in his estimate of men, and open, manly and frank in his treatment of all, he made lasting friends who loved him to the end.[24]

Reason to Believe

David Whitmer was one of the Three Witnesses to the Book of Mormon. He said that an angel had shown him the plates. The translation was completed at his parent's home, and he had intimate knowledge of the whole process. He was there when the Church was organized and saw firsthand many miracles related to the coming forth of the Book of Mormon.

For over fifty years, David remained outside of the Church and disagreed with many of the teachings and practices of Joseph Smith. During his time outside the Church, many Latter-day Saints and those of other faiths visited him to ask about his Book of Mormon testimony. He never once wavered from his testimony of what he saw and heard. When someone accused him of denying his testimony, he actually got prominent people in the community to sign a document to testify that he was a man of integrity. He reiterated to the world his testimony of the Book of Mormon. He later bore this testimony on his deathbed. What on earth would prompt someone to do all of this if he were lying? The only compelling reason I can think of for his persistent story is that he had indeed seen the angel and the plates and heard the voice of God.

Notes

1. *Richmond Democrat*, 2 February 1888, in "David Whitmer," *The Historical Record* 7, Andrew Jenson, ed. (Oct 1888), 622–24.
2. "The Book of Mormon," *Chicago Tribune,* 17 December 1885, vol. 45, 3.
3. David Whitmer, Interview with the Kansas City Journal, June 5, 1881, in *The Latter-Day Saints Millennial Star*, vol. 43, 422.
4. Ibid.
5. Ibid., 423.
6. *Church History in the Fulness of Times*,(Salt Lake City: Church of Jesus Christ of Latter-day Saints, 1989), 56–57.
7. Lyndon Cook, ed., *David Whitmer Interviews: A Restoration Witness* (Orem, Utah: Grandin Book Co. 1991), 123.
8. Joseph Smith, *History of the Church of Jesus Christ of Latter-day Saints*, ed. B. H. Roberts, 2nd ed. rev., 7 vols. (Salt Lake City: The Church of Jesus Christ of Latter-day Saints, 1932–1951), 1:48.
9. Andrew Jenson, *Latter-day Saint Biographical Encyclopedia* (Salt Lake City: The Deseret News, 1901), 267.
10. Ibid., 283.
11. Richard L. Anderson, "Reuben Miller, Recorder of Oliver Cowdery's Reaffirmations," *BYU Studies,* 1968, 8:277.
12. David Whitmer, *An Address to All Believers in Christ by a Witness to the Divine Authenticity of the Book of Mormon* (Richmond, MO, 1887), 12.
13. Ibid., 32.
14. "David Whitmer Interview," *Millennial Star*, vol. 40, no. 49, 50, September 17, 1878.
15. *History of the Church*, 1:77–78.
16. Ibid., 1:79.
17. Lucy Mack Smith, *History of Joseph Smith*, ed. Preston Nibley, (Salt Lake City: Bookcraft, 1958), 168.

18. William McLellin to Relatives, 4 August 1832, typescript, RLDS Archives.

19. John P. Greene, *Facts Relative to the Expulsion of the Mormons from the State of Missouri, under the "Exterminating Order"* (Cincinnati: R. P. Brooks, 1839), 17.

20. *Richmond Conservator Report,* 26 Jan. 1888, quoted in Lyndon W. Cook, ed., *David Whitmer Interviews: A Restoration Witness* (Orem, Utah: Grandin Book Company, 1993), 95–96.

21. David Whitmer, interview with the *Kansas City Journal,* June 1, 1881, in Lyndon Cook, ed., *David Whitmer Interviews: A Restoration Witness,* 63.

22. David Whitmer, *An Address to All Believers in Christ: By a Witness to the Divine Authenticity of the Book of Mormon* (1887), 8.

23. *Richmond Conservator Report,* 26 January 1888, quoted in Lyndon W. Cook ed., *David Whitmer Interviews: A Restoration Witness,* (Orem, Utah: Grandin Book Company, 1993), 226.

24. *Richmond Democrat,* 2 February 1888, quoted in Eldin Ricks, *The Case of the Book of Mormon Witnesses* (Salt Lake City: Deseret News Press, 1971), 16.

Chapter 20: The Character of Joseph Smith

"Joseph Smith is undoubtedly one of the greatest characters of the age. He indicates as much talent, originality, and moral courage as Mahomet, Odin, or any of the great spirits that have hitherto produced the revolutions of past ages. In the present infidel, irreligious, material, ideal, geological, animal-magnetic age of the world, some such singular prophet as Joseph Smith is required to preserve the principle of faith, and to plant some new germs of civilization that may come to maturity in a thousand years."[1]

—*New York Herald* (1842)

Since the day Joseph Smith first said that an angel appeared to him and led him to gold plates that he translated, both he and the Book of Mormon have been on trial. In the court of public opinion, he has been called both a mighty prophet of God and a cunning fraud. Now there are millions of people who have lined up on both sides. The Book of Mormon has been presented as crucial evidence that he is telling the truth.

President Gordon B. Hinckley made this statement about the Book of Mormon: "Through all of these years critics have tried to explain it. They have spoken against it. They have ridiculed it. But it has outlived them all, and its influence today is greater than at any time in its history."[2]

In any trial, the prosecution tries to destroy the relevance of the evidence and the character of the defendant. The Book of Mormon is the evidence that Joseph Smith was telling the truth. After almost two hundred years, both sides are still presenting evidence with no final verdict reached from the critics' point of view. When a person's honesty is in question during a trial, the defense will call in character witnesses to let the court know a little about the person on trial. By definition, a character witness is "a person who testifies in a trial on behalf of a person as to that person's good ethical qualities and morality both by the personal knowledge of the witness and the person's reputation in the community. Such testimony is primarily relevant when the party's honesty or morality is an issue, particularly in most criminal cases and civil cases such as fraud."[3]

For those who are still trying to decide whether Joseph Smith was a prophet and the Book of Mormon is true, it would help to learn a little more about him from those who knew him best. Those who are able to observe an individual are far more likely to paint an accurate picture than are his or her enemies. The following are recorded testimonies from such people who actually knew Joseph Smith personally and observed him firsthand:

George Q. Cannon

"It was the author's privilege thus to meet the Prophet for the first time. The occasion was the arrival of a large company of Latter-day Saints at the upper landing at Nauvoo. The general conference of the Church was in session and large numbers crowded to the landing place to welcome the emigrants. Nearly every prominent man in the community was there. Familiar with the names of all and the persons of many of the prominent elders, the author sought with a boy's curiosity and eagerness to discover those whom he knew, and especially to get sight of the Prophet and his brother Hyrum, neither of whom he had ever met. When his eyes fell upon the Prophet, without a word from anyone to point him out, or any reason to separate him from others who stood around, he knew him instantly. He would have known him among ten thousand. There was that about him, which, to the author's eyes, distinguished him from all the men he had ever seen."[4]

Lydia Knight

"Next morning many were the curious glances that I cast at this strange man who dared to call himself a prophet. I saw a tall, well-built form, with the carriage of an Apollo; brown hair, handsome blue eyes, which seemed to dive down to the innermost thoughts with their sharp, penetrating gaze; a striking countenance, and with manners at once majestic yet gentle, dignified yet exceedingly pleasant."[5]

L. O. Littlefield (Zion's Camp)

"While there the men were paraded outside of the camp for exercise and instruction. This was an unpleasant feature for me, as I was too young and too small of stature to act with the men. This created within me, as I remember, some lonesome reflections. I sat down on a rock where the men were passing, the better to observe their movements. While thus seated, the prophet Joseph Smith, who happened to be passing by in quite a hurry, noticed me.

"He stepped to where I sat alone. It might have been my isolated position that attracted him. I know not the motive; but that man, who to me appeared so good and so Godlike, really halted in his hurry to notice me—only a little boy. Placing one of his hands upon my head, he said: 'Well, bub, is there no place for you?'

"This recognition from the man who I then knew was a Prophet of God created within me a tumult of emotions. I could make him no reply. My young heart was filled with joy to me unspeakable."[6]

Mary Jane Lytle

"I knew the Prophet Joseph Smith. Many times when we were out on the playground at school, he would stop and talk with us. He always shook hands with the girls and played marbles with the boys. He was a great favorite among the children."[7]

Mary Frost Adams

"While he was acting as mayor of the city, a colored man named Anthony was arrested for selling liquor on Sunday, contrary to law. He pleaded that the reason he had done so was that he might raise the money to purchase the freedom of a dear child held as a slave in a Southern State. . . . Joseph said, 'I am sorry, Anthony, but the law must be observed, and we will have to impose a fine.'

"The next day Brother Joseph presented Anthony with a fine horse, directing him to sell it, and use the money obtained for the purchase of the child."[8]

William Taylor

"Never in all my life have I seen anything more beautiful than the striking example of brotherly love and devotion felt for each other by Joseph and Hyrum. I witnessed this many, many times. No matter how often or when or where they met, it was always with the same expression of supreme joy."[9]

John W. Hess

"I never saw another man like Joseph. There was something heavenly and angelic in his looks that I never witnessed in the countenance of any other person. I was fourteen years old when the Prophet came to stay at our home. During the thirteen days he was with us, I learned to love him more dearly than any other person I ever met, including my mother and father."[10]

Lyman L. Woods

"I have seen him on a white horse wearing the uniform of a general. . . . He was leading a parade of the legion and looked like a god."[11]

Mary Alice Lambert

"I was fourteen when I first saw the Prophet. I knew him the instant my eyes rested upon him, and at that moment I received my testimony that he was a prophet of God, for I never had such a feeling as thrilled my being. He was not pointed out to me. I knew him from all the other men, and, child that I was, I knew I saw a prophet of God." [12]

Edwin Holden

"In 1838 Joseph and some of the young men were playing various outdoor games, among which was a game of ball. By and by they began to get weary. He saw it, and calling them together he said: 'Let us build a log cabin.' So off they went, Joseph and the young men, to build a log cabin for a widow woman. Such was Joseph's way, always assisting in whatever he could."[13]

Mosiah Hancock

"He always had a smile for his friends and was always cheerful."[14]

Mary Ann Winters

"I saw him on parade at the head of the Nauvoo Legion, looking noble and grand as a leader could do. His commanding presence could be discerned above all others, and all eyes were centered on him, as he rode back and forth giving the commands of his office."[15]

John Taylor

"Joseph Smith, the Prophet and Seer of the Lord, has done more, save Jesus only, for the salvation of men in this world, than any other man that ever lived in it" (D&C 135:3).

Parley P. Pratt

"I have known him when chained and surrounded with armed murderers and assassins who were heaping upon him every possible insult and abuse, rise up in the majesty of a son of God and rebuke them, in the name of Jesus Christ, till they quailed before him, dropped their weapons, and, on their knees, begged his pardon, and ceased their abuse."[16]

Emmeline B. Wells

"At last the boat reached the upper landing, and a crowd of people were coming toward the bank of the river. As we stepped ashore the crowd advanced, and I could see one person who towered away and above all the others around him; in fact I did not see distinctly any others. His majestic bearing, so entirely different from anyone I had ever seen (and I had seen many superior men) was more than a surprise. It was as if I beheld a vision; I seemed to be lifted off my feet, to be as it were walking in the air, and paying no heed whatever to those around me. I made my way through the crowd, then I saw this man whom I had noticed, because of his lofty appearance, shaking hands with all the people, men, women, and children. Before I was aware of it he came to me, and when he took my hand, I was simply electrified,—thrilled through and through to the tips of my fingers, and every part of my body, as if some magic elixir had given me new life and vitality. I am sure that for a few minutes I was not conscious of motion. I think I stood still, I did not want to speak, or be spoken to. I was overwhelmed with indefinable emotion."[17]

Margarette McIntire Burgess

"Joseph's wife, Sister Emma, had lost a young babe. My mother having twin baby girls, the Prophet came to see if she would let him have one of them. Of course it was rather against her feelings, but she finally consented for him to take one of them, providing he would bring it home each night. This he did punctually himself, and also came after it each morning. One evening he did not come with it at the usual time, and mother went down to the Mansion to see what was the matter, and there sat the Prophet with the baby wrapped up in a little silk quilt. He was trotting it on his knee, and singing to it to get it quiet before starting out, as it had been fretting. The child soon became quiet when my mother took it, and the Prophet came up home with her.

"Next morning when he came after the baby, mother handed him Sarah, the other baby. They looked so much alike that strangers could not tell them apart; but as Mother passed him the other baby he shook his head and said, 'This is not my little Mary.'

"Then she took Mary from the cradle and gave her to him, and he smilingly carried her home with him. The baby Mary had a very mild disposition, while Sarah was quite cross and fretful, and by this my mother could distinguish them one from the other, though generally people could not tell them apart. But our Prophet soon knew which was the borrowed baby.

"After his wife became better in health he did not take our baby anymore, but often came in to caress her and play with her. . . . When, after a time, the little one died, he grieved as if he had lost one of his own. I remember seeing him embrace the little cold form and say, 'Mary, oh my dear little Mary!' "[18]

George A. Smith

"Joseph wrapped his arms around me and pressed me to his bosom and said, 'George A., I love you as I do my own life.' "[19]

Mary Ellen Kimball

"The last time I saw the Prophet, he was on his way to Carthage jail. He and his brother Hyrum were on horseback, also Brothers John Taylor and Willard Richards. They stopped opposite Sister Clawson's house, at the house of Brother Rosecrans. We were on the porch and could hear every word he said. He asked for a drink of water. Some few remarks passed between them which I do not remember. But one sentence I well remember. After bidding goodbye, he said to Brother Rosecrans, 'If I never see you again, or if I never come back, remember that I love you.'"[20]

Willard Richards

"Before Joseph went to the Carthage Jail, he said to Dr. Richards: 'If we go into the cell, will you go in with us?' The doctor answered, 'Brother Joseph you did not ask me to cross the river with you—you did not ask me to come to Carthage—you did not ask me to come to jail with you—and do you think I would forsake you now? But I will tell you what I will do; if you are condemned to be hung for treason, I will be hung in your stead, and you shall go free.' Joseph said, 'You cannot.' The doctor replied, 'I will.'"[21]

William Taylor

"It is impossible for me to express my feelings in regard to this period of my life. I have never known the same joy and satisfaction in the companionship of any other person . . . that I felt with him. . . . He was always the most companionable and loveable of men."[22]

Enoch E. Dodge

"Every Saint who knew him loved him, and would have been willing to lay down his life for him if it had been necessary."[23]

Mary Alice Lambert

"The love the Saints had for him was inexpressible. They would willingly have laid down their lives for him. If he was to talk, every task would be laid aside that they might listen to his words. He was not an ordinary man. Saints and sinners alike felt and recognized a power and influence which he carried with him. It was impossible to meet him and not be impressed by the strength of his personality and influence."[24]

Amasa M. Lyman

"When he grasped my hand in that cordial way (known to those who have met him in the honest simplicity of truth), I felt as one of old in the presence of the Lord; my strength seemed to be gone, so that it required an effort on my part to stand on my feet; but in all this there was no fear, but the serenity and peace of heaven pervaded my soul, and the still small voice of the spirit whispered its living testimony in the depths of my soul, where it has ever remained, that he was the man of God."[25]

Wilford Woodruff

"I have felt to rejoice exceedingly in what I saw of brother Joseph, for in his public and private career he carried with him the Spirit of the Almighty, and he manifested a greatness of soul which I had never seen in any other man."[26]

Lucy Mack Smith

"How often I have parted every bed in the house for the accommodation of the brethren, and then laid a single blanket on the floor for my husband and myself, while Joseph and Emma slept upon the same floor, with nothing but their cloaks for both bed and bedding."[27]

Josiah Quincy Jr.

"It is by no means improbable that some future textbook, for the use of generations yet unborn, will contain a question something like this: What historical American of the nineteenth century has exerted the most powerful influence upon the destinies of his countrymen? And it is by no means impossible that the answer to that interrogatory may be thus written: Joseph Smith, the Mormon Prophet. And the reply, absurd as it doubtless seems to most men now living, may be an obvious commonplace to their descendants."[28]

James B. Bracken

"I never saw a nobler looking or acting man than Joseph Smith appeared on that occasion."[29]

Daniel D. McArthur

"To me he seemed to possess more power and force of character than any ordinary man. I would look upon him when he was with hundreds of other men, and he would appear greater than ever."[30]

Angus M. Cannon

"He was one of the grandest samples of manhood that I ever saw walk or ride at the head of a legion of men. In listening to him as he has addressed the Saints his words have so affected me that I would rise upon my feet in the agitation that would take hold of my mind."[31]

M. L. Davis (member of Congress, in a letter to his wife)

"I went last evening to hear 'Joe Smith,' the celebrated 'Mormon,' expound his doctrine. I, with several others, had a desire to understand his tenets as explained by himself. He is not an educated man; but he is a plain, sensible, strong-minded man. Everything he says is said in a manner to leave an impression that he is sincere."[32]

George A. Smith

"In consequence of the influence exerted by General Doniphan, General Lucas hesitated to execute the sentence of his court-martial, and he delivered Joseph Smith and his associates into the charge of General Moses Wilson, who was instructed to take them to Jackson County and there put them to death. I heard General Wilson, some years after, speaking of this circumstance. He was telling some gentlemen about having Joseph Smith a prisoner in chains in his possession, and said he—'He was a very remarkable man. I carried him into my house, a prisoner in chains and in less than two hours my wife loved him better than she did me.'"[33]

Eliza R. Snow

"His expansive mind grasped the great plan of salvation, and solved the mystic problem of man's destiny; he was in possession of keys that unlocked the past and the future, with its successions of eternities; yet in his devotions he was as humble as a little child. Three times a day he had family worship; and these precious seasons of sacred household service truly seemed a foretaste of celestial happiness."[34]

United States Artillery Officer (1842)

"The Smiths are not without talent, and are said to be as brave as lions. Joseph, the chief, is a noble-looking fellow, a Mahomet every inch of him. . . . The city of Nauvoo contains about ten thousand souls, and is rapidly increasing. It is well laid out, and the municipal affairs appear to be well conducted. The adjoining country is a beautiful prairie. Who will say that the Mormon Prophet is not among the great spirits of the age?"[35]

Masonic Grand Master of Illinois

"During my stay of three days, I became well acquainted with their principal men, and more particularly with their Prophet. . . . I found them hospitable, polite, well-informed and liberal. With Joseph Smith, the hospitality of whose house I kindly received, I was well pleased; of course on the subject of religion, we widely differed, but he appeared to be quite as willing to permit me to enjoy my right of opinion, as I think we all ought to be to let the Mormons enjoy theirs; but instead of the ignorant and tyrannical upstart, judge my surprise at finding him a sensible, intelligent, companionable and gentlemanly man. In frequent conversations with him he gave me every information that I desired, and appeared to be only pleased at being able to do so. He appears to be much respected by all the people about him, and has their entire confidence."[36]

George Q. Cannon

"Think of what he passed through! Think of his afflictions, and think of his dauntless character! Did any one ever see him falter? Did any one ever see him flinch? Did any one ever see any lack in him of the power necessary to enable him to stand with dignity in the midst of his enemies, or lacking in dignity in the performance of his duties as a servant of the living God? God gave him peculiar power in this respect. He was filled with integrity to God; with such integrity as was not known among men. He was like an angel of God among them. Notwithstanding all that he had to endure, and the peculiar circumstances in which he was so often placed, and the great responsibility that weighed constantly upon him, he never faltered; the feeling of fear or trembling never crossed him—at least he never exhibited it in his feelings or actions. God sustained him to the very last, and was with him, and bore him off triumphant even in his death."[37]

Wilford Woodruff

"No greater prophet than Joseph Smith ever lived on the face of the earth save Jesus Christ."[38]

These men and women knew Joseph Smith in many different circumstances. Some observed his behavior with children and saw compassion and energy. Some told of their experience with him as a political or military leader and described his dignity. Some were awed by his countenance. Some experienced his congenial nature and friendship. Some were with him when extreme persecution, scorn, and abuse fell upon them and they saw calm, righteous power and peace. Some knew him from close association and reported his great love, tenderness, and prophetic nature. But all saw him as an extraordinary man of integrity, spiritual strength, and faith. Joseph Smith was admired, loved, and revered by those who knew him best.

Reason to Believe

It seems to be an established fact that high-profile leaders are going to have some who love them and others who dislike them or even despise them. Think about those who have served as president of the United States, for example. No matter who occupies that office, some of the population love and admire him while others dislike him immensely, and certain people fall somewhere in-between. These feelings often come from the political party or personal views of the individual.

Influential religious leaders are often looked at in a similar way through the lens of a person's religious affiliation or indoctrination. It is difficult to know what a person is really like when you have so many contradicting opinions being expressed about them. I think the best way to determine a person's true character is to see what those who know him or her best have to say.

Over the years, I've read many statements by those who knew Joseph Smith on a close, personal level. I have enclosed merely a few of those statements in this chapter. I believe these statements together paint a picture of the kind of person Joseph Smith really was. Why would honorable men like John Taylor, Brigham Young, and Wilford Woodruff say he is the greatest prophet who ever lived with the exception of Jesus Christ if he was a fraud? One reason I believe that Joseph Smith was not a fraud and did not make up the Book of Mormon himself is because of what those closest to him had to say about his character.

Notes

1. Quoted in George Q. Cannon, *The Life of Joseph Smith* (Salt Lake City: Juvenile Instructor Office, 1888), 345.
2. Gordon B. Hinckley, "Stone Cut Out of the Mountain," Conference Report, October 2007.
3. "Character Witness," http://legal-dictionary.thefreedictionary. com.
4. George Q. Cannon, *The Life of Joseph Smith* (Salt Lake City: Juvenile Instructor Office, 1888), 26.
5. Susa Young Gates, *Lydia Knight's History* (Salt Lake City: Juvenile Instructor Office, 1883), 14–23.
6. Lyman O. Littlefield, *"The Prophet Joseph Smith in Zion's Camp"* (Salt Lake City: *Juvenile Instructor* 27, no. 1, 1892,) 56–57.
7. "A Biographical Sketch of the Life of Mary Jane Lytle," *Mormon Diaries,* XVI, 90.
8. Mary F. Adams, "Joseph Smith, the Prophet" (*Young Woman's Journal* 17, no. 12 December 1906), 538.
9. William Taylor, "Joseph Smith the Prophet," (*Young Woman's Journal* 17, no. 12, December 1906), 548.
10. John W. Hess, *Recollections of the Prophet Joseph Smith,* (Salt Lake City: *Juvenile Instructor* 27, no. 10, 1892), 302–3.
11. Hyrum L. Andrus, *Joseph Smith: the Man and the Seer* (Salt Lake City: Deseret Book, 1960), 5.
12. Mary A. Lambert, "Joseph Smith the Prophet" (*Young Woman's Journal* 16, no. 12, December 1905), 554.
13. Edwin Holden, "Recollections of the Prophet Joseph Smith" (*Juvenile Instructor* 27, March 1892), 153.
14. Mosiah L. Hancock, *The Life Story of Mosiah Hancock* (Provo, Utah: Brigham Young University, 1956), 3.
15. Mary Ann Winters, "Joseph Smith, the Prophet" (*Young Woman's Journal,* 16 December 1905), 558.

16. Parley P. Pratt, *Autobiography of Parley P. Pratt* (Salt Lake City: Deseret Book, 1874), 47.

17. Emmeline B. Wells, "Joseph Smith, the Prophet" (*Young Woman's Journal* 16, no. 12, December 1905), 555.

18. Margarette Burgess, "Recollections of the Prophet Joseph Smith" (*Juvenile Instructor* 27, January 1892), 66–67.

19. Hyrum L. Andrus, *Joseph Smith: the Man and the Seer* (Salt Lake City: Deseret Book, 1960), 43.

20. Mary Ellen Kimball, "Recollections of the Prophet Joseph Smith" (*Juvenile Instructor*, no. 16, 15 August 1892), 490–91.

21. Joseph Smith, *History of The Church of Jesus Christ of Latter-day Saints*, ed. B. H. Roberts, 2nd ed. rev., 7 vols. (Salt Lake City: The Church of Jesus Christ of Latter-day Saints, 1932–1951), VI, 616.

22. William Taylor, "Joseph Smith, the Prophet" (*Young Woman's Journal* 17, no. 12 December 1906), 548.

23. Enoch E. Dodge, "Joseph Smith, the Prophet" (*Young Woman's Journal* 17, no. 12, December 1906), 544.

24. Mary Alice Lambert, "Joseph Smith, the Prophet" (*Young Woman's Journal* 16, no. 12, December 1905), 544.

25. Amasa Lyman, "Amasa Lyman's History," *Latter-day Saints' Millennial Star* 27, no. 30, 29 July 1865), 473.

26. Wilford Woodruff, *Journal of Discourses,* 26 vols. (Liverpool: F. D. Richards & Sons, 1851–1886), 7:101.

27. Lucy Mack Smith, *History of Joseph Smith by His Mother*, ed. Preston Nibley (Salt Lake City: Bookcraft, 1954), 190–91, 231–32.

28. Josiah Quincy, Jr., *Figures of the Past* (Boston: Roberts Brothers, 1883), 376.

29. James B. Bracken, "Recollections of the Prophet Joseph Smith" (Salt Lake City: *Juvenile Instructor* 27, no. 7, 1 April 1892), 203.

30. Daniel D. McArthur, "Recollections of the Prophet Joseph Smith" (Salt Lake City: *Juvenile Instructor* 27, no. 4, 15 February 1892), 128.

31. Angus Cannon, "Joseph Smith, the Prophet" (*Young Women's Journal* 17, December 1906), 546.

32. Preston Nibley, *Joseph Smith, the Prophet* (Salt Lake City: Deseret News Press, 1944), 335.

33. George A. Smith, *Journal of Discourses,* 26 vols. (Liverpool: F. D. Richards & Sons, 1851–1886), 17:92–93.

34. Edward W. Tullidge, *The Women of Mormondom* (New York: Tullidge & Crandall, 1877), 66.

35. Henry Mayhew, *History of the Mormons: Or, Latter-day Saints* (Buffalo, New York: Miller, Orton and Mulligan, 1854), 147.

36. George Q. Cannon, *The Life of Joseph Smith* (Salt Lake City: Juvenile Instructor Office, 1888), 331.

37. George Q. Cannon, *Journal of Discourses,* 26 vols. (Liverpool: F. D. Richards & Sons, 1851–1886), 23:36.

38. Wilford Woodruff, *Journal of Discourses,* 26 vols. (Liverpool: F. D. Richards & Sons, 1851–1886), 21:317.

Chapter 21: What Joseph Smith Left Behind

"That Joseph Smith is beyond compare the greatest leader of modern times is a proposition that needs no comment."[1]

—Hugh Nibley

There is at least one thing that both believers and nonbelievers should be able to agree on about Joseph Smith: he is either a prophet and the Book of Mormon is true or he was not and the book is not true. I cannot come up with any scenarios where it could be anything different than those two choices because of what he claimed. He said that an angel named Moroni appeared to him and gave him ancient plates to translate. This either happened or it did not. Joseph Fielding Smith put it this way: "Mormonism, as it is called, must stand or fall on the story of Joseph Smith. He was either a prophet of God, divinely called, properly appointed and commissioned, or he was one of the biggest frauds this world has ever seen. There is no middle ground."[2]

If these events really happened, they prove that there is a God and that He speaks to people in our day. The experience Joseph shared about the Father and the Son appearing to him in the First Vision is different from the experiences with Moroni. We only have his word that the First Vision actually happened. However, when he claims to have been visited by an angel who delivered ancient records, that is much different. Why? Because in March of 1830, a book was published that Joseph Smith claimed to be the translated version of those ancient records. For believers, it is proof that his claims are true.

For nonbelievers, the challenge to logically explain where the book came from begins. Since that time, millions have gained a testimony that it is true. And nonbelievers put forth their conflicting theories to explain the book's origin.

When driving toward the Austin airport, for many months I saw a billboard with a three-word quote that I love. It is by the American business magnate and philanthropist John D. Rockefeller and simply states, "Leave something behind." That short statement has had a major impact on me. What will I leave behind? What will you leave behind? I believe that quote can help determine whether Joseph Smith is a prophet or a fraud. Jesus Christ gave us a perfect guide to determine if someone is a true or false prophet.

Matthew 7

15 Beware of false prophets, which come to you in sheep's clothing, but inwardly they are ravening wolves.

16 Ye shall know them by their fruits. Do men gather grapes of thorns, or figs of thistles?

17 Even so every good tree bringeth forth good fruit; but a corrupt tree bringeth forth evil fruit.

18 A good tree cannot bring forth evil fruit, neither can a corrupt tree bring forth good fruit.

19 Every tree that bringeth not forth good fruit is hewn down, and cast into the fire.

20 Wherefore by their fruits ye shall know them.

In different words, Jean de La Fontaine said, "By the work one knows the workman."[3] In many cases, false prophets tend to have great followings and adoring fans throughout their lifetimes. False prophets are revealed over time by examining the lives of those who follow their teachings. If the fruit is bad, the leader was bad. On the other hand, true prophets often receive tremendous opposition and mocking from the masses. But upon examination, you can see good fruit in those who follow the principles they taught. Albert Einstein validated this when he said, "Great spirits have always encountered violent opposition from mediocre minds."[4]

The criteria for determining true prophets from false ones does not seem to have anything to do with the number of followers they have. Great leaders will always have followers because so few have the desire or the capability to be leaders. The key is to see if good is the result of following their philosophies and teachings.

Evidence throughout history shows that most people tend to be followers rather than leaders. Because of this inclination, whenever a charismatic leader steps to the stage, plenty of individuals are willing to follow his or her lead. This leaning seems to especially hold true in the areas of entertainment, politics, and religion. And it doesn't seem to matter whether the leader is wicked or righteous. Dennis Peer once said, "One measure of leadership is the caliber of people who choose to follow you."[5] Let's briefly look at a few charismatic leaders and use the Lord's guideline concerning "fruit."

Adolph Hitler

In 1925, Adolph Hitler, an obscure politician born in Austria, released the first volume of his book *Mein Kampf.* It received little attention at first. The book was the autobiographical manifesto of an angry ranting man that outlined his political ideology and future plans for Germany. Hitler gave ominous hints about his idea to use force against those of Jewish descent when he said, "In the same way the Jew will never spontaneously give up his march towards the goal of world dictatorship or repress his external urge. He can be thrown back on his road only by forces that are exterior to him, for his instinct towards world domination will die out only with himself."[6]

His book caught on and led to one of the darkest series of events in human history. Most historians now agree that approximately six million Jews were systematically killed under the direction of Adolf Hitler and the Nazi Party in German-occupied territories. The fruits produced by the teachings of Adolph Hitler and his book *Mein Kampf* were horrendous. Using the guideline given by Christ in Matthew 7, we see that this manuscript produced an abundance of evil fruit.

Karl Marx

As was mentioned earlier, in 1848 a small book was published in England by political theorist Karl Marx, assisted by Friedrich Engels. The *Communist Manifesto* is recognized as one of the most influential political manuscripts in history. This book contains the political theories of Marx and his views on the nature of society and politics. Propositions in the book include:

- Abolition of property in the land and application of all rents on land to public purposes
- A heavy progressive or graduated income tax
- Abolition of all right of inheritance
- Centralization of credit in the hands of the state by means of a national bank
- Extension of factories and instruments of production owned by the state
- A more equitable distribution of the population over the country
- Free education for all children in public schools

Marx was virtually unknown during his lifetime, but his teachings began the major communist movements after his death. A quick look at the leaders who embraced his philosophy should let us determine if his teachings produced good fruit. Among his more famous followers were Vladimir Lenin, Joseph Stalin, Nikita Khrushchev, Mao Zedong, Kim Il-Sung, Pol Pot, Ho Chi Minh, Erich Honecke, and Fidel Castro. Most communist governments were formed after the violent overthrow of the existing government.

In 1999, the Harvard University Press published an American edition of a book called *The Black Book of Communism: Crimes, Terror, Repression*. It was written by several European scholars and edited by Stéphane Courtois. In the introduction of the book, Courtois said that "Communist regimes . . . turned mass crime into a full-blown system of government."[7] The research teams estimate that communist governments over the years have killed nearly one hundred million people. The fruits produced by *The Communist Manifesto* are horrific. Using the guideline given by Christ in Matthew 7, we see that the document produced an abundance of evil fruit.

Thomas Jefferson

Between June 11 and June 28, 1776, Thomas Jefferson drafted a document called The Declaration of Independence, and the Continental Congress adopted this document on July 4, 1776. The American people of the time wanted a different form of government. Their intent behind that desire was one inspired by God. In the document, Jefferson expressed the convictions of good people everywhere with these enduring words:

> We hold these truths to be self-evident, that all men are created equal, that they are endowed by their Creator with certain unalienable Rights, that among these are Life, Liberty and the pursuit of Happiness.—That to secure these rights, Governments are instituted among Men, deriving their just powers from the consent of the governed,— That whenever any Form of Government becomes destructive of these ends, it is the Right of the People to alter or to abolish it, and to institute new Government, laying its foundation on such principles and organizing its powers in such form, as to them shall seem most likely to effect their Safety and Happiness.[8]

The fruits of the document Jefferson drafted have blessed the lives of hundreds of millions of people, not only in America but also throughout the world. On April 29, 1962, President John F. Kennedy spoke at a dinner honoring the Nobel Prize winners of the Western Hemisphere: "I want to tell you how welcome you are to the White House. I think this is the most extraordinary collection of talent, of human knowledge, that has ever been gathered together at the White House, with the possible exception of when Thomas Jefferson dined alone."[9] Using the guideline given by Christ in Matthew 7, we see that the document drafted by Jefferson produced an abundance of good fruit.

Joseph Smith

It has now been over two hundred years since Joseph Smith was born. We have had plenty of time to examine his life and teachings and those who followed him. We can also look closely at the people today who look to him as a true prophet of God. By the same token, we can look closely at those who chose to be bitter enemies of him and the church he organized. "By their fruits" should apply to our day as much as it did in the days of Christ.

Surely no one, either friend or foe, could possibly argue in good faith that Joseph Smith was not a remarkable leader. The fact that religious leaders and fanatics of his day did everything in their power to stop him and eventually kill him does not prove whether he was a true or false prophet anymore than it did in the days that Jesus Christ ministered on earth. The true test comes from the fruit produced by the teachings he left behind.

In March of 1830, the Book of Mormon was published and released to the world. Joseph Smith made no claims to writing the book. Using the guidelines that the Lord gave us, we should be able to decipher whether Joseph Smith was a prophet and the Book of Mormon is true by looking at the teachings and the fruit produced. If what he claims is true, following his teachings and the words of the book he left behind will produce good fruit like no other. But if he wrote the book, he was a false prophet and evil fruit should follow.

Before buying into the teachings of any individual or group, we should know the characters of the people involved. Applying this concept to the Book of Mormon should encourage all to learn more about Joseph Smith. George Q. Cannon once said, "No wicked man could write such a book as this; and no good man would write it, unless it were true and he were commanded of God to do so."[10]

If I wanted to study the life of the great civil rights leader Martin Luther King Jr., I would not go to the publications or websites produced by the Ku Klux Klan. And if I want to know about Joseph Smith, I should not turn to anti-Mormon publications or websites. I should seek out the things he talked about and ask myself if following his teachings would lead to good fruit or evil fruit.

The Book of Mormon contains truths that produce good fruit. Anyone who searches it prayerfully with real intent and lives by its teachings will come closer to God. Joseph Smith also left behind his personal teachings through sermons and writings for all to examine and ponder. The following are a few statements that reveal volumes about his intent and the kind of man he was.

- "Salvation could not come to the world without the mediation of Jesus Christ."[11]
- "A man filled with the love of God, is not content with blessing his family alone, but ranges through the whole world, anxious to bless the whole human race."[12]
- "Let us realize that we are not to live to ourselves, but to God; by so doing the greatest blessings will rest upon us both in time and in eternity."[13]
- "Men not unfrequently forget that they are dependent upon heaven for every blessing which they are permitted to enjoy."[14]

- "God judges men according to the use they make of the light which He gives them."[15]
- "It is one of the first principles of my life, and one that I have cultivated from my childhood, having been taught it by my father, to allow everyone the liberty of conscience."[16]
- "If we would secure and cultivate the love of others, we must love others, even our enemies as well as friends."[17]
- "I have no enmity against any man. I love you all; but I hate some of your deeds."[18]
- "Stand by the Constitution of your country; observe its principles."[19]
- "Fathers should be kind to their children."[20]
- "The Constitution of the United States is a glorious standard; it is founded in the wisdom of God. It is a heavenly banner."[21]
- "Happiness is the object and design of our existence; and will be the end thereof, if we pursue the path that leads to it; and this path is virtue, uprightness, faithfulness, holiness, and keeping all the commandments of God."[22]
- "I love that man better who swears a stream as long as my arm yet deals justice to his neighbors and mercifully deals his substance to the poor, than the long, smooth-faced hypocrite."[23]
- "We are not willing to idle any time away which can be spent to useful purposes."[24]
- "Words and language are inadequate to express the gratitude that I owe to God for having given me so honorable a parentage."[25]
- "One of the grand fundamental principles of Mormonism is to receive truth, let it come from whence it may."[26]
- "The best way to obtain truth and wisdom is not to ask from books, but to go to God in prayer, and obtain divine teaching."[27]

Joseph Smith taught about the love of God and mankind, liberty, industriousness, and receiving light from the Lord. He pointed out kindness, happiness, gratitude, and holiness. How could anyone come to the conclusion that these personal teachings would lead to bad fruit?

But it is not just the Book of Mormon and personal teachings that Joseph left behind that demonstrate his fruit, but also a list of accomplishments that rivals any in history. Over the years, I have tried to think of a way to summarize his achievements in a concise manner. I finally decided to construct his résumé. It is by no means complete, but I hope it will show some of the things he left behind during the thirty-eight short years he was allowed to live.

Joseph Smith Jr.

Basic Information

- Residence: Nauvoo, Illinois
- Birthplace: Sharon, Vermont
- Age: Thirty-eight years old
- Born: December 23, 1805

Education

- Approximately three years of formal education
- Independently studied all the following languages: Hebrew, German, Egyptian, and Reformed Egyptian
- Established the School of the Prophets in 1833 (for both theological and secular learning)
- Helped establish the University of Nauvoo in 1841 (among first municipal universities in United States)

Publications

- Book of Mormon (1830), Palmyra, NY: E. B. Grandin
- Book of Commandments (1833), Independence, MO: W. W. Phelps Co.
- Doctrine and Covenants (1835), Kirtland, OH: Fredrick G. Williams Co.
- Pearl of Great Price (1851), Liverpool, England: compiled by Franklin D. Richards

  - Book of Moses (1830)
  - Book of Abraham (1835–1842)
  - Matthew 24
  - Writings of Joseph Smith

- Inspired Translation of the Bible (1830–1833)
- *History of the Church* (DHC) began at his direction
- Articles of Faith (1842)

Church Organization

- Aaronic Priesthood (1829)
- Melchizedek Priesthood (1829)
- Organized the Church of Jesus Christ of Latter-day Saints on April 6, 1830
- Presiding Councils:
  - Bishop (1830)
  - First Presidency (1833)
  - Patriarch (1833)
  - High Council (1834)
  - Council of Twelve (1835)
  - Council of Seventy (1835)
- Aaronic and Melchizedek Quorum
  - Size, offices, and organization (1830 and 1835)
  - Duties of elders, priests, teachers, and deacons (1830)
- Requirements for Church admission and duties of members (1830 and 1835)
- Home teaching program (1830)
- Blessing of children (1830)
- Sacramental prayers (1830)
- Church judicial system (1830 and 1835)
- Gathering of Israel (1836)
- Stakes: Kirtland, OH (1834); Clay County, MO (1834); and Nauvoo, IL (1839)
- Ward: Nauvoo, Illinois (1840s)
- Sealing keys (1836)

Public Speaker

- Gave many public speeches in the United States and Canada on various topics
- Presented redress petitions for Missouri to Congress in Washington, D.C.
- Delivered the King Follett Address in 1844. Called "one of the truly remarkable sermons ever preached in America" by literary critic Harold Bloom[28]
- Was able to quote long passages from memory (for example, D&C 76; D&C 132)

Missionary Activity and Gathering of Israel
- Started formal missionary work in 1830
- Sent missionaries all throughout the United States, Canada, England, Europe, and Polynesia
- Personal missionary work in various parts of the Eastern United States and Canada
- Gathered thousands of converts to Kirtland, Jackson County, and Nauvoo
- Sent Apostle Orson Hyde to dedicate the Holy Land in 1841 for the return of the Jews
- The Church had grown to 26,146 members by 1844

Temple Builder
- Established the true purpose of temples
- Ordinances for the living and dead
  - Baptisms for the dead
  - Washings and anointing
  - Temple endowment
  - Sealing of couples and families
- Site was selected and dedicated for temple in Independence, MO (1831)
- Kirtland Temple dedicated (1836)
- Site was selected and dedicated for temple in Far West, MO (1837)
- Nauvoo Temple (began under his direction, being constructed at his death)

Newspaper Publisher
- *Evening and Morning Star* (Independence, MO, from 1832–1833; Kirtland, OH, from 1833–1834)
- *Messenger and Advocate* (Kirtland, OH, from 1834–1837)
- *The Elders Journal* (Kirtland, OH, and Far West, MO from 1837–1838)
- *Wasp* (Nauvoo, IL, from 1842–1843)
- *Times and Seasons* (Nauvoo, IL, from 1839–1846)
- *Nauvoo Neighbor* (Nauvoo, IL, from 1843–1845)

Public Service

- City councilman of Nauvoo, IL
- Mayor of Nauvoo, IL
- Candidate for president of the United States in 1844; platform included:
  - Territorial expansion
  - Liberation of slaves
  - National banking system
  - Prison reform

Military Leader

- Established pattern for and led Zion's camp; the pattern was later used in exodus to Utah
- Lieutenant General of Nauvoo Legion (commanded 2,500+ uniformed men)

Dietician

- Announced a revolutionary diet plan known as the Word of Wisdom in 1833

Women's Rights Activist

- Organized the women's Relief Society in 1842

Truths Revealed

- God appears to man in our day
- There are three distinct individuals in the Godhead
- God the Father and Jesus Christ have bodies of flesh and bone
- The Holy Ghost is a spirit personage
- All mortals are the spiritual offspring of God the Father
- We have a Mother in Heaven
- Jesus Christ is the spiritual brother of all mankind
- Jesus Christ is the literal firstborn Son of God the Father
- There are three degrees of glory in the hereafter
- All people lived in a premortal state before being born on earth
- Mortals have the potential to be gods in the eternities
- Priesthood authority has been restored to the earth
- Men are saved by grace after all they can do

- The Church of Jesus Christ is the only true church on the earth
- The Church is to be governed by the law of common consent
- Life on earth is only for a short time period in an eternal existence
- The Garden of Eden was in Jackson County, Missouri
- Adam helped to create the earth under the direction of Jesus Christ
- Man will be punished for their own sins and not for Adam's transgression
- Every man who has a calling to minister was ordained in the premortal existence
- The gospel will be preached on every continent before the Second Coming
- A third of the host of heaven rejected the Lord's plan and followed Lucifer
- The center of God's plan is the Atonement of Jesus Christ
- The age of accountability is eight years of age
- The gift of the Holy Ghost is given by the laying on of hands
- The Bible is the word of God as far as it is translated correctly
- Zion (the New Jerusalem) will one day be built on the American continent
- Though the Atonement of Jesus Christ, all mankind may be saved by obedience
- Descendants of Abraham through Joseph migrated from Jerusalem to America
- The Book of Mormon is the most correct book on earth and a second witness of Christ
- The Book of Mormon will bring individuals closer to God than any other book
- Individuals existed as "intelligences" independent of God
- The first principle of the gospel is faith
- The second principle of the gospel is repentance
- The third principle of the gospel is baptism by immersion
- The fourth principle of gospel is the laying on of hands for the gift of Holy Ghost
- This earth was created for us mortals to get a body and to be tested

- The Lord's plan of salvation allows mortals the opportunity to progress
- Mortals are given agency in order to accept or reject the plan of salvation
- Children are to be named and blessed by one having authority
- Patriarchal blessings are given to help individuals fulfill their life missions
- Jesus Christ created worlds without number
- A man must be called of God and given authority to administer ordinances
- The gift of tongues, prophecy, revelation, visions, and healing exist in modern times
- There will be a literal gathering of Israel and the lost ten tribes will return
- Jesus Christ will reign personally on the earth during the Millennium
- The earth will be renewed and receive its paradisiacal glory
- Two elders have the authority to anoint and bless the sick
- Individuals are called and set apart by those in authority to serve in the Church
- Vicarious ordinances are performed for those who have departed this life
- People are to be subject to their kings, presidents, rulers, and magistrates
- All should obey, honor, and sustain the law
- People should seek out all things virtuous, lovely, or of good report or praiseworthy
- The true Church has same organization as Christ's ancient Church
- We have living prophets on the earth today
- The U.S. Constitution is a divinely inspired document
- Mortals have the right to personal revelation
- Tobacco and alcohol are not good for people
- An angel of God does not have wings
- The body and spirit are the soul of man
- Those who die before the age of accountability inherit the celestial kingdom

- There are two priesthoods: the Aaronic and Melchizedek
- Plus many more eternal truths

This constructed résumé is filled with remarkable and varied accomplishments. It shows that Joseph Smith managed temporal affairs efficiently while also being a spiritual leader. It is remarkable how much he accomplished in such a short period of time.

Reason to Believe

What Joseph Smith left behind is nearly incomprehensible. Surely he should be considered one of the greatest polymaths to have ever lived. He accomplished it all while being driven from place to place, facing countless frivolous lawsuits, having close friends betray him, and being imprisoned. Throw in being the mayor of one of the largest cities in Illinois, running for the U.S. presidency, and governing a church that had grown to over 26,000 people at the time of his death. And all that while trying to be a husband and father and provide for his family. Brigham Young said, "He passed a short life of sorrow and trouble, surrounded by enemies who sought day and night to destroy him. . . . He was hunted unremittingly."[29] I believe no man could have achieved what Joseph Smith did without God's help. His grand accomplishments, done with the Lord's aid, are those of a true prophet.

Notes

1. Hugh Nibley, "Leaders and Managers," BYU Speeches, 19 August 1983.
2. Joseph Fielding Smith, *Doctrines of Salvation*, comp. Bruce R. McConkie (Salt Lake City: Bookcraft, 1954), 188.
3. Jean de La Fontaine, *Civilization's Quotations: Life's Ideal* (New York: Algora Publishing, 2002), 207.
4. Albert Einstein, Letter to Morris Cohen, 19 March 1940.
5. Dennis A. Peer, *Classic Wisdom for the Professional Life* (Nashville, Tennessee: Thomas Nelson Inc., 2010), 104.
6. Adolf, Hitler, *Mein Kampf* (LaVargne, Tennessee: Bottom of the Hill Publishing, 2010), 557.
7. *The Black Book of Communism: Crimes, Terror, Repression,* ed. Stéphane Courtois (Cambridge, MA: Harvard University Press, 1999), 2.

8. Thomas Jefferson, *Declaration of Independence* (Washington D.C., National Archives).

9. John F. Kennedy, "Remarks at a Dinner Honoring Nobel Prize Winners of the Western Hemisphere," 29 April 1962, *The American Presidency Project.* See www.presidency.uscb.edu.

10. George Q. Cannon, quoted in "The Twelve Apostles," in Andrew Jenson, ed., *The Historical Record* (Salt Lake City: Andrew Jenson, 1890), 6:175.

11. Joseph Smith, *History of The Church of Jesus Christ of Latter-day Saints*, ed. B. H. Roberts, 2nd ed. rev., 7 vols. (Salt Lake City: The Church of Jesus Christ of Latter-day Saints, 1932–1951), 5:555.

12. *History of the Church,* 4:227.

13. Ibid., 4:231.

14. Ibid., 2:23–24.

15. Ibid., 5:401.

16. Ibid., 6:56.

17. Ibid., 5:498.

18. Ibid., 6:317.

19. Ibid., 2:455.

20. Ibid., 2:263.

21. Ibid., 3: 305.

22. Ibid., 5:134.

23. Ibid., 5:401.

24. Ibid., 1:369.

25. Ibid., 5:126.

26. Ibid., 5:499.

27. Ibid., 4:425.

28. Richard Lyman Bushman, *Joseph Smith: Rough Stone Rolling* (New York: Knopf, 2005), 533.

29. Brigham Young, *Discourses of Brigham Young*, ed. John A. Widtsoe (Salt Lake City: Deseret Book, 1954), 464.

Chapter 22: Impact of the Book of Mormon

"I feel certain that if, in our homes, parents will read from the Book of Mormon prayerfully and regularly, both by themselves and with their children, the spirit of that great book will come to permeate our homes and all who dwell therein. The spirit of reverence will increase; mutual respect and consideration for each other will grow. The spirit of contention will depart. Parents will counsel their children in greater love and wisdom. Children will be more responsive and submissive to the counsel of their parents. Righteousness will increase. Faith, hope, and charity—the pure love of Christ—will abound in our homes and lives, bringing in their wake peace, joy, and happiness."[1]

—Marion G. Romney

At the age of nineteen, I was drafted into the United States Army during the Vietnam era. The month I entered also happened to have the highest number of deaths of the entire war: 2,415. It was a frightening time. Though I was raised in the Church, I did not have a strong testimony and had no idea what the future held for me.

During my two years of active duty, I read a few chapters of the small military copy of the Book of Mormon that I had received from my bishop but never with a strong desire to know whether or not it was true.

Upon release from active duty, I decided to get serious about what I really did and did not believe. During this time I attended a talk given by Don Lind, a U.S. astronaut working at NASA in Houston,

Texas. He was also a former naval aviator, and he had a PhD in high-energy nuclear physics from the University of California, Berkeley.

His talk had a more powerful effect on me than any talk I had ever heard, before or since. The topic that night was the Book of Mormon. He was passionate about his subject and presented persuasive evidence that no uneducated farm boy could have possibly written the book. I don't think anyone who listened to him that night doubted that he had a strong testimony that the Book of Mormon was divinely inspired. Several times, I was overcome with emotion as he spoke. I wondered how this book could have such an astounding impact on a brilliant scientist—unless it really was true.

As I walked away afterward, however, I did not feel uplifted. I felt discouraged and depressed that I had grown up in the Church and had never even taken the time to read the Book of Mormon cover to cover to find out for myself if it was true. I was weighed down with guilt for every mistake I ever made. Don Lind made such a powerful case concerning the truthfulness of the Book of Mormon that it defied logic for me to try and argue with it. However, despite the evidence he presented, I did not have a testimony that it was true. What his talk did for me was create a desire to know for myself. I opened the pages and read "I, Nephi, having been born of goodly parents . . ." for the umpteenth time. But this time was different. This time I really did want to know for myself. I remember praying at the end of each page and asking, "Did Joseph Smith write this?"

During this time, I browsed through a college catalogue from Brigham Young University. Looking at the faculty in the religion department, I noticed that many of these professors had degrees from prestigious universities. For some reason, the idea popped into my mind to write to several of them at their BYU addresses. For the most part, I picked the ones who had written books that were on my mother's bookshelf. I did not know a lot about Truman Madsen or any of the others I wrote to other than that they were respected scholars who had authored books.

In my letter, I told them I was trying to gain my own testimony of the Book of Mormon and wondered if they would share their feelings concerning it. Looking back, I'm embarrassed to say that my letter was handwritten and then duplicated several times with no name at the top or bottom. I wrote their names in at the top and signed my name at the bottom of each letter.

I still cannot believe these busy men all responded to a terribly written letter from some unknown young single adult from Texas. But soon I had a file full of letters from respected scholars with advanced degrees sharing their testimonies of the Book of Mormon. I treasure those letters to this day.

The following is the one I received from the well-known religious scholar, Hugh Nibley. He, like Don Lind, had a PhD from Berkeley and had a brilliant mind. According to his colleagues, while doing research he liked to read his primary and secondary sources in their original languages. It has been reported that in addition to English, he could read Egyptian, Dutch, Arabic, French, Coptic, Greek, German, Old Norse, Italian, Hebrew, Russian, Latin, and other languages. Here is his letter to me:

Dear Brother Wright,

The Book of Mormon, the record of "a lonesome and a solemn people," is the story of a few lonely men who had good reason to despair of the human race in their generation but never stopped importuning the Lord to tell them what was best to do and to support them in it. Lehi, Nephi, the Brother of Jared, Abinadi, Moroni, Mormon, Ether, etc.—there is hardly a major character in the book who does not stand most of the time completely alone, as popular as a lone bicycle rider going the wrong way on the freeway during rush hour. That is the stock situation in the Book of Mormon, and if you look carefully you will find that it is also the normal order of things in every dispensation of the Gospel. Even being in the Church, as Alma found out, does not change things very much, since we are still a long ways from Zion. From which we can conclude that no small part of our testing during this time of probation is to how we behave when we are completely on our own. An exhilarating and a frightening situation—but what else can we expect if this is to be a REAL test? It is reassuring to know in this age of desperate conformity that God has _his_ people in unlikely places, so that "the foundation of God standeth sure, having this seal, "The Lord only knoweth them that are his" (2 Timothy 2:19). With all the evidences around us today as the prophecies rush into fulfillment, one is tempted to ask, "Who needs a testimony?" Answer: We all do, since without it the evidence though frightening, doesn't make much sense; today I feel as if I were "all testimony"—no other thought occupies me at all. The time is very short. Thank you for your note, and don't weaken!

With much urgency and respect, Hugh Nibley

When I received the letters, I was reading the Book of Mormon with real intent, and it was beginning to affect me in a powerful way. Those letters created within me an even stronger desire to know if it was really true. It made absolutely no sense to me that an uneducated boy could possibly write a book that could fool brilliant scholars like Hugh Nibley. I continued my careful reading of the Book of Mormon, and the more I read, the more convinced I became that neither Joseph Smith alone, nor with a co-conspirator's help, could have written it.

I can still remember clearly the day I was reading in the book of Alma and came to these words: "Now, if ye give place, that a seed may be planted in your heart, behold, if it be a true seed, or a good seed, if ye do not cast it out by your unbelief, that ye will resist the Spirit of the Lord, behold, it will begin to swell within your breasts" (Alma 32:28). When I read those words, I got really emotional. I knew that I had planted a seed by reading the Book of Mormon with real intent.

Then I read, "And when you feel these swelling motions, ye will begin to say within yourselves—It must needs be that this is a good seed, or that the word is good, for it beginneth to enlarge my soul; yea, it beginneth to enlighten my understanding, yea, it beginneth to be delicious to me" (Alma 32:28). I was feeling the "swelling motions" he spoke about more and more as I read, and I knew it was good. I also realized that reading those words truly did "enlighten my understanding" and began "to be delicious to me." At the end of the last page of the Book of Mormon, I again asked if Joseph Smith wrote the book, and an overwhelming feeling came over me that he did not write it but translated it by the gift and power of God. I noticed also that by reading the book, I was getting closer to God and felt much better about myself. I discovered that the statement made by Joseph Smith was true when he said, "I told the brethren that the Book of Mormon was the most correct of any book on earth, and the keystone of our religion, and a man would get nearer to God by abiding by its precepts, than by any other book."[2]

At about this time, I was taking a Dale Carnegie public speaking course in Beaumont, Texas. I was the youngest in a large class filled with executives, top salesmen, and two CEOs of large companies. Every week, our trainer taught us different teaching techniques, and then we stood and gave a short talk in front of the entire group. I felt rather intimidated during the first few weeks of the class. I noticed, however, that the more my testimony grew of the Book of Mormon, the more confidence I had when speaking in public.

At the end of the course, our assignment was to give a much longer talk on anything we felt passionate about. We knew for weeks that this talk was coming up and that it should be our best. I tried to think of a topic I felt strongly about but nothing came to mind. Finally, one day this thought popped into my mind: *Why don't you talk about the Book of Mormon?* I then thought to myself, *I wouldn't do that in front of those people for any amount of money!* I knew some of the most successful people in the class belonged to a religion that had anti-Mormon literature in the foyers of their church buildings. I tried my best to think of another topic, but absolutely nothing came to mind. I finally gave into the feeling that wouldn't go away and decided to talk about Joseph Smith and the Book of Mormon.

As my final talk approached, I became extremely nervous and yet somehow more confident at the same time. I decided if I was going to do it, I might as well go all out. I brought copies of the Book of Mormon to give to everyone in the class. As I stood in front of my classmates, I felt totally confident, and I think everyone in the class would have agreed that I was passionate about my subject, regardless of how they felt about the topic or my speaking ability.

When I finished, I was worried that the speakers who followed would blast me. It didn't help that the next person to speak was the top salesman for the largest beer and wine distributor in Southeast Texas. When Jerry stood, he said, "I'm not going to give the talk I prepared tonight. After Randal's talk, I want to say something else." It didn't surprise me that someone would have negative things to say about my speaking on a religious topic, especially about the Book of Mormon, in a Dale Carnegie public speaking class. However, he shocked me when he admitted to the group that he was also a "Mormon," but had not been living his life as he should. He then told us that he'd be returning to church and sat down without giving his talk.

Jerry did exactly what he said he was going to do and came back to church. He also read the Book of Mormon with real intent and gained a testimony of it himself. He quit his job with the beer and wine distribution company and found a new line of work. The next year, I got married and moved to Utah to attend Brigham Young University. During my last year of school, Jerry and his wife moved right next door to us in Provo so he could finish his degree. I moved back to Texas after graduation, and a few years later he did the same. We served in a bishopric together. I think both of us would say that the Book of Mormon has had a powerful impact on our lives and has helped motivate us to be better.

Over the years I have read many testimonies in various Church publications about the impact that the Book of Mormon has had on individuals worldwide. I would like to share a few that I have observed or heard firsthand.

Letter from Japan

Several years ago, I went to the mailbox and saw a letter addressed to the "Wright Family" from someone with an address in Japan. Since I didn't know anyone in Japan and had never been there before, I had no idea who had sent it or how they had gotten our address. Here is the letter:

Dear Wright Family,

How do you do? My name is Chikako. I am Japanese. I met the sister missionaries on the street and the next day I went to church. This was three weeks ago. The sisters taught me about the plan of salvation and the Church. I learned a lot of new things. I would like to introduce myself. There are six people in my family (father, mother, little brother, grandfather and grandmother). I am 20 years old, and am a student at the Yamagata Women's Community College. I study Japanese literature. I will graduate soon, so school tests are soon. I am studying very much. Japan is very cold. Is Texas, cold? Please take care of yourself.

I live in Iwate-Ken. Iwate-Ken is very nice. Please come and see me. I was given a Book of Mormon from your family. Thank you very much. It is a real treat to me. The Book of Mormon is a help to know the truth. Once again, thank you for the Book of Mormon and helping me to know the truth. I was baptized on January 23 at the Yamagata Ward. I am very happy.

Chikako

At first I was confused and had no idea what she was talking about. Finally, I realized what had happened. A few years before we received the letter from Chikako, President Ezra Taft Benson gave his classic Book of Mormon talk in general conference. In that talk, he said,

> We must flood the earth with the Book of Mormon—and get out from under God's condemnation for having treated it lightly. (See D&C 84:54–58.) . . . I do not know fully why God has preserved my life to this age, but I do know this: That for the present hour He has revealed to me the absolute need for us to move the Book of Mormon forward now in a marvelous manner. You must help with this burden and with this blessing which He has placed on the whole Church, even all the children of Zion.[3]

Our ward leaders had encouraged members to write testimonies in several copies of the Book of Mormon and hand them in to the ward mission leader. It had been a few years since we had done that, and I had forgotten all about it. Our books were sent to a mission in Japan and sat in the mission office until they were needed.

This experience reminded me of a statement made by President Heber J. Grant many years before: "The Book of Mormon is the great, the grand, the most wonderful missionary that we have."[4] I have personally observed the truth of that statement many times over the years.

James Jr. and Nephi

As a Church Educational System coordinator, I was responsible for interviewing individuals to teach early-morning seminary. I knew when I asked James to be an early morning seminary teacher that it would not be easy for him. As an employee in his father-in-law's thriving business, he had a tremendous workload. Seminary, after all, started at six a.m. five days a week every day that school was in session. However, his priesthood leaders felt that he would have an incredible influence for good with the teenagers in the ward.

As we talked, he appeared shocked that he had been asked. He then listed the things he had going and told me that he would not be able to accept the assignment at this point in his life. When I heard how many hours he worked and the other elements of his life, I empathized with him. I told him to go home and talk to his family about it and then call me the next day with his final decision.

When he called me later that night and told me that he would be glad to teach, I was quite surprised. I asked what had changed since our earlier meeting. He explained the calling to his wife and asked what she thought about it. After reminding him of everything he had going on, she said he should absolutely not teach the seminary class.

While they were still talking about it, her parents who owned the business he worked for came to visit. James told his in-laws—faithful Church members—that he had been asked to teach seminary. His father-in-law, his boss, told him that they were far too busy at work for him to take on that responsibility. His mother-in-law agreed and remarked that there were plenty of good people in the ward who could do it. Since James didn't think he could teach anyway, having his wife and in-laws agree gave him the resolve to call me and say no.

But while they were still talking about all the reasons he should give me as to why it would be impossible for him to teach at the time, eight-year-old James Jr. walked in. After listening to the conversation for a moment, he asked what they were talking about. His father said, "Son, I was asked to teach early-morning seminary, but I am not going to do it. It starts at six a.m. and requires lots of preparation. I just don't have the time for it."

James Sr. began talking to his wife and in-laws again when the son interrupted, "In Primary, my teacher taught us about Nephi in the Book of Mormon. Nephi said he would go and do what the Lord said, even when it was hard." There was silence in the room for a moment. Then everyone in the room agreed that James should call to tell me he would teach seminary. He became an excellent seminary teacher and had a great impact on his students.

It is interesting that the Book of Mormon has appeal to all age groups. In this case, an eight-year-old boy remembered a specific lesson from the Book of Mormon and then shared it with his family. That moment had meaning far beyond the living room of their home.

Chinese PhD Student

While serving in the mission presidency of the Texas San Antonio Mission, I often was called on to do what is called "second interviews." These interviews are required when those desiring baptism have been involved in a serious sin in the past. I can still remember one interview I conducted with a sister I'll call Wang Li from Beijing, China. She came to the United States on a student visa and was a PhD student in English at the University of Texas–Austin. It was clear after talking to her for only a few minutes that she was extremely bright. I was interested to hear about her life growing up under a communist government in mainland China. She told me that from the time she was a little girl, she had totally bought into the party line and grew up believing there was no God. All during her undergraduate studies, she thought those who believed in God were misguided and gullible.

While pursuing her master's degree in English from a prestigious university, a classmate convinced her that she needed to read the Bible because it was such an important part of the English language. Wang Li then looked me in the eyes and said, "The Bible touched my heart, and I became a Christian."

I then asked her how she became interested in The Church of Jesus Christ of Latter-day Saints. She said that two missionaries had knocked on her door and briefly told her about the Book of Mormon. She was intrigued and accepted the book and their challenge to read it. Her motivation was only that it could help with her English reading skills. She began reading and then became engrossed and read it from cover to cover.

I'll never forget what she said next. Looking me in the eyes again, she said, "The Bible touched my heart. The Book of Mormon touched my soul. I want to be baptized." Those words went through me like electricity and strengthened my own testimony of the Book of Mormon.

Here we have a brilliant PhD student and former atheist who had no exposure to the Book of Mormon before coming to Texas. In fact, she had never even heard of it until two young elders knocked on her door and challenged her to read it. As she read the book with no preconceived notions, it made a deep impression. What a wonderful experience, to get to be involved in her baptism.

The Book of Mormon has an amazing ability to change people for the better. How could a religious fraud write a book that has that kind of impact on people?

Mongolian Seminary Class

While working for the Church Educational System, I loved hearing about our leaders' trips to foreign countries. I remember well when our zone administrator shared with us an experience he had in Mongolia.

At the time of his visit, the Church had only been established in that country for a few years and had about eight hundred members in total. According to our administrator, they had two CES missionary couples with 235 enrolled institute students and forty-two who were enrolled in seminary. During his trip, he was able to visit a seminary class with fourteen students in attendance. Over half of the students had been members of the Church for less than a year. At that time, only small portions of the Book of Mormon were translated into Mongolian. During the class, he asked the students how many had a testimony of the Book of Mormon. All fourteen students raised their hands.

He then asked one of the seminary students how he could know that the Book of Mormon was true if he had only read a small portion of it. The young man said, "It's like a piece of cake. You can take one bite and know if the rest of the cake is good."

Fireworks Going Off

I once spoke at a local youth conference in Euphrata, Washington. Several of the youth bore their testimonies about the truthfulness of the Book of Mormon. I loved the following comment from one of the fourteen-year-old boys who stood to bear his testimony.

He said to all those present, "I didn't want to tell anyone about the Book of Mormon until I had read it for myself. I didn't want to rely on my parent's testimonies. When I finished the entire Book of Mormon, I knelt by my bed and asked if it was true. When I asked that question, it was like fireworks going off inside of me, and I knew that it was true." He added that once he gained his own testimony, he felt comfortable bearing witness to others.

Marriott Hotel Stay

In July 2007, a young man named Lance came to my door at the Austin Institute and introduced himself. He said that he had been baptized the month before and asked about institute classes. He was obviously a bright, good-looking nineteen-year-old who joined the Church while working in Washington, D.C. for the U.S. House of Representatives.

I asked how he got interested in the Church. I expected him to tell me about a girl, but that was not the case. He said that when he was eight years old, he stayed with his family at a Marriott Hotel. While looking through the drawers in the room, he found a Book of Mormon. Without his parent's knowledge, he stuffed the book into his bag and took it home. When he got back to his home in Dallas, Texas, he put it in a little chest that contained his personal things.

He forgot about the book until he was fifteen and saw it while cleaning out his chest. He decided to read it, and told me when he did that, he gained a testimony that it was true. He found out that it was a publication of the Church of Jesus Christ of Latter-day Saints and told his parents that he wanted to be baptized. They were extremely upset with him and absolutely forbade it. I asked if he had any LDS friends in his school at the time, and he said he didn't know any members.

From the time he read the Book of Mormon at age fifteen, his desire was to be baptized. When he arrived in Washington, D.C., he started attending Church and was baptized by the bishop of the ward he attended. Coincidently, the bishop was an executive with Marriott. I asked if his parents were aware that he had joined the Church. He said they were, and they were still upset with him. I then asked him what his father did for a living. He told me his dad was the minister of a large southern Protestant church in Dallas.

Reason to Believe

As I think about these experiences, it makes me wonder how many convert baptisms we would have without the Book of Mormon. Even with the story of the First Vision and the Bible, I doubt that our missionaries would come close to the number of convert baptisms we have with it. Joseph Smith said, "Take away the Book of Mormon and the revelations and where is our religion? We have none."[5] What a miracle that a book published in America in 1830 has the power to change people all over the world, regardless of age, race, education, socioeconomic class, previous religious affiliation, or traditions. For this reason, I believe it is from God and not man.

Notes

1. Marion G. Romney, "The Book of Mormon," *Ensign,* May 1980, 67.
2. Joseph Smith, *History of The Church of Jesus Christ of Latter-day Saints*, ed. B. H. Roberts, 2nd ed. rev., 7 vols. (Salt Lake City: The Church of Jesus Christ of Latter-day Saints, 1932–1951), 4:461.
3. Ezra Taft Benson, "A Sacred Responsibility," *Ensign,* November 1988, 78.
4. Heber J. Grant, *Conference Report*, April 1837, 126.
5. *History of the Church,* 2:52.

Chapter 23: Lessons Learned from the Book of Mormon

"The Book of Mormon was written for us today. God is the author of the book. It is a record of a fallen people, compiled by inspired men for our blessing today. Those people never had the book—it was meant for us. Mormon, the ancient prophet after whom the book is named, abridged centuries of records. God, who knows the end from the beginning, told him what to include in his abridgment that we would need for our day. Mormon turned the records over to his son Moroni, the last recorder; and Moroni, writing over 1,500 years ago but speaking to us today, states: 'Behold, I speak unto you as if ye were present, and yet ye are not. But behold, Jesus Christ hath shown you unto me, and I know your doing.' (Mormon 8:35.)"[1]

—Ezra Taft Benson

One of the most powerful ways to read the Book of Mormon is to ask, "What lesson can I learn from this verse?" When Mormon was compiling the record, he looked back on records from the beginning of the Nephite history. He also had the brass plates, which contained the sacred history from Adam to Jeremiah. Along with these were the plates of Ether and the thousand-year record of the Nephites. Everything he included in the final product was meant for our day.

Each time I have read the Book of Mormon, I've tried to look for lessons to apply to my life and to our day. I would like to share just a few of them.

Love Your Enemy

While the Lamanites were intent on robbing, plundering, and killing the Nephites to recover their "rights" of rule and government, the righteous Nephites were intent on bringing the Lamanites back into the fold of God. Both groups carried on their traditions from the start of the Book of Mormon until the end. As Nephi closes out his record, he says, "For I pray continually for them by day, and mine eyes water my pillow by night, because of them" (2 Nephi 33:3). And in the last chapter of the entire book, Moroni says, "Now I, Moroni, write somewhat as seemeth me good; and I write unto *my brethren, the Lamanites*" (Moroni 10:1; emphasis added).

Think about what happened to the Nephite nation and to Moroni's family and friends thirty-six years earlier. Describing his situation, he said, "My father hath been slain in battle, and all my kinsfolk, and I have not friends nor whither to go" (Mormon 8:5). Imagine Moroni being years alone after everyone he loved was killed, engraving on metal records his inspiring words for his "brethren, the Lamanites." Moroni is one of the greatest examples in history of someone who achieved Christlike characteristics. But it just wasn't Nephi and Moroni who grew to love their enemy. Consider these other examples:

Jacob: Jacob 4 (emphasis added)

3 Now in this thing we do rejoice; and we labor diligently to engraven these words upon plates, hoping that *our beloved brethren* and our children will receive them with thankful hearts, and look upon them that they may learn with joy and not with sorrow, neither with contempt, concerning their first parents.

Enos: Enos 1 (emphasis added)

11 And after I, Enos, had heard these words, my faith began to be unshaken in the Lord; and I prayed unto him with many long strugglings for *my brethren, the Lamanites.*

Jarom: Jarom 1 (emphasis added)

2 And as these plates are small, and as these things are written for the intent of the benefit of *our brethren the Lamanites*, wherefore, it must needs be that I write a little.

King Benjamin: Mosiah 1 (emphasis added)

5 I say unto you, my sons, were it not for these things, which have been kept and preserved by the hand of God, that we might read

and understand of his mysteries, and have his commandments always before our eyes, that even our fathers would have dwindled in unbelief, and we should have been like unto *our brethren, the Lamanites*, who know nothing concerning these things, or even do not believe them when they are taught them, because of the traditions of their fathers, which are not correct.

Ammon: Alma 26 (emphasis added)

3 Behold, I answer for you; for *our brethren, the Lamanites*, were in darkness, yea, even in the darkest abyss, but behold, how many of them are brought to behold the marvelous light of God! And this is the blessing which hath been bestowed upon us, that we have been made instruments in the hands of God to bring about this great work.

Moroni: Moroni 1 (emphasis added)

4 Wherefore, I write a few more things, contrary to that which I had supposed; for I had supposed not to have written any more; but I write a few more things, that perhaps they may be of worth unto *my brethren, the Lamanites*, in some future day, according to the will of the Lord.

After pondering these verses, I'm encouraged to think that it is possible in this life to learn to love your enemies. If these men could have love in their hearts for people who actively sought to destroy them, it should be possible for us to love those whose offenses are minor in comparison.

Fate of the Wicked in the Book of Mormon

The Lord has allowed righteous men and women to die at the hands of the wicked to seal their testimonies. These individuals are referred to as martyrs, those willing to suffer death rather than renounce their religious beliefs. Christ himself was crucified at the hands of the wicked. The first known Christian martyr was Stephen, who was accused of blasphemy and stoned to death. Tradition says that many of the original Twelve Apostles also died as martyrs. In the Book of Mormon, we read of Abinadi, Gideon, and Mormon dying at the hands of the wicked. In modern Church history, wicked men assassinated Joseph Smith and his brother Hyrum in Carthage, Illinois, in 1844. There are others, including women and children, who died a martyr's death because of their religious beliefs.

Others throughout recorded history have died in disgraceful, shameful, dishonorable, or humiliating ways. In the Book of Mormon, there seems to be a consistent theme with those who fight against the prophets of God. While we don't know the fate of all of the wicked men in the Nephite record, we do know what happened to several. From these, we learn that "the devil will not support his children at the last day" (Alma 30:60). Let's look at a few to see the pattern.

Laban: A wicked Jewish man of power, wealth, and influence. He attempted to have Nephi and his brothers murdered after stealing their gold, silver, and precious things.

1 Nephi 4:18: "Therefore I did obey the voice of the Spirit, and took Laban by the hair of the head, and I smote off his head with his own sword."

Sherem: Sherem was an anti-Christ that contended against Jacob concerning the law of Moses and the coming of Christ. He accused Jacob of blasphemy and asked for a sign.

Jacob 7:20: "And it came to pass that when he had said these words he could say no more, and he gave up the ghost."

King Noah: A lazy, immoral, egotistical king who spent his time drinking and in riotous living. He had the prophet Abinadi burned at the stake.

Mosiah 19:20: "And the king commanded them that they should not return; and they were angry with the king, and caused that he should suffer, even unto death by fire."

Nehor: Founder of the apostate sect who introduced priestcraft to the Nephites and tried to enforce it by the sword. He killed Gideon, a old righteous man.

Alma 1:15: "His name was Nehor; and they carried him upon the top of the hill Manti, and there . . . acknowledge, between the heavens and the earth, that what he had taught to the people was contrary to the word of God; and there he suffered an ignominious death."

Amlici: The leader of a group of Nephite dissenters who was made a king by his followers. He armed his people and led them to battle against his brethren.

Alma 2:31: "Now when Alma had said these words he contended again with Amlici; and he was strengthened, insomuch that he slew Amlici with the sword."

Korihor: An anti-Christ who was a critic of the Christian religion. He was responsible for leading many people to commit sin, and he contended with Alma and demanded a sign.

Alma 30:59: "As he went forth among the . . . Zoramites . . . and as he went forth amongst them, behold, he was run upon and trodden down, even until he was dead."

Zerahemnah: Chief captain of the Lamanite army who inspired his soldiers to fight against the army of Helaman. He attempted to kill Captain Moroni, and then begged for mercy when he failed.

Alma 44:13: "And it came to pass that the soldier who stood by, who smote off the scalp of Zerahemnah."

Amalickiah: A Nephite traitor who sought to destroy the Church of God. He became the Lamanite king through deceit and murder and promised to drink the blood of Moroni.

Alma 51:34: "And it came to pass that Teancum stole privily into the tent of the king, and put a javelin to his heart; and he did cause the death of the king immediately."

Ammoron: A Nephite apostate and the brother of Amalickiah. He became king of the Lamanites when his brother was killed.

Alma 62:36: "And it came to pass that Teancum in his anger did go forth into the camp of the Lamanites. . . . And he went forth with a cord, from place to place, insomuch that he did find the king; and he did cast a javelin at him, which did pierce him near the heart."

Morianton: Leader of the people involved in land dispute with the people of Lehi. When Morianton tried to flee to the land northward, he was cut off and compelled to return.

Alma 50:35: "And so stubborn were the people of Morianton, (being inspired by his wickedness and his flattering words) that a battle commenced between them, in the which Teancum did slay Morianton and defeat his army, and took them prisoners."

Pachus: The king of a group of Nephite dissenters who drove the freemen out of the land of Zarahemla and took possession of the land.

Alma 62:8: "And behold, Pachus was slain and his men were taken prisoners, and Pahoran was restored to his judgment-seat."

Kishkumen: Formed a secret band of murderers and plunderers later known as the Gadianton robbers. He also personally assassinated Pahoran and tried to kill Helaman.

Helaman 2:9: "Now this did please Kishkumen exceedingly, for he did suppose that he should accomplish his design; but behold, the servant of Helaman, as they were going forth unto the judgment-seat, did stab Kishkumen even to the heart, that he fell dead without a groan."

Paanchi: After the death of Pahoran, an election was held and Pahoran Jr. was chosen as chief judge. Paanchi, his brother, was angry and was about to stir up his followers to rebellion when he was taken and tried.

Helaman 1:8: "And it came to pass as he was about to do this, behold, he was taken, and was tried according to the voice of the people, and condemned unto death."

Coriantumr: A Nephite apostate who defected and became the leader of the Lamanite army. He personally killed Pacumeni, the chief judge.

Helaman 1:30: "And it came to pass that Moronihah did head them in their retreat, and did give unto them battle, insomuch that it became an exceedingly bloody battle; yea, many were slain, and among the number who were slain Coriantumr was also found."

Giddianhi: Governor of the secret society of Gadianton robbers. He demanded that all the Nephites yield up their cities, lands, and possessions or be destroyed.

3 Nephi 4:14: "And it came to pass that Giddianhi, who had stood and fought with boldness, was pursued as he fled; and being weary because of his much fighting he was overtaken and slain. And thus was the end of Giddianhi the robber."

Zemnarihah: Replaced Giddianhi as the leader of the wicked Gadianton robbers. He lead an attack against the Nephites before commanding his forces to withdraw.

3 Nephi 4:28: "And their leader, Zemnarihah, was taken and hanged upon a tree, yea, even upon the top thereof until he was dead."

Jacob: Leader of the Lamanite army who was a descendant of Zoram. He had an unconquerable spirit and led his army with fury against the armies of Captain Moroni.

Alma 52:35: "And it came to pass that they fought on both hands with exceeding fury; and there were many slain on both sides; yea, and Moroni was wounded and Jacob was killed."

Though not everyone who rejects the prophets and fights against them will die a violent death, there is a consistent pattern in the Book of Mormon for those who did. Their fight against righteousness was devastating to them on several levels. While the mortal body may live, a part of the spirit seems to die and the person often becomes past feeling as to spiritual things.

Places of Their Homes

It is interesting how people refer to places they or their ancestors have lived in the past. For example, when I asked my wife to name some of the places we have resided, she had a name for each home. She was consistent in having a name for each house, but she was totally inconsistent in how she named them. Some of my names for the same houses match hers, and some are different. These are the names and the rationale for each name:

- *The 809 State house* – street address
- *The Clark's house* – last name of owners
- *The Orem house* – city where located
- *The Shugie house* – nickname of owner
- *The Yellow house* – color of house
- *The Corbett house* – street name
- *The Cherry Creek house* – subdivision

The Book of Mormon writers had a somewhat similar method when describing where they or their ancestors once lived. In most cases, the writers consistently used the phrase *the land of* . . . preceding the actual place they were referring to. This phrase is used in 358 different verses, and some of those verses included the phrase up to four times. Many of the events in the Book of Mormon revolve around three areas:

- The land where Lehi's family first landed and lived until the death of Lehi
- The land where Nephi fled with his followers after the death of Lehi
- The land and city of Zarahemla where Mosiah took a group from the land of Nephi

The places and names of their homes had significance to them. The consistent references to the places where they established their homes are evidence of the strong link to their heritage. Here are three of the ways Book of Mormon writers referred to lands where they or their ancestors once lived:

"the land of their [our] first inheritance"

Zeniff: Mosiah 10 (emphasis added)

13 And again, that they were wronged while in *the land of their first inheritance*, after they had crossed the sea, and all this because that Nephi was more faithful in keeping the commandments of the Lord—therefore he was favored of the Lord.

Mormon: Alma 22 (emphasis added)

28 Now, the more idle part of the Lamanites lived in the wilderness, and dwelt in tents; and they were spread through the wilderness on the west, in the land of Nephi; yea, and also on the west of the land of Zarahemla, in the borders by the seashore, and on the west in the land of Nephi, in *the place of their fathers' first inheritance*, and thus bordering along by the seashore.

Captain Moroni: Alma 54 (emphasis added)

12 And behold, if ye do not this, I will come against you with my armies; yea, even I will arm my women and my children, and I will come against you, and I will follow you even into your own land, which is *the land of our first inheritance*; yea, and it shall be blood for blood, yea, life for life; and I will give you battle even until you are destroyed from off the face of the earth.

The phrase *the land of our first inheritance* apparently refers to the land where Lehi and his family first landed, which is different than the land of Nephi.

"the land of Nephi"

Amaleki: Omni 1 (emphasis added)

27 And now I would speak somewhat concerning a certain number who went up into the wilderness to return to *the land of Nephi*; for there was a large number who were desirous to possess *the land of their inheritance*.

Ammon: Alma 26 (emphasis added)

23 Now do ye remember, my brethren, that we said unto our brethren in the land of Zarahemla, we go up to *the land of Nephi*, to preach unto our brethren, the Lamanites, and they laughed us to scorn?

Mormon: Mosiah 7 (emphasis added)

6 And Ammon took three of his brethren, and their names were Amaleki, Helem, and Hem, and they went down into *the land of Nephi*.

The phrase *the land of Nephi* is used fifty-five times in the Book of Mormon by various individuals, but mostly it is used by Mormon. Amaleki refers to the land of Nephi as the land of their inheritance and not the land were the group first landed.

"the land of our fathers"

Zeniff: Mosiah 9 (emphasis added)

4 Nevertheless, after many days' wandering in the wilderness we pitched our tents in the place where our brethren were slain, which was near to *the land of our fathers*.

Zeniff: Mosiah 10 (emphasis added)

3 And it came to pass that we did inherit *the land of our fathers* for many years, yea, for the space of twenty and two years.

Zeniff is the only one who used the phrase *the land of our fathers*, but he used it four different times in his writings. It appears that he was referring to the land of Nephi rather than the place where they first landed.

It is significant that the Old Testament uses *the land of . . .* in 548 verses in the same manner the Book of Mormon does. I've never heard anyone use the phrase *the land of . . .* to identify the place where they once lived. Imagine telling someone that you used to live in "the land of Utah" or "the land of Provo." It is also hard to imagine Joseph Smith saying that he once lived in "the land of Vermont" or "the land of Palmyra."

Family Influence and Tradition

With university degrees in family studies, I am always interested in the influence that parents have on their posterity. In the Book of Mormon, you can see that influence multiple times. The things that families said and did were passed from generation to generation. Nephi and Laman had such powerful influences on their descendants that they were still calling themselves Nephites and Lamanites after a thousand years. Look closely at the individuals and their language in the following quotations to see if you catch a pattern.

"and I make an end"

Jacob: Jacob 7 (emphasis added)

27 And I, Jacob, saw that I must soon go down to my grave; wherefore, I said unto my son Enos: Take these plates. And I told him the things which my brother Nephi had commanded me, and he promised obedience unto the commands. *And I make an end* of my writing upon these plates.

Omni: Omni 1 (emphasis added)

3 And it came to pass that two hundred and seventy and six years had passed away, and we had many seasons of peace; and we had many seasons of serious war and bloodshed. Yea, and in fine, two hundred and eighty and two years had passed away, and I had kept these plates according to the commandments of my fathers; and I conferred them upon my son Amaron. *And I make an end.*

Chemish: Omni 1 (emphasis added)

9 Now I, Chemish, write what few things I write, in the same book with my brother; for behold, I saw the last which he wrote, that he wrote it with his own hand; and he wrote it in the day that he delivered them unto me. And after this manner we keep the records, for it is according to the commandments of our fathers. *And I make an end.*

Abinadom: Omni 1 (emphasis added)

11 And behold, the record of this people is engraven upon plates which is had by the kings, according to the generations; and I know of no revelation save that which has been written, neither prophecy; wherefore, that which is sufficient is written. *And I make an end.*

Amaleki: Omini 1:30 (emphasis added)

30 And I, Amaleki, had a brother, who also went with them; and I have not since known concerning them. And I am about to lie down in my grave; and these plates are full. *And I make an end* of my speaking.

Of the 153 voices with speaking parts in the Book of Mormon, the phrase *and I make an end* is only used by five individuals. It is never used in the Old Testament or New Testament. Did you notice anything from these verses that teaches a lesson about the influence of families? Remember that the descendants of Nephi recorded most of this record, but for a time Jacob and his descendants kept it. Notice that four of the individuals who used the phrase *and I make an end* were Jacob's direct descendants and are the only writers who used the phrase. The lesson I learned from this is that our words can have an influence upon our descendants. Our choice of words matters because our children remember them, no matter how insignificant they may seem at the time. The words we speak should always be uplifting and faith-promoting.

"being over-zealous"
Zeniff: Mosiah 9 (emphasis added)

3 And yet, I *being over-zealous to inherit the land of* our *fathers*, collected as many as were desirous to go up to possess the land, and started again on our journey into the wilderness to go up to the land; but we were smitten with famine and sore afflictions; for we were slow to remember the Lord our God.

Limhi: Mosiah 7 (emphasis added)

21 And ye all are witnesses this day, that Zeniff, who was made king over this people, he *being over-zealous to inherit the land of* his *fathers*, therefore being deceived by the cunning and craftiness of king Laman, who having entered into a treaty with king Zeniff, and having yielded up into his hands the possessions of a part of the land, or even the city of Lehi-Nephi, and the city of Shilom; and the land round about.

In Mosiah 7:21, Limhi spoke about his grandfather Zeniff and used the exact phrase that his grandfather had previously used. It seems obvious to me that he had read his grandfather's journal. Through this example and others in the Book of Mormon, the importance of keeping a written record for our posterity is powerfully illustrated.

"he was dressed in a white robe"
Lehi: 1 Nephi 8 (emphasis added)

5 And it came to pass that I saw a man, *and he was dressed in a white robe*; and he came and stood before me.

Nephi: 1 Nephi 14 (emphasis added)

19 And I looked and beheld a man, *and he was dressed in a white robe*.

Mormon: 3 Nephi 11 (emphasis added)

8 And it came to pass, as they understood they cast their eyes up again towards heaven; and behold, they saw a Man descending out

of heaven; *and he was clothed in a white robe*; and he came down and stood in the midst of them.

A tradition of family righteousness is apparent in these visions. Lehi saw a man dressed in a white robe in his dream. Later, his son Nephi saw a man dressed in a white robe in a vision. In both cases, the person was the Savior. When Christ appeared to the Nephites in the Americas, He wore a white robe. I have learned from examples like these that past prophets were able to clearly see, in vision, the coming of the Savior to fulfill His mortal mission. This teaches me that prophets in our day can also know that the Savior is coming again for His Millennial reign and that I need to be ready.

Reason to Believe

The number of valuable lessons for us to discover in the Book of Mormon is remarkable. I'm convinced that a person could spend every day for the rest of his life reading the book and never discover everything there is to learn. Some of the most valuable lessons are pointed out by the writers with phrases such as *and thus we see that . . .*

However, the book has so many layers that these lessons just keep coming and coming if we are willing to pay the price to look for the treasures it contains. As I have considered the hundreds of valuable lessons I have learned from the Book of Mormon, it becomes more and more unreasonable to believe, or even consider, that Joseph Smith wrote it.

Notes

1. Ezra Taft Benson, "The Book of Mormon Is the Word of God," *Ensign*, May 1975, 63.

Chapter 24: The Nephi Model for Overcoming Personal Weakness

"No one should deny the importance of circumstances, yet in the final analysis the most important thing is how we react to the circumstances."[1]

—Spencer W. Kimball

Several years ago, I attended a testimony meeting in a southern state and watched an old lady being helped up to the stand. I didn't know how old she was at the time, but I learned later that she was approaching her ninetieth birthday. She told how she was baptized when she was eight years old. Then she made an interesting comment: "I never missed a day of church until I got married. We had some visitors come in from the East, and I wanted to take them and do something fun. The only day we had was Sunday. I wanted to take them to the beach in the worst way but knew we would have to miss church."

I expected to hear "I didn't give into that temptation" from this beautiful sister because her countenance showed she was a follower of Jesus Christ. But she said, "I talked to my husband and said, 'Let's take them to the beach.'" He said okay.

A bit surprised, I thought to myself, *Oh, don't say that. My children are here with me. Let's hear a positive story! Well, if she went, then surely she had a bad time.*

I was surprised again when she exclaimed, "I just want everyone here to know that I had a *glorious* time at the beach that day!"

No, don't say that! I thought. *You're not supposed to admit that in testimony meeting!*

She continued, "The next day, however, I didn't feel so good. Later on, two missionaries came over to visit. One of them looked at me and said, 'Sister Ashcraft, you don't feel so good, do you?'

'No, I don't,' I said.

'You feel like H-E-double hockey sticks, don't you?'

'Yes, I do.'

'It's because you didn't go to church yesterday.'

'Yes, I know,'" she said. And then she said she had never missed another Sunday meeting since that time.

I was shocked at how many years that represented. Often when we give into our weaknesses, we feel guilty afterward, like Sister Ashcraft did. How unusual, however, that she gave into the temptation to miss church when she first married but never gave in to that temptation again. In fact, that is extraordinary!

Would it not be wonderful to say, "When I first got married, I gave into the temptation to procrastinate, but I have never done it again?" Usually, we give into a weakness over and over again. We all choose things that make us feel bad about ourselves and we need to change. Then why don't we? Perhaps one reason is because it is hard to fully admit our weaknesses. We have built-in defense mechanisms that try to keep us emotionally balanced. When we do wrong things, we regret doing so, but subconsciously our defenses try to stabilize these feelings by making us justify or forget about our mistakes. Unfortunately, this often leads to rationalization and not change.

Every person born into this world—Jesus Christ excepted—has weaknesses. Paul said in Romans, "For all have sinned, and come short of the glory of God" (Romans 3:23). However, just because we all have sinned does not mean we cannot change with the Lord's help.

So how can we change and be better? Let's look at Nephi. In his life, he developed many strengths, talents, and skills. He was a record keeper who even made his own metal plates to engrave upon. He was also a ship builder, city planner, temple builder, leader, teacher, and prophet. The influence that Nephi had on his posterity across the years is amazing. Approximately 452 years after Lehi left Jerusalem, we read, "But there was one among them whose name was Alma, he also being a descendant of Nephi" (Mosiah 17:2). Why was it pointed out that he was a descendant of Nephi instead of Lehi, or the others in his long direct line? And after 922 years, we read, "And I, Mormon, being a descendant of Nephi" (Mormon 1:5). How strange that after a thousand years, these people were still calling themselves Nephites. He must have been a powerful leader and example!

In my mind, Nephi seemed practically perfect: obedient, talented, skilled. And yet, at one point in his life, even Nephi was almost ruined by sin. When I first read about his sin, I thought to myself, *Nephi, sin? No, he was next to perfect. He was an ideal man.* And yet, we are told that he had a guilty conscience that took away his peace. We read that Nephi wept often because of his sin and that he even became depressed over this weakness. This led to Nephi's slacking off in his spiritual responsibilities. It began to play on his physical health and gave Satan a place in his heart. Nephi's sin was not trivial. In fact, it was extremely serious.

In 2 Nephi 4:27, Nephi shares with readers the sin that brought him so much unhappiness and discouragement: it was anger toward his brothers. Fortunately, in that same chapter he provides for his readers an incredible model for overcoming sin and weaknesses. I have put what he taught into a seven-step plan. If Nephi were alive today, I believe he could write a book about how to overcome weaknesses that would be a best seller.

Step 1: Keep a journal.

In 2 Nephi 4:15, Nephi says, "And upon these [plates] I write the things of my soul." The first thing we need to do if we are going to overcome our weaknesses is connected to this. Many therapists have discovered the power of writing in a journal to help those they counsel to conquer weaknesses. We all can benefit from doing as Nephi did and writing down the things of our soul. Remember that Nephi kept two journals. One was on large plates, where he recorded the more historical record, and the other on small plates, where he kept a spiritual record of the things of his soul. President Spencer W. Kimball said, "Every person should keep a journal and every person can keep a journal. It should be an enlightening one and should bring great blessings and happiness to the families. If there is anyone here who isn't doing so, *will you repent today* and change—change your life?"[2]

Why did Nephi keep a journal? Obviously, the Lord commanded him to write down his experiences and revelations to benefit himself, his posterity, and the millions of other people who would read his written words. Does He command us to do the same? Absolutely.

Are we doing that? Think how we profit from keeping a journal. Journals serve as an aid to avoid sin and temptation. Think about writing in your journal for your children, grandchildren, and your great-grandchildren to read:

- "Today, I watched a really graphic R-rated movie. It had a lot of immorality, violence, and profanity, but it just portrayed real life."
- "I got kicked out of the gym today for yelling at the officials at my son's basketball game."
- "I swore at a phone solicitor because I'm sick of him calling me."
- "I went on a pornographic website today so I could see what was out there."

Would you record such things in your journal for your descendants to read? If you or I would feel uncomfortable recording anything for our loved ones or others to read, it is most likely not something we should be doing. Journals provide protection from and awareness of sin.

Journals also allow us to see behaviors that lead to success or to failure in our goal to become more like Christ. I recently read a journal entry I made many years ago: "Got up early today and said my prayers. I then went jogging, came back in, read my scriptures, and planned the day." At the end of the entry, I wrote, "I had a marvelous day." I discovered a pattern I needed to follow if I wanted to dramatically increase my chances of having "marvelous" days. Keeping a journal provides us with a powerful tool for identifying behaviors that lead to happiness and those that lead to failure and remorse.

Challenge 1: Keep a personal journal for your own benefit and for the benefit of your posterity.

Step 2: Make a list of your strengths.

It is easy to get down on ourselves and not realize the strengths we all have. Perhaps we feel if we admit to having certain strengths that we are being prideful. I feel certain that Nephi is not trying to be prideful or arrogant in the least when he indirectly told his readers some of his strengths. While he was struggling with anger, he was still doing several things right. Look closely at what he said:

2 Nephi 4

15 My soul delighteth in the scriptures.

15 My heart pondereth them, and writeth them for the learning and the profit of my children.

16 My soul delighteth in the things of the Lord.

16 My heart pondereth continually upon the things which I have seen and heard.

24 By day have I waxed bold in mighty prayer before him.

24 My voice have I sent up on high.

32 My heart is broken and my spirit is contrite.

34 I have trusted in thee.

Nephi listed his strengths and reminded himself that he was still a good person. He was not bragging but also was not hiding the fact that he was trying to be good. And yet he still had faults that were weighing him down. We can be good too, even with weaknesses.

Sometimes, it seems as hard to admit that we have strengths as it is to admit we have weaknesses. When I tried to make a list of my strengths, it was difficult at first. I wrote a couple of things, and then I just went blank. I could not think of one other thing I was good at. I finally went to the temple recommend questions about the Word of Wisdom. I asked myself, *Do you smoke? No. Do you drink? No, I don't drink.* I was stretching here, trying to come up with something I was strong in. Then I thought, *Not everybody in the world could say they didn't do those things.* So maybe those were strengths. *Are you faithful to your wife? Yes, I'm totally faithfully to her.*

I wrote it all down. I continued to write and then asked, *Heavenly Father, if I have any more strengths, please help me list them.* And I started writing more and more. In fact, I wrote down sixty things that I thought I was at least okay in. I did not do it to bolster my pride. Then I had a thought: *Satan hates this, doesn't he?* He does not want us to point out the things we are doing right.

Challenge 2: Pray and ask Heavenly Father to help you list as many strengths as you can.

Step 3: Make a list of your weaknesses.

After listing the strengths that you have, you are ready to identify your weaknesses and take responsibility for them. It is time to admit that we have weaknesses, and probably a lot more than we realize. Be careful, though, when Satan whispers things like, "You have so many weaknesses that you'll never make it, so don't even try." That is why we list our strengths first. By recognizing our good points, it allows us to look more closely at our weaknesses and write them down without getting down on ourselves.

Nephi probably had more faults than just anger, but he only revealed the one that apparently was holding him back the most. Do you have one weakness that is holding you back more than any other? Which one on the list is it?

One thing that holds many people back from overcoming faults is the tendency to blame other people or circumstances for their weaknesses. Nephi could have easily said, "The reason I have an anger problem is because . . ." However, he takes full responsibility for his feelings and doesn't blame his anger on others. "Nevertheless, notwithstanding the great goodness of the Lord, in showing me his great and marvelous works, my heart exclaimeth: O wretched man that I am! Yea, my heart sorroweth because of my flesh; my soul grieveth because of mine iniquities" (2 Nephi 4:17).

As an undergraduate at BYU years ago, I had an organizational behavior class taught by Stephen R. Covey. One day, a classmate came in before class and said, "Brother Covey, I'm not going to be in class on Thursday because I have to go to a tennis tournament in Albuquerque."

I can still remember our professor looking at him and saying, "No, you don't have to go to Albuquerque. You choose to go."

The student retorted, "You don't understand. I'm on the tennis team, and we have a tournament that I have to attend."

Brother Covey calmly replied, "No, you don't have to go. You choose to go rather than come to my class."

The student finally said, "I have a tennis tournament on Thursday that I choose to go to rather than come to your class."

Brother Covey said, "If I were on the tennis team, that's exactly what I would choose to do. But remember not to blame tennis for your choices."

It was a powerful moment for me, and I have thought about it many times over the years. What a great message! We need to quit blaming the tennis team, our parents, the weather, and every other circumstance and step back like Nephi did to make our own choices and take responsibility for them. As I started listing areas where I needed to improve, I decided to pray for help. I said, "Heavenly Father, if I have any weaknesses, you can go ahead and point them out. I'm okay with hearing them now since I have already listed sixty positive things."

I remember spending an entire week listing weaknesses when they came into my mind. The list became much larger than I had anticipated. By day two, my list was getting long. While driving to a YSA activity being held at the institute building, I thought, *Heavenly Father, I'll be okay if you let me know more weaknesses I need to work on.* The floodgates were opened that night and I saw weaknesses that I had not even considered before. I remember thinking, *Okay, you can cut it off now!* But it wasn't over. Let's just say my list of weaknesses increased dramatically.

Nephi could easily say that he was justified in his anger. After all, his two oldest brothers beat him with a rod and tried to kill him on four different occasions. They mocked him constantly and were disrespectful to his parents, his wife, and his children. They accused him of being power-hungry. They tied him up and wanted to leave him for dead. With this kind of treatment, the vast majority of people would be angry. Usually we react like a boomerang. If you want someone to slap you, the quickest way is to slap him or her, right? If you are not friendly, people are not friendly back.

Nephi did not give in to the boomerang effect. He did not try to kill his brothers. He did not tie them up. He never took revenge. Yet, something happened that made him angry. Nephi was close to his father. They shared visions. They were both prophets and record keepers. You can imagine the bond they felt as they shared years together in spiritual callings. They spent a huge amount of time working together to try to help Laman and Lemuel, but to no avail.

How did Laman and Lemuel take their father's death? "And it came to pass that not many days after his [Lehi's] death, Laman and Lemuel and the sons of Ishmael were angry with me" (2 Nephi 4:13). They didn't even appear to mourn their father's death. The fact that Laman and Lemuel couldn't even respect their dead father and go through the grieving process appears to have been the final straw for Nephi. Most people would probably think Nephi was justified in his anger. But he probably remembered that he chose to be angry. His father had taught, "Wherefore, men are free according to the flesh; and all things are given them which are expedient unto man. And they are free to choose liberty and eternal life, through the great Mediator of all men, or to choose captivity and death, according to the captivity and power of the devil; for he seeketh that all men might be miserable like unto himself" (2 Nephi 2:27). Nephi knew that his anger, his weakness was ultimately his own choice, just like ours are.

Challenge 3: Pray for help in identifying your weaknesses, write them down, and take ownership of them. Identify one that seems to be holding you back the most.

Step 4: Write out your testimony and your blessings.

Throughout his writings, Nephi bore testimony of the things he knew to be true, along with his blessings, or the things he was grateful for. Consider the phrases he used:

2 Nephi 4

19 I know in whom I have trusted.

20 My God hath been my support.

20 He hath led me through mine afflictions in the wilderness.

20 He hath preserved me upon the waters of the great deep.

21 He hath filled me with his love, even unto the consuming of my flesh.

22 He hath confounded mine enemies, unto the causing of them to quake before me.

23 He hath heard my cry by day.

23 He hath given me knowledge by visions in the night-time.

24 Angels came down and ministered unto me.

24 Upon the wings of his Spirit hath my body been carried away.

25 Mine eyes have beheld great things, yea, even too great for man.

35 I know that God will give liberally to him that asketh.

35 My God will give me, if I ask not amiss.

Nephi had a strong testimony and much to be thankful for. We all have much to be thankful for. I hope that we too have a testimony of the gospel of Jesus Christ. Have you ever written out the things you are grateful for and your testimony of the things you know to be true? Doing so will help you see the big picture and motivate you to change, as needed.

Now consider this scenario. Imagine Nephi getting angry at Laman and Lemuel because they were disrespectful during the time of Lehi's death. He let it get to him, and then got down on himself because of his weakness. He thought he was a wretched man and gave in far too easily to temptation.

One day, he reread the written account of when the angel appeared and saved Sam and him from the beating they got from their older brothers. Next, he read about seeing the discovery and colonization of America, the coming forth of the Book of Mormon, and the building of Zion in the last days. As he continued, he recalled securing food for the starving group, building a ship with the Lord's help, making tools, and quieting a storm while traveling to the promised land.

Do you think he would still be angry after contemplating the great blessings he had been given? That is one of the benefits of keeping personal records, recording our testimonies, and listing the blessings we are grateful for.

Challenge 4: Write down your testimony of the things you know to be true and the things you are grateful for.

Step 5: List the price you pay for your weaknesses.

We often hear people talk about the price that must be paid to accomplish something of worth. If we want to be in great physical shape, it will not happen by just putting on exercise clothes and watching other people work out. To get into shape, we have to pay a price. However, once we pay the price we enjoy better health and increased joy and satisfaction.

There is also a tremendous price to pay for having weaknesses like anger. Unless a person overcomes that weakness, joy and satisfaction will not increase. The positive thing about listing the short and long range consequences we are paying for our weaknesses is that it can wake us up and give us the motivation needed to change.

Let's see the price that Nephi paid for the anger he felt:

2 Nephi 4

17 O wretched man that I am!

17 Yea, my heart sorroweth because of my flesh.

17 My soul grieveth because of mine iniquities.

19 I am encompassed about, because of temptations and sins which do so easily beset me.

19 My heart groaneth because of my sins.

26 My heart weep[s] and my soul linger[s] in the valley of sorrow.

26 My flesh waste away.

26 My strength slacken.

27 I yield to sin.

27 I give way to temptations.

27 The evil one have place in my heart.

27 To destroy my peace and afflict my soul.

28 Droop in sin.

Nephi appears to actually have been depressed because of his anger, and it even affected him physically since his "strength slacken[ed]." When someone has an anger problem, it can affect many areas of life. Anger can damage or destroy marriages and parent-child relationships. It can damage the self-esteem of the person who struggles with it, plus those around them. It can cause others to lose respect for the person. It has now been shown to damage our health. And it will kill the Spirit, a consequence that could ultimately cost a person eternally. Other sins and weaknesses can have a similar devastating impact.

Challenge 5: Make a list of the short and long-term consequences you and others are paying for your weakness.

Step 6: Ask why you have the weaknesses you do.

Nephi taught us the importance of asking "why" questions. For example, when he had angry feelings, he asked himself why he allowed those feeling to destroy his happiness.

2 Nephi 4

26 Why should my heart weep[?]

26 [Why should] my soul linger in the valley of sorrow[?]

26 [Why should] my flesh waste away[?]

26 [Why should] my strength slacken, because of mine afflictions?

27 Why should I yield to sin, because of my flesh?

27 Why should I give way to temptations, that the evil one have place in my heart[?]

27 Why am I angry because of mine enemy?

Everyone has weaknesses and faults. Have you ever asked yourself why you have those faults? Where you born with them? Were there experiences in your life that led to them? Have you been incorrectly indoctrinated to believe certain things? I am sure many people never even ask themselves why they believe or act in certain ways.

While attending BYU, I took a sociology class taught by Reed Bradford. During the semester, we received an assignment to write a ten-page paper on why we were the way we were.

I'll never forget the difficulty I had writing that paper. I had never before thought about why I thought and acted the way I did. I spent weeks examining myself closely and focused on the many weaknesses I had. I wondered why I would get so worried if my wife were not home when I thought she would be. I finally realized something from my past.

When I was growing up, my parents owned their own business. They worked long, hard hours every day. When they went to bed at night, they were often exhausted. My brother was four years older than me and my sister two years older. I never went to bed when they were out with friends or on dates. If they were fifteen minutes later than I thought they would be, I tried to say in my mind that they must have run out of gas. If they were thirty minutes late, they must have been in a fender bender. If they were an hour late, they surely had been killed. My brother and sister got killed (in my mind) almost every weekend for years. It was terrible! It finally dawned on me that when my wife was a little late, I was reliving the past. I needed to change this weakness.

Challenge 6: Spend some time asking yourself why you are the way you are.

Step 7: Wake up to your weaknesses and commit to change.

Nephi came to the point where he had had enough of his brothers' disrespect. I think he felt tired of being angry and of what it was doing to him. After all, it was destroying his peace and his physical vitality. At some point, he made commitments to himself and to the Lord to overcome the anger he had in his heart.

2 Nephi 4

Commits to Self

28 Awake, my soul!

28 No longer droop in sin.

28 Rejoice, O my heart.

28 Give place no more for the enemy of my soul.

29 Do not anger again because of mine enemies.

29 Do not slacken my strength because of mine afflictions.

30 Rejoice, O my heart.

30 Cry unto the Lord.

Commits to the Lord

30 O Lord, I will praise thee forever.

30 My soul will rejoice in thee, my God, and the rock of my salvation.

34 O Lord, I have trusted in thee, and I will trust in thee forever.

34 I will not put my trust in the arm of flesh.

35 I will lift up my voice unto thee.

35 I will cry unto thee, my God, the rock of my righteousness.

35 My voice shall forever ascend up unto thee, my rock and mine everlasting God.

Asks Specific Questions

31 O Lord, wilt thou redeem my soul?

31 Wilt thou deliver me out of the hands of mine enemies?

31 Wilt thou make me that I may shake at the appearance of sin?

32 May the gates of hell be shut continually before me.

32 O Lord, wilt thou not shut the gates of thy righteousness before me.

33 O Lord, wilt thou encircle me around in the robe of thy righteousness[?]

33 O Lord, wilt thou make a way for mine escape before mine enemies[?]

33 Wilt thou make my path straight before me[?]

33 Wilt thou not place a stumbling block in my way [?]

33 [Wilt thou] clear my way before me [?]

33 [Wilt thou] hedge not up my way, but the ways of mine enemy[?]

After Nephi realized what his weakness was doing to him, he woke up. I think he realized he was blaming his brothers' anger toward him for his own anger. He obviously realized that he could not control his brothers' feelings, but he was free to choose how he responded to their actions. Once he awoke to what was happening to him because of his choices, he made commitments to change.

What he did next is powerful. He asked the Lord specific questions. This is one of the most potent things any of us can do. Because Joseph Smith asked which church was true, he received the First Vision. Because he asked if there is just a heaven and hell, he received D&C 76. "If thou shalt ask, thou shalt receive revelation upon revelation" (D&C 42:61). Imagine writing down something along the lines of, "Heavenly Father, how can I overcome my tendency to . . . ?" Once we ask the Lord a question, we need to listen for the answers and write them down.

Challenge 7: Wake up to the weaknesses that you have and make the necessary commitments to yourself and the Lord to change. Ask the Lord questions and write down the answers.

Nephi Was Successful

Did Nephi finally overcome his problem? Yes! "But behold, there are many that harden their hearts against the Holy Spirit [Laman, Lemuel, and others], that it hath no place in them; wherefore, they cast many things away which are written and esteem them as things of naught. But I, Nephi, have written what I have written, and I esteem it as of great worth, and especially unto my people. For I pray continually for them by day, and mine eyes water my pillow by night, because of them; and I cry unto my God in faith, and I know that he will hear my cry" (2 Nephi 33:2–3). We can overcome any of our weaknesses too if we will use the seven-step plan used by Nephi.

Reason to Believe

The things that Nephi did to overcome his feelings of anger are inspiring. Over the years, I have shared the seven-step plan from Nephi, and many have experienced amazing results. I do not believe that Joseph Smith, at such an early age and with such little experience in life, could possibly have come up with such an exceptional plan for overcoming personal weakness. For this reason too, I believe he did not write the Book of Mormon but translated it by revelation.

Notes

1. Spencer W. Kimball, *The Teachings of Spencer W. Kimball*, ed. Edward L. Kimball (Salt Lake City: Bookcraft, 1982), 161.
2. Spencer W. Kimball, "Let Us Move Forward and Upward," *Ensign*, May 1979, 84.

Chapter 25: The Alma 5 Challenge

"For 179 years this book has been examined and attacked, denied and deconstructed, targeted and torn apart like perhaps no other book in modern religious history—perhaps like no other book in any religious history. And still it stands."[1]

—Jeffrey R. Holland

On July 20, 1969, all the world heard the historic words from Neil Armstrong, "The Eagle has landed." News organizations immediately flashed the words: "Men on the moon." This was (and still is) an achievement of gigantic proportion, something that could only have been dreamed about in generations past. It is still difficult to believe that it happened. It was an accomplishment that required the combined knowledge and skills of many dedicated researchers.

But according to some, man never actually ever landed on the moon. By this line of reasoning, the Apollo program and all six manned moon landings were hoaxes staged by NASA and other groups. Even today, after overwhelming evidence that it indeed did happen, various surveys estimate that between six and twenty percent of Americans do not believe the moon landings ever occurred.

According to a number of conspiracy theorists, NASA, along with other organizations and certain individuals, deliberately misled the public by faking physical evidence like the rock samples, photos, and live transmissions. According to some critics, Stanley Kubrick, the acclaimed film director, screenwriter, producer, and cinematographer, was approached by U.S. government officials who convinced him to help deceive the public into thinking the moon landings actually took place. Kubrick had produced and directed the film "2001: A Space Odyssey" and was a genius who possibly could have pulled it off. With the help of Kubrick, as the theories say, the whole event was nothing but a clever plan carried out in a film studio.

These theorists claim the motive behind the hoax was that the United States government wanted to win the space race with Russia at all costs. By convincing the world that Americans had actually landed on the moon, it would send a powerful message to Russia that the United States had superior technology. That, of course, would discourage them from even trying to keep up with the only true superpower.

For some of those who believe the landings never happened, it appears that no amount of evidence can convince them that man landed on the moon. Instead of being at least open to the possibility, they only look for every scrap of "evidence" to show that it never really transpired. To prove their point, they present these kinds of details:

- The flag appeared to be fluttering on the atmosphere-free moon
- The flag was brightly lit when it is not facing any light
- There was no impact crater where they landed
- There were multiple light sources that were not explained
- There is an unexplained object reflecting off the astronaut's helmet
- There is a lack of stars in the distance in all of the pictures

Once people become convinced of a conspiracy, it can be quite difficult to persuade them otherwise. From their point of view, in the case of the moon landing, those who believe men actually landed on the moon are the ones who are naïve and misled. On the other side of the debate, the U.S. government has presented strong evidence that man has indeed walked on the moon.

In 2009, I was fascinated by photos taken by NASA's Lunar Reconnaissance Orbiter (LRO) that clearly show the Apollo landing site, including the TV camera, Lunar Module descent stage, and even Neil Armstrong's footsteps. In 2012, images were released that showed five of the six Apollo missions' American flags are still standing on the moon. The Apollo 11 flag was accidently blown over by the takeoff rocket's exhaust.[2]

Another compelling argument that the moon landing actually occurred is the fact these twelve men testified that they had personally walked on the moon.

- Neil Armstrong
- Buzz Aldrin Jr.
- Pete Conrad
- Alan Bean
- Alan Shepard
- Edgar Mitchell
- David Scott
- James Irwin
- John Young
- Charles Duke
- Eugene Cernan
- Harrison Schmitt

It is interesting that neither the new photographic evidence nor the testimony of these twelve men has convinced all conspiracy theorists that the moon landing was not a hoax. They say things like, "pictures can be altered." Or, "all twelve of these witnesses were astronauts, so they would lose their jobs and their prestige if they told the truth." And, "those who worked on the space program at NASA were either involved in the hoax or were deceived, like the millions watching the events on live TV."

Over the years, I have heard many of the arguments from those who do not believe the moon landings ever occurred. I have also considered the government's case that it really did happen. After pondering all the evidence on both sides, I believe man really did walk on the moon. Critics would call me a gullible fool, but I still believe it happened.

Along the same lines, I have talked to and read the views of many critics who believe the Book of Mormon is a hoax. Many believe that Joseph Smith's motive for producing the Book of Mormon was to make money. A few months after its publication, an Ohio newspaper published this:

> The only opinion we have of the origin of this Golden Bible, is that
> Mr. Cowdery and Mr. Smith the reputed author, have taken the old
> Bible to keep up a train of circumstances, and by altering names
> and language have produced the string of jargon called the 'Book of
> Mormon,' with the intention of making money by the sale of their
> Books; and being aware they would not sell unless an excitement and
> curiosity could be raised in the public mind.[3]

As soon as the Book of Mormon was published, critics mocked
both it and Joseph Smith relentlessly. Some of the most vocal and
intolerant opinions came from the ministers of the day. For example,
prominent religious leader Alexander Campbell said, "Smith, its real
author, as ignorant and impudent a knave as ever wrote a book."[4]
Those views continue unabated today, even though we supposedly live
in a day when it is not politically correct to be intolerant of another's
race or beliefs.

A modern critic asked how any "rational thinking" individual could
believe that the Book of Mormon is anything other than a hoax written
to deceive people? What an excellent question and one that everyone
should ask! How is it that rational thinking people *can* believe?

My wife and I recently moved out of a ward that included seven
individuals with PhDs, two doctors, three attorneys, a dentist, a
number of successful business owners, multiple individuals with
master's degrees in business and engineering, and people in other
prestigious professions. Our new ward and the two that border it
to the west include a former Heisman Trophy winner, an MVP of
the National Baseball League, multiple doctors, dentists, attorneys,
CEOs, executives, professors, counselors, and other notable people.
I think, by any standard, they would be considered rational thinkers.
How is it that they all believe the Book of Mormon is true?

A little more than nine months after the Book of Mormon was
published, Joseph Smith's hometown newspaper wrote, "We have
long been waiting, with considerable anxiety, to see some of our
contemporaries attempt to explain the immediate causes, which
produced that anomaly in religion and literature, which has most
strikingly excited the curiosity of our friends at a distance, generally
known under the cognomen of the Book of Mormon, or the Gold
Bible."[5] Now, 185 years later, critics are still trying to come to an

agreement that explains how this book came to be. But there is still no consensus to explain its origin.

Louis C. Midgley, the professor emeritus of political science at Brigham Young University, wrote an article about the theories proposed concerning the source of the Book of Mormon. He said,

> The theories of the critics on the authorship of the Book of Mormon tend to fall into four general categories:
> The initial Smith Theory, which theorizes that Joseph Smith wrote the book as a conscious fraud.
> Later psychological variations on the Smith Theory, in which Joseph Smith wrote the book under the influence of some sort of paranoia or demonic possession or dissociative illusion; in some cases the critics conclude that Joseph knew that the book so produced was a modern fraud, while others conclude that it is a modern book that Joseph himself believed was ancient.
> A conspiracy theory, which holds that Joseph Smith had the help of someone like Sidney Rigdon in creating the book as a conscious fraud, probably borrowing from some other source, such as the Spalding manuscript.
> A divine fiction theory, the most recent variation on the Smith Theory, which holds that Joseph Smith wrote the book while under some sort of "religious inspiration," so that while it is modern fiction, it at least holds some religious value.[6]

Elder Jeffrey R. Holland summarized critics' explanations for the origin of the Book of Mormon:

> Failed theories about its origins have been born and parroted and have died—from Ethan Smith to Solomon Spaulding to deranged paranoid to cunning genius. None of these frankly pathetic answers for this book has ever withstood examination because there is no other answer than the one Joseph gave as its young unlearned translator. In this I stand with my own great-grandfather, who said simply enough, "No wicked man could write such a book as this; and no good man would write it, unless it were true and he were commanded of God to do so."[7]

Perhaps the rationally thinking critic should ask why we are still waiting for the definitive answer to explain the Book of Mormon, other than the explanation Joseph Smith gave. President Gordon B. Hinckley said this of the book: "Through all of these years critics have tried to explain it. They have spoken against it. They have ridiculed it. But it has outlived them all, and its influence today is greater than at any time in its history."[8]

While many are waiting for a plausible alternate explanation, maybe we should look at the evidence that it is true. To me, there is a multitude of excellent reasons to believe that Joseph Smith could not have written the Book of Mormon, either alone or with help. Perhaps, the most powerful evidence of all that it is true is the book itself. The one thing that both critics and believers should be able to agree on is that the book did not fall out of the sky. Joseph Smith either wrote it himself (or with help from others) or he translated it from the Nephite record. There are not a lot of other possibilities.

I have asked myself if Joseph Smith himself could possibly have produced such a complex, inspiring book that touches me so deeply and with such dramatic impact. Each time, the answer has been that there is no way he could have done that. I realize that critics have their own evidence for believing it is not divine, just as those who do not believe the moon landing occurred have their reasons for not believing. Both sides believe they have sufficient evidence to feel justified in their beliefs. After examining the evidence, I believe the Book of Mormon is a divinely inspired translation of an ancient record.

Even though I have many reasons to believe the Book of Mormon is true, the main one is that I have taken the challenge issued by Moroni at the end of the book. He said, "And when ye shall receive these things, I would exhort you that ye would ask God, the Eternal Father, in the name of Christ, if these things are not true; and if ye shall ask with a sincere heart, with real intent, having faith in Christ, he will manifest the truth of it unto you, by the power of the Holy Ghost" (Moroni 10:4).

I have included in this book some rational reasons, in addition to the spiritual reasons, that led to my belief that the Book of Mormon is true. Just working on this book has dramatically increased my testimony of its truthfulness. Even working on a computer with access to vast amounts of material on the Internet, this project has taken hundreds of hours over several years. Almost daily, I find myself thinking of the time spent on this endeavor and the things left undone because of it. Then I think about the amount of time that it took to translate and then publish the

Book of Mormon—an incredibly short amount of time that produced this masterpiece of religious literature. Richard L. Bushman said,

> John Welch and Tim Rathbone estimate that there were sixty-three translating days available from Oliver Cowdery's start as secretary on 7 April 1829 to the end of June when the title page was published in the Wayne Sentinel. That comes to eight pages of printed text a day—a marvelous production rate for any writer and a stupendous one for an uneducated twenty-three-year-old who, according to his wife, could scarcely write a coherent letter.[9]

I have often thought about the testimonies of the twelve men who testified to the world under oath that they had seen the plates from which the Book of Mormon was translated. It took courage to sign their names. They would appear with their testimonies in every copy of the book. They knew that they would be mocked and persecuted for it. I cannot imagine signing my name to something that would ruin my reputation if it were not true. And yet they did it, and none of them ever denied what they had seen. Here are the names of those who allowed their testimonies to be published to the world:

- Joseph Smith Jr.
- Oliver Cowdery
- David Whitmer
- Martin Harris
- Christian Whitmer
- Jacob Whitmer
- Peter Whitmer Jr.
- John Whitmer
- Hiram Page
- Joseph Smith Sr.
- Hyrum Smith
- Samuel Smith

The testimonies of these twelve men have likely not convinced doubters to believe any more than the testimonies of the twelve astronauts who walked on the moon have convinced the conspiracy theorists that it actually happened. Critics who were shocked that any rational thinker could be a believer also say that outside the Church, not one scholar or scientist takes the Book of Mormon seriously.

To me, this statement doesn't seem all that rational. It is a broad generalization based on limited knowledge. This person obviously did not get input from every scholar and scientist about their views of the Book of Mormon to form that conclusion. Perhaps a more accurate and rational statement could read like this: "Outside the thousands of scholars and scientists who believe the Book of Mormon to be true, not one non-believing critic takes the Book of Mormon seriously." It could probably also be said with a high degree of accuracy that not one person in the world who believes the moon landing to be a staged, government-sponsored hoax believes that man actually landed on the moon.

I have no illusions that what I say will have any influence whatsoever on those who have their minds made up about the Book of Mormon. One of the critics said that the Book of Mormon is nothing but a clumsy sham that no intelligent person would ever consider wasting their time on. And yet millions of intelligent people spend their time reading, studying, and pondering its pages every day.

Consider this: One of the most universally admired masterpieces of world architecture is the Taj Mahal, located in Agra, India. Shah Jahan had it constructed between 1632 and 1654 as a memorial to his wife, Mumtaz Mahal. If critics wanted to put a negative spin on this building, they would certainly be going against the positive views of more than three million visitors per year. Here is a sample of opinions found on *TripAdvisor.com* about this magnificent building:

Excellent (6,080 remarks)

"It is truly the most beautiful building in the world."

"This is an astounding building. You have to see it to understand the power it has."

"Words really can't express the utter magnificence of the Taj Mahal."

"Your jaws are guaranteed to drop. It is awe-inspiring."

"I have seen it three times now, and it still gives me goosebumps."

"The place is simply breathtaking! Definitely a must-do when you are in India!"[10]

You may wonder what the Taj Mahal has to do with the Book of Mormon. Over the years and through countless testimony meetings, personal conversations, and teaching Book of Mormon classes multiple times for the Church Educational System, I have found that people who search the book diligently with real intent often have a similar experience to that of the 6,080 visitors who rated the Taj Mahal as being excellent on *TripAdvisor.com.*

However, not everyone sees the Taj Mahal the same way. Here are a few examples from the twenty-four people who rated the building as being a terrible place to visit.

Terrible (24 remarks)

"Never been so disappointed in my entire life."

"Please do not waste any time seeing this; the greatest letdown ever."

"Overall the experience was one worth forgetting, I would not go back."

"Overall pathetic place to visit."

"Never, never spend your hard-earned money to see Taj Mahal."[11]

I wonder if these negative comments say more about the person writing them than they do about the building. To me, the Book of Mormon is the Taj Mahal of books. When I read it with real intent, I always feel like those who loved the Taj Mahal. The Book of Mormon is "breathtaking" and the "most beautiful" book in the world to me. I believe it is "an astounding" book, and it is hard for me to describe the "power it has" had on my life. I've read it multiple times and it "still gives me goosebumps."

I wish I could convince people who have never read the Book of Mormon with real intent to just read it with an open mind and to at least consider the possibility that it may be true. Even with critics trying to destroy its influence, it continues to have a dramatic impact on many of those who open its covers and read. Brigham Young made this profound statement many years ago: "How many witnesses has the Book of Mormon? Hundreds and thousands are now living upon the earth, who testify of its truth."[12] Since then, millions of witnesses have born their testimony of its truthfulness.

Many years ago, I took religion classes from Hugh Nibley, who was a professor at Brigham Young University. As many know, he was a brilliant religious scholar and researcher of the history and languages of the Middle East. Sometimes he gave his students a challenge, a thought-provoking exercise. No one ever stepped forward to accept it. The following text explains the challenge:

Since Joseph Smith was younger than most of you and not nearly so experienced or well-educated as any of you at the time he copyrighted the Book of Mormon, it should not be too much to ask you to hand in by the end of the semester (which will give you more time than he had) a paper of, say, five to six hundred pages in length. Call it a sacred book if you will, and give it the form of a history. Tell of a community of wandering Jews in ancient times; have all sorts of characters in your story, and involve them in all sorts of public and private vicissitudes; give them names—hundreds of them—pretending that they are real Hebrew and Egyptian names of circa 600 BC; be lavish with cultural and technical details—manners and customs, arts and industries, political and religious institutions, rites, and traditions, include long and complicated military and economic histories; have your narrative cover a thousand years without any large gaps; keep a number of interrelated local histories going at once; feel free to introduce religious controversy and philosophical discussion, but always in a plausible setting; observe the appropriate literary conventions and explain the derivation and transmission of your varied historical materials.

Above all, do not ever contradict yourself! For now we come to the really hard part of this little assignment. You and I know that you are making this all up—we have our little joke—but just the same you are going to be required to have your paper published when you finish it, not as fiction or romance, but as a true history! After you have handed it in you may make no changes in it (in this class we always use the first edition of the Book of Mormon); what is more, you are to invite any and all scholars to read and criticize your work freely, explaining to them that it is a sacred book on a par with the Bible. If they seem over-skeptical, you might tell them that you translated the book from original records by the aid of the Urim and Thummim—they will love that! Further to allay their misgivings, you might tell them that the original manuscript was on golden plates, and that you got the plates from an angel. Now go to work and good luck!

To date no student has carried out this assignment, which, of course, was not meant seriously. But why not? If anybody could write the Book of Mormon, as we have been so often assured, it is high time that somebody, some devoted and learned minister of the gospel, let us say, performed the invaluable public service of showing the world that it can be done.[13]

While I don't believe that Hugh Nibley ever expected a student to accept the challenge, it does bring up some of the reasons why no vocal critic has ever attempted to write a similar book, even though many contend that Joseph Smith wrote it and that it would not have been that difficult to do. Now, with the help of technology that is light years ahead of the day in which the book came forth, you would think that someone would step forward to attempt it.

I would like to propose a far easier challenge than the one Hugh Nibley offered for those who believe that Joseph Smith wrote the book, or that he and some accomplices wrote it. As discussed in previous chapters, the major writers in the Book of Mormon had their own unique ways of expressing themselves. They used phrases that were original with them. All of the speakers said things that do not appear anywhere else. This fact gives credit to the Book of Mormon's claimed origin, and it further shows that the vast majority of the book could not have been copied from any other source.

Several sermons delivered by individuals appear to be provided in their entirety in the Book of Mormon. Consider one sermon (found in Alma chapter 5) given by Alma, the son of Alma. By dividing this sermon into four- or seven-word phrases, we can recognize Alma's originality. I found over two hundred of these short phrases that are not found anywhere in the Old Testament, the New Testament, or the Apocrypha. In fact, none of these phrases are used anywhere else in the Book of Mormon. Those included here are only used by Alma in this sermon and are not found in any of his other writings. Here is a sample of seventy-five of these short phrases from that sermon.

- having power and authority from God (v. 3)
- by the mercy and power of God (v. 4)
- the captivity of your fathers (v. 6)
- his mercy and long-suffering towards them (v. 6)
- delivered their souls from hell (v. 6)
- behold, he changed their hearts (v. 7)
- awakened them out of a deep sleep (v. 7)
- they were in the midst of darkness (v. 7)
- their souls were illuminated (v. 7)
- by the light of the everlasting word (v. 7)
- encircled about by the bands of death (v. 7)
- everlasting destruction did await them (v. 7)
- the chains of hell which encircled them (v. 9)
- they did sing redeeming love (v. 9)
- yea, and also the chains of hell (v. 10)

- and was he not a holy prophet (v. 11)
- a mighty change wrought in his heart (v. 12)
- trust in the true and living God (v. 13)
- they were faithful until the end (v. 13)
- have ye spiritually been born of God (v. 14)
- received his image in your countenances (v. 14)
- do ye exercise faith in the redemption (v. 15)
- look forward with an eye of faith (v. 15)
- this mortal body raised in immortality (v. 15)
- this corruption raised in incorruption (v. 15)
- brought before the tribunal of God (v. 18)
- your souls filled with guilt and remorse (v. 18)
- perfect remembrance of all your wickedness (v. 18)
- can ye look up to God at that day (v. 19)
- a pure heart and clean hands (v. 19)
- engraven upon your countenances (v. 19)
- his garments are washed white (v. 21)
- to redeem his people from their sins (v. 21)
- what will these things testify against you (v. 22)
- and are spotless pure and white (v. 24)
- the children of the kingdom of the devil (v. 25)
- sing the song of redeeming love (v. 26)
- keeping yourselves blameless before God (v. 27)
- made white through the blood of Christ (v. 27)
- behold, are ye stripped of pride (v. 28)
- I would that he should prepare quickly (v. 29)
- wo unto all ye workers of iniquity (v. 32)
- the arms of mercy are extended (v. 33)
- repent and I will receive you (v. 33)
- the bread and the waters of life (v. 34)
- bring forth works of righteousness (v. 35)
- puffed up in the vain things (v. 37)
- the good shepherd doth call you (v. 38)
- a child of the devil (v. 39)
- whatsoever is good cometh from God (v. 40)
- whatsoever is evil cometh from the devil (v. 40)
- for his wages he receiveth death (v. 42)
- being dead unto all good works (v. 42)

- the manifestation of the Spirit of God (v. 47)
- I know that Jesus Christ shall come (v. 48)
- full of grace and mercy and truth (v. 48)
- the order after which I am called (v. 49)
- to preach unto my beloved brethren (v. 49)
- they must repent and be born again (v. 49)
- yea thus saith the Spirit (v. 50)
- the Holy One hath spoken it (v. 52)
- trample the Holy One under your feet (v. 53)
- puffed up in the pride of your hearts (v. 53)
- sanctified by the Holy Spirit (v. 54)
- come ye out from the wicked (v. 57)
- touch not their unclean things (v. 57)
- their names shall be blotted out (v. 57)
- the word of God may be fulfilled (v. 57)
- an inheritance at my right hand (v. 58)
- that the wolves enter not (v. 59)
- if a wolf enter his flock (v. 59)
- the good shepherd doth call after you (v. 60)
- if you will hearken unto his voice (v. 60)
- suffer no ravenous wolf to enter (v. 60)
- I speak by way of invitation (v. 62)

If Joseph Smith wrote the Book of Mormon, it means that he invented over two hundred original phrases to use in the Alma speech alone. I would like to propose two separate challenges to choose from for anyone who believes that Joseph Smith wrote the Book of Mormon. My hope is that if anyone accepts one of the challenges and is unable to complete it, he or she will read the book with real intent and ask the Lord in prayer if it is true. The challenge, of course, needs to be completed in sixty-three working days. This challenge should be far easier than the one proposed by Hugh Nibley and infinitely more simple than producing a Book of Mormon equivalent.

- Option 1: Write an inspiring religious speech of any length using King James Bible language. For your speech, you must plagiarize the Book of Mormon using all seventy five of the short phrases included above that Alma used in his address, found in Alma 5.

- Option 2: Write an inspiring religious speech of any length that includes a minimum of seventy-five original phrases (being four to seven words in length) that have never been used by anyone before. You cannot use a search engine for help in completing the challenge.

Reason to Believe

Many critics seem to think that anyone who believes the Book of Mormon to be the word of God is an ignorant, irrational fool who has been deceived or indoctrinated, or is just uninformed. If not, they would not believe the book to be true. It does not seem to matter what socioeconomic class a believer comes from or whether they are a high school dropout or a brilliant PhD researcher. If they believe, they cannot be a rational thinker. In critics' minds, believers just have not seen the latest and greatest theory of the Book of Mormon's origin or haven't heard that one little-known telling tidbit of information of early Church history.

And yet, all any critic needs to do to prove this is produce a similar work to show how easy it would be to have written the book. You would think that someone would step forward and try it because they would receive heroic acclaim worldwide. But no one has attempted it in over 185 years. I believe that if anyone could write a work similar to the Book of Mormon, it would have been done by now.

Based on the rate that Joseph was translating, he would have produced the sermon found in Alma 5 in less than a day. I will be extremely surprised if anyone actually steps forward and completes either of the two challenges listed above in even sixty-three working days. If no one completes the simple challenge to produce another Alma 5 using the guidelines in the challenge, I believe we can rest assured that an uneducated farm boy could not do it either. That should lead to the rational conclusion that Joseph Smith could not have possibly written the Book of Mormon.

Notes

1. Jeffrey R. Holland, "Safety for the Soul," *Conference Report*, October 2009.
2. "Apollo Moon flags still standing, images show," BBC News (London: BBC), July 30, 2012.

3. "The Golden Bible," *Ashtabula (Ohio) Journal*, 4 December 1830, quoting the *Cleveland Herald*.

4. "Delusions," *Millennial Harbinger* 22 (7 February 1831), 84–96.

5. *The Reflector*, Palmyra, New York, (6 January 1831), 76.

6. Louis C. Midgely, "Who Really Wrote the Book of Mormon? The Critics and Their Theories," in *Book of Mormon Authorship Revisited: Evidence for Ancient Origins,* ed. Noel B. Reynolds (Provo, Utah: Maxwell Institute, 1997).

7. Jeffrey R. Holland, "Safety for the Soul," *Conference Report*, October 2009.

8. Gordon B. Hinckley, *Conference Report,* "The Stone Cut Out of the Mountain," October 2007.

9. Richard L. Bushman, "The Recovery of the Book of Mormon," in *Book of Mormon Authorship Revisited: Evidence for Ancient Origins,* ed. Noel B. Reynolds (Provo, Utah: Maxwell Institute, 1997), 23.

10. TripAdvisor.com.

11. Ibid.

12. *Journal of Discourses*, 26 vols. (Liverpool: F. D. Richards & Sons, 1851–1886), 10:326.

13. Hugh Nibley, "The Prophetic Book of Mormon," *Collected Works of Hugh Nibley*, vol. 8 (Salt Lake City: Deseret Book, 2010), 221–22.

Chapter 26: Both Good and Evil

"Young Joseph was told that his name would be 'both good and evil spoken of' throughout the world (Joseph Smith—History 1:33). Except from a divine source, how audacious a statement! Yet his contemporary religious leaders, then much better known than Joseph, have faded into the footnotes of history, while the work of Joseph Smith grows constantly and globally."[1]

—Neal A. Maxwell

It is hard to imagine anything more difficult than to be known for good and evil throughout the world. Those in world history who have risen to fame are either associated with good *or* evil, not good *and* evil. In most cases, those known for evil committed horrific crimes against humanity. Adolph Hitler, Pol Pot, and Joseph Stalin are well known, but their names are almost always associated only with evil. These three were responsible for the needless deaths of untold millions of innocent men, women, and children. Those known for good have often done remarkable acts of selfless service, overcome tremendous obstacles in their way, taught life-changing principles, or left behind inventions that have blessed all of mankind. Mother Theresa, Helen Keller, Thomas Edison, and Mohandas Gandhi are a few examples of individuals known worldwide, and they are almost exclusively associated with good. Of all the billions of people who have lived on earth, how many are known for both good and evil?

Few fit into this category. When they do, it is usually because those who are in authority feel threatened by that individual. As a result, they call the person who is the threat evil. After that, they indoctrinate their followers and others with similar attitudes and claims about the evil in that individual. Their followers continue in the tradition and spread that characterization of evil. Long after the "evil" person dies, people begin to realize the full extent of good the person has actually done.

One such individual who fits this pattern is William Tyndale. Born in 1494 near Gloucestershire, England, he was an excellent scholar, theologian, and linguist. He received a master's degree at twenty-one from Oxford University and also studied at Cambridge. Most sources report that he could speak and write eight languages and was quite proficient in Greek. Over time, he published his religious views, which were considered heretical by the Roman Catholic Church, King Henry VIII, and the Church of England.

Tyndale lived in a time when only the clergy were considered to be qualified to read and interpret the Bible. It was a forbidden book to laymen. Tyndale came to the attention of church authorities because of his support of Martin Luther's reform movement and for his desire to translate the Bible into English. The clergy were vehemently opposed to the idea of making the Bible available to the masses. Reportedly, one orthodox priest who condemned the idea of an English translation said, "We are better to be without God's laws than the Pope's." Tynsdale replied, "I defy the Pope and all his laws. If God spares my life ere many years I will cause the boy that drives the plough to know more of the scriptures than you!"[2]

Even though Tyndale faced extreme opposition from both church and political authorities, he was not deterred and spent much of his adult life working on an English translation of the Bible. Because of persecution and threats, Tyndale fled England and spent several years living in poverty and constant danger. Because of his obsession to complete this translation, he became one of the most wanted men in Europe. He was constantly on the run to avoid capture while he tried to complete the work that consumed him.

He finished the English translation of the New Testament and had it published in the German city of Worms in 1525. He later produced a revised version of the New Testament and continued his translation of the Old Testament. His translation was so precise that some scholars believe that the vast majority of the King James Bible can be attributed to his work. He is appropriately known as the "Father of the English Bible."

Before he could completely finish his work on the Old Testament, he was betrayed to the authorities in Belgium by Henry Phillips, a person he believed to be his friend. After spending time in prison, he was condemned to death for heresy. Tyndale became one of the few people in history to be known for both good and evil; evil by those who wanted to maintain their power and prestige, and (over time) good by the untold millions who have had their lives changed for the better because of his work. He is now viewed as a martyr because he was killed for his religious beliefs. The word *martyr* comes from a Greek word meaning witness.

William Tyndale knew he was called of God to do a special work and would not back down, even in the face of death. Just before he was put to death, he was given a moment to pray. John Foxe, an English historian, reported that Tyndale cried out, "Lord, open the King of England's eyes!"[3] He was then strangled by the executioner and burned at the stake. The king never opened his eyes, but untold millions have done so because one man had the courage to stand up against the religious and political authorities of his day.

Over three hundred years after Tyndale's birth, another religious reformer was born who would also come to infuriate the religious and political authorities of his day. However, he was not educated at Oxford or Cambridge and was not fluent in eight languages, or considered a linguistic genius at all. His name was Joseph Smith, and he was just an ordinary, uneducated boy who grew up plowing fields in Vermont and New York.

How did such a common boy get put on the infinitely small list of individuals who are known for good and evil? What horrific crimes against humanity did Joseph commit to be viewed as both throughout the world? It seems his offenses were similar to those committed by Tyndale. His works also irritated the religious and political authorities of his day. Considered a heretic by many, Joseph claimed that God the Father and His Son Jesus Christ personally appeared to him. He also claimed that an angel named Moroni was sent from God to call him to a special work on September 21, 1823. Describing that event, he said: "He called me by name, and said unto me that he was a messenger sent from the presence of God to me, and that his name was Moroni; that God had a work for me to do; and that my name should be had for good and evil among all nations, kindreds, and tongues, or that it should be both good and evil spoken of among all people" (Joseph Smith—History 1:33).

Joseph Smith, like Tyndale, also translated into English an ancient religious record that testified of Jesus Christ. This infuriated many of the political and religious leaders and their followers in his day. It was heresy in the eyes of some because the Lord already had a bible and people did not need any more bibles. However, Joseph would not back down from his claims that the book was "translated by the gift and power of God" (D&C 135:3), no matter how much he was ridiculed, persecuted, or threatened.

Some thought that he was worthy of death because of his "evil" actions. One such man was William G. "Parson" Brownlow, a minister, newspaper editor, and politician. He eventually served as the governor of Tennessee and then as a U.S. Senator. When he learned that Joseph Smith had been killed at the Carthage jail, he said in his paper, *The Jonesborough Whig*: "Some of the public Journals of the country, we are sorry to see, regret the death of that blasphemous wretch Joe Smith, the Mormon Prophet. Our deliberate judgement is, that he ought to have been dead ten years ago, and that those who at length have deprived him of his life, have done the cause of God, and of the country, good service. Smith was killed, as he should have been. . . . Three Cheers to the brave company who shot him to pieces!"[4]

Alexander Campbell was another ordained minister who viewed Joseph Smith as evil. Perhaps his hatred can be traced to the fact that he lost many of his members to the preaching of LDS missionaries. His reaction to the Prophet's death is reminiscent of the priest-inspired crowds shouting to Pilate, who asked, "What will ye then that I shall do unto him whom ye call the King of the Jews? And they cried out again, Crucify him" (Mark 15:12–13).

Here are Campbell's words:

> Joseph Smith and his brother Hiram have been providentially cut off in the midst of their diabolical career. They were most lawlessly and mobocratically put to death. . . . But the money-digger, the juggler, and the founder of the Golden Bible delusion, has been hurried away in the midst of his madness to his final account. "He died not as a righteous man dieth." The hand of the Lord was heavy upon him.

An outlaw himself, God cut him off by outlaws. He requited him according to his works. He was not persecuted, unless to punish a traitor, a public plunderer, a marauder, be persecution! The killing of Robespierre was not murder. It was the outrages of the Mormons that brought upon the head of their leader the arm of justice. The phrenzy of a fanatic cannot make out of the affair persecution, Religion or religious opinions had nothing to do with it. It was neither more nor less than the assassination of one whose career was in open rebellion against God and man.[5]

It is interesting that Campbell would compare Joseph Smith to Maximilien Robespierre. Robespierre was the French politician known as the architect of the Reign of Terror during the French Revolution. He encouraged the execution of tens of thousands of enemies of the Revolution. Most of them were beheaded with the guillotine, while others were summary executed, meaning they were killed immediately, without the benefit of a trial. The Terror ended after Robespierre himself and twenty-one followers were guillotined before a cheering crowd in Paris.

Some authorities in Joseph Smith's day thought he too was guilty of crimes that were worthy of death. After studying his life for many years, I find that both his teachings and his actions reflect that of a man who only wanted to be good and to teach others to do the same. Of course, he was not without faults, but those closest to him saw a man trying to live by the following code of conduct: "We believe in being honest, true, chaste, benevolent, virtuous, and in doing good to all men; indeed, we may say that we follow the admonition of Paul—We believe all things, we hope all things, we have endured many things, and hope to be able to endure all things. If there is anything virtuous, lovely, or of good report or praiseworthy, we seek after these things."[6]

The fulfillment of Moroni's prophecy that stated people would deem Joseph Smith as evil began almost immediately after he claimed to see the Father and the Son. It increased dramatically when word got out that he had seen an angel and was translating a golden bible into the English language. Religious leaders led a smear campaign of epic proportions against him, and the political authorities soon joined in. James A. Cullimore said, "The Prophet was tried and tested and suffered many indignities. He was falsely arrested 42 times but was always cleared by the law of the land. He was tarred and feathered. He spent nearly six months in Liberty Jail in terrible conditions and with food not fit for humans."[7]

While many religious and political leaders and their followers claimed the Prophet was evil, others considered him to be a mighty prophet who was as good and noble a man as had ever lived on earth. Here is a description of him by Emmeline B. Wells, who knew him well: "He [Joseph Smith] was beyond my comprehension. The power of God rested upon him to such a degree that on many occasions he seemed transfigured. His expression was mild and almost childlike in repose; and when addressing the people, who loved him it seemed to adoration, the glory of his countenance was beyond description."[8]

Several years ago, I was invited to attend a meeting for the area directors of the Church Educational System. It was held the week after October general conference in Utah. Attending that meeting were those who supervised multiple seminaries and institutes throughout the world. I was fascinated to be in the same room with these good and honorable men from nations like Russia, Hong Kong, Japan, Bolivia, Nigeria, South Korea, Mexico, Brazil, Germany, England, Chile, South Africa, and many more.

Toward the end of the week, we saw a new film about the life of Joseph Smith and the coming forth of the Book of Mormon. At one point in the film, his often-quoted statement in the Wentworth Letter was read: "No unhallowed hand can stop the work from progressing; persecutions may rage, mobs may combine, armies may assemble, calumny may defame, but the truth of God will go forth boldly, nobly, and independent, till it has penetrated every continent, visited every clime, swept every country, and sounded in every ear, till the purposes of God shall be accomplished, and the great Jehovah shall say the work is done."[9]

The film showed large, high-speed presses printing copies of the Book of Mormon. Sitting toward the front, I turned around and viewed almost everyone in the room. Many silently wiped tears away. I focused on the area director from western Africa. He had tears streaming down his face. I contemplated the explosive growth of the Church occurring in many areas of Africa because of good people like him.

Suddenly, I was overwhelmed with emotion as I realized that I was literally seeing the fulfillment of the prophecy made by Joseph Smith concerning the gospel going to every country. Every man in that room had a testimony of the Book of Mormon and knew that book had helped them become good and honorable men. They were the embodiment of the scripture: "Wherefore by their fruits ye shall know them" (Matthew 7:20). They collectively had responsibility for every country in the world. The gospel *is* going forth boldly, nobly, and independently, and it *is* penetrating every clime. The following statement made by the Prophet Joseph Smith is being proven true: "I told the brethren that the Book of Mormon was the most correct of any book on earth, and the keystone of our religion, and a man would get nearer to God by abiding by its precepts, than by any other book."[10]

The film concluded with a dramatic and realistic portrayal of the martyrdom of the Prophet Joseph and his brother Hyrum. A reverent feeling permeated the room as we all realized that these men proved they were good by being willing to lay down their lives for the gospel. I have always admired those willing to courageously stand up for worthy causes when they faced tremendous opposition from the world. I am in awe, however, of those who have been willing to give their lives for the gospel of Jesus Christ. Valiant men like Abinadi, Peter, James, Stephen, Paul, William Tyndale, and many other men and women are great examples of that goodness. Their values would not let them deny what they knew to be true, regardless of the consequences of espousing those beliefs.

Is there anything you value enough to be willing to die for it, as these men did? Obviously, William Tyndale was not only willing to *risk* his life for his belief that the Bible should be available in the English language, but he also was willing to *give* his life for that cause. Abinadi, Paul, and many others also demonstrated their goodness through their commitment to give their lives for their testimonies of the gospel. Even more impressive to me is the fact that some of these martyrs were given an opportunity to recant what they believed to save their lives, but they refused to do so.

Joseph Smith was also placed in the same unenviable position of having civil and religious authorities hating him and considering him evil. He commented on his situation: "By the power of God I translated the Book of Mormon from hieroglyphics, the knowledge of which was lost to the world, in which wonderful event I stood alone, an unlearned youth, to combat the worldly wisdom and multiplied ignorance of eighteen centuries, with a new revelation."[11]

He suffered great persecution as others learned about his visions, and when he took possession of the plates for the translation, things got even worse. But even with severe persecution, regardless of the consequences, Joseph Smith would not deny the fact that he had seen a vision. Joseph said he felt like Paul, who related the account of his vision to King Agrippa with few believing him. In the Joseph Smith—History, he said,

> Some said he was dishonest, others said he was mad; and he was ridiculed and reviled. But all this did not destroy the reality of his vision. He had seen a vision, he knew he had, and all the persecution under heaven could not make it otherwise; and though they should persecute him unto death, yet he knew, and would know to his latest breath.
>
> So it was with me. I had actually seen a light, and in the midst of that light I saw two Personages, and they did in reality speak to me; and though I was hated and persecuted for saying that I had seen a vision, yet it was true; and while they were persecuting me, reviling me, and speaking all manner of evil against me falsely for so saying, I was led to say in my heart: Why persecute me for telling the truth? I have actually seen a vision; and who am I that I can withstand God, or why does the world think to make me deny what I have actually seen? For I had seen a vision; I knew it, and I knew that God knew it, and I could not deny it, neither dared I do it; at least I knew that by so doing I would offend God, and come under condemnation. (Joseph Smith—History 1:24–25)

Brigham Young knew the extremely difficult situation that Joseph found himself in because of the things he taught and claimed to have seen. He said,

> Our situation is peculiar at the present time. Has it not been peculiar ever since Joseph found the plates? The circumstances that surrounded him when he found the plates were singular and strange. He passed a short life of sorrow and trouble, surrounded by enemies who sought day

and night to destroy him. If a thousand hounds were on this Temple Block, let loose on one rabbit, it would not be a bad illustration of the situation at times of the Prophet Joseph. He was hunted unremittingly.[12]

The fact that Joseph was willing to suffer so much for the sake of the gospel and ultimately go to Carthage to face a certain death is a powerful testimony that he was telling the truth. What would be the point of going through all these things for a lie? There can be little doubt that he knew he was going to die if he went to Carthage.

Consider these statements as Joseph Smith spoke to the Apostles, his wife, and his devoted followers before his martyrdom:

"Some have supposed that Brother Joseph could not die; but this is a mistake: it is true there have been times when I have had the promise of my life to accomplish such and such things, but, having now accomplished those things, I have not at present any lease of my life, I am as liable to die as other men."[13]

"Brethren, the Lord bids me hasten the work in which we are engaged. . . . Some important scene is near to take place. It may be that my enemies will kill me. And in case they should, and the keys and power which rest on me not be imparted to you, they will be lost from the earth. But if I can only succeed in placing them upon your heads, then let me fall a victim to murderous hands if God will suffer it, and I can go with all pleasure and satisfaction, knowing that my work is done, and the foundation laid on which the kingdom of God is to be reared in this dispensation of the fulness of times."[14]

"I advised my brother Hyrum to take his family on the next steamboat and go to Cincinnati. Hyrum replied, 'Joseph, I can't leave you.' Whereupon I said to the company present, 'I wish I could get Hyrum out of the way, so that he may live to avenge my blood.'"[15]

"I do not regard my own life. I am ready to be offered a sacrifice for this people; for what can our enemies do? Only kill the body, and their power is then at an end. Stand firm, my friends; never flinch. Do not seek to save your lives, for he that is afraid to die for the truth, will lose eternal life. Hold out to the end, and we shall be resurrected and become like Gods, and reign in celestial kingdoms, principalities, and eternal dominions."[16]

"I am going like a lamb to the slaughter; but I am calm as a summer's morning; I have a conscience void of offense towards God, and towards all men. I shall die innocent, and it shall yet be said of me—he was murdered in cold blood" (D&C 135:4).

"I am very much resigned to my lot, knowing I am justified and have done the best that could be done. Give my love to the children and all my friends."[17]

"I roll the burden and responsibility of leading this church off from my shoulders onto yours. Now, round up your shoulders and stand under it like men; for the Lord is going to let me rest awhile."[18]

It is interesting that Joseph would use the phrase *the Lord is going to let me rest awhile* when giving responsibility to the Twelve Apostles. Keep that phrase in mind as you read the following experience recorded by Jasper Henry Lawn, a member of the Reorganized Church of Jesus Christ of Latter Day Saints (RLDS):

> My father was one of the guards, placed by Governor Ford at Carthage Jail, the day before Joseph and Hyrum Smith were martyred; and heard each of them speak from the stairway to the guard below. And when Hyrum spoke, he told them to take their pencil and note down Revelation the sixth chapter, from the ninth to the eleventh verses inclusive. For said he, "That is now about to be fulfilled." My father made a note of it at once, and was so much affected by what he had both seen and heard while there, that as soon as he was released from duty that evening, he came home and read those three verses to my mother, and turned down the leaf. The above incident was told me by my mother, some years afterward, as nearly as I can remember as related. And she showed the bible to me, with the verses marked, and the leaf down. I have his bible now just as he left it in 1847; when he died."[19]

Here are the verses that Jasper Lawn said Hyrum asked the prison guards to write down:

Revelation 6

9 And when he had opened the fifth seal, I saw under the altar the souls of them that were slain for the word of God, and for the testimony which they held:

10 And they cried with a loud voice, saying, How long, O Lord, holy and true, dost thou not judge and avenge our blood on them that dwell on the earth?

11 And white robes were given unto every one of them; and it was said unto them, that they should rest yet for a little season, until their fellowservants also and their brethren, that should be killed as they were, should be fulfilled.

Lucy Mack Smith, the mother of the Prophet and his brother Hyrum, went through emotional turmoil like few women have been required to endure. The martyrdom of her two sons was almost more than she could bear. She gave this heart-wrenching description of seeing her sons for the first time after their deaths:

> After the corpses were washed and dressed in their burial clothes, we were allowed to see them. I had for a long time braced every nerve, roused every energy of my soul and called upon God to strengthen me, but when I entered the room and saw my murdered sons extended both at once before my eyes and heard the sobs and groans of my family and the cries of "Father! Husband! Brothers!" from the lips of their wives, children, brothers and sisters, it was too much; I sank back, crying to the Lord in the agony of my soul, "My God, my God, why hast thou forsaken this family!" A voice replied, "I have taken them to myself, that they might have rest." . . . How my mind flew through every scene of sorrow and distress which we had passed, together, in which they had shown the innocence and sympathy which filled their guileless hearts. As I looked upon their peaceful, smiling countenances, I seemed almost to hear them say, "Mother, weep not for us, we have overcome the world by love; we carried to them the gospel, that their souls might be saved; they slew us for our testimony, and thus placed us beyond their power; their ascendency is for a moment, ours is an eternal triumph."[20]

Joseph Smith and his faithful brother Hyrum completed the mission they were sent to earth to perform. John Taylor said, "To seal the testimony of this book and the Book of Mormon, we announce the martyrdom of Joseph Smith the Prophet, and Hyrum Smith the Patriarch" (D&C 135:1).

Eliza R. Snow said the following in tribute to Joseph: "He boldly and bravely confronted the false traditions, superstitions, religions, bigotry and ignorance of the world—proved himself true to every heaven-revealed principle—true to his brethren and true to God, then sealed his testimony with his blood."[21]

Today, millions of people worldwide sing with enthusiasm the beloved hymn "Praise to the Man" in honor of Joseph Smith. They see him as not just a good man but a great man. Others still view him as an evil man and refuse to even consider his good qualities and the good that comes to those who follow the teachings revealed to him. There is one thing, however, that both the believer and the nonbeliever should agree on. Both should concur that the prophecy made by Moroni on September 21, 1823, about Joseph Smith's name being known for good and evil throughout the world is literally being fulfilled.

Reason to Believe

Why would Joseph and Hyrum be willing to lay down their lives for a lie? Jeffery R. Holland made this thought-provoking observation:

> Never mind that their wives are about to be widows and their children fatherless. Never mind that their little band of followers will yet be "houseless, friendless and homeless" and that their children will leave footprints of blood across frozen rivers and an untamed prairie floor. Never mind that legions will die and other legions live declaring in the four quarters of this earth that they know the Book of Mormon and the Church which espouses it to be true. Disregard all of that, and tell me whether in this hour of death these two men would enter the presence of their Eternal Judge quoting from and finding solace in a book which, if not the very word of God, would brand them as imposters and charlatans until the end of time? *They would not do that!* They were willing to die rather than deny the divine origin and the eternal truthfulness of the Book of Mormon.[22]

Few people are ever put in a position where they have to choose between their cause and their lives. Abinadi, William Tyndale, Joseph Smith, and others across history were willing to die rather than renounce their testimonies, making them icons of good men. At the time the Prophet Joseph went to Carthage, he had four young children, and Emma was pregnant with another. Joseph was only thirty-eight years old and had everything to live for. He was the mayor of one of the largest cities in Illinois and was loved by thousands. Hyrum left behind six living children and his wife, Mary Fielding Smith, one of the great women in Church history.

What could possibly be the motive for Joseph to voluntarily go like a lamb to the slaughter? If his motive were to get rich from the Book of Mormon, surely he would have realized after fourteen years in print that it didn't work. If he were seeking fame, how would going to be murdered in cold blood help that goal?

If anyone would haven known that Joseph Smith was lying about the coming forth of the Book of Mormon, it would have been Hyrum. If it were a lie, why would he read from it for comfort the night before they were killed? If Joseph, either alone or with the help of co-conspirators, wrote the Book of Mormon, it is hard to believe that he would bear his testimony of its truthfulness to the Carthage Jail guards the same night (Wednesday, June 26, 1844).

> During the evening the Patriarch Hyrum Smith read and commented upon extracts from the Book of Mormon, on the imprisonments and deliverance of the servants of God for the Gospel's sake. Joseph bore a powerful testimony to the guards of the divine authenticity of the Book of Mormon, restoration of the Gospel, the administration of angels, and that the kingdom of God was again established upon the earth, for the sake of which he was then incarcerated in that prison, and not because he had violated any law of God or man.[23]

What kind of husband, father, son, or brother would lie about something that would cause his immediate family immense suffering because they believed what he told them? If he made the whole thing up for money, fame, power, or whatever other reason, why would he continue the lie when everyone he loved suffered so much because of it? Not only did his family suffer, but also his close personal friends and thousands of believers who had joined the Church.

What could possibly be his motive for doing so? There's really only one answer: because it was true.

What Joseph accomplished in just a few short years is perhaps unequalled in history, and yet his critics act as if there were nothing extraordinary about it. Of course, accomplishing great things does not make someone a prophet. Fortunately, the Lord allowed tangible evidence to be left behind to prove that Joseph was a good man and a prophet of God. The Book of Mormon is that proof. It is true.

Notes

1. Neal A. Maxwell, "Joseph, the Seer," *Ensign*, November 1983, 54.
2. William Tyndale, from *Foxe's Book of Martyrs* by John Foxe (England: John Day, 1563).
3. Ibid.
4. David A. Copeland, *The Antebellum Era: Primary Documents on Events from 1820 to 1860*, (Westport, CT: Greenwood Press), 2003, 245–46.
5. "Death of J. Smith, the Mormon Imposter," *The Millennial Harbinger*, third series, vol. I. Bethany, VA, September 1844, no. 9.
6. Joseph Smith, *History of The Church of Jesus Christ of Latter-day Saints*, ed. B. H. Roberts, 2nd ed. rev., 7 vols. (Salt Lake City: The Church of Jesus Christ of Latter-day Saints, 1932–1951) 4:541.
7. James Cullimore, "Joseph Smith, the Mormon Prophet," Devotional, BYU, 4 January 1977, speeches.byu.edu.
8. "Joseph Smith, the Prophet," *Young Woman's Journal*, December 1905, 556.
9. "The Wentworth Letter," *Times and Seasons* 3, 1 March 1842, 709.
10. *History of the Church*, 4:461.
11. Ibid. 6:74.
12. Brigham Young, *Discourses of Brigham Young*, ed. John A. Widtsoe (Salt Lake City: Deseret Book, 1954), 464.
13. *History of the Church*, 4:587.
14. "Declaration of the Twelve Apostles, " undated draft, reporting on March 1844 meeting; in Brigham Young, Office Files 1832–1878, Church Archives.
15. Lyman O. Littlefield, *The Martyrs: A Sketch of the Lives and a Full Account of the Martyrdom of Joseph and Hyrum Smith*, (Salt Lake City: Juvenile Instructor's Office, 1882), 58.
16. *History of the Church*, 6:500.
17. "Letter from Joseph Smith to Emma Smith, June 27, 1844," Carthage Jail, Carthage, Illinois; Community of Christ Archives, Independence, Missouri; copy in Church Archives.

18. Quoted in "Declaration of the Twelve Apostles," undated draft, reporting on March 1844 meeting; in Brigham Young, Office Files 1832–1878, Church Archives, The Church of Jesus Christ of Latter-day Saints, Salt Lake City, Utah.

19. J. H. Lawn, *Autobiography of Elder J. H. Lawn*, 3; owned by Arthur Hawley. See also *Autumn Leaves* 22:60–61.

20. *History of Joseph Smith*, 324–25.

21. "Anniversary Tribute to the Memory of President Joseph Smith," *Woman's Exponent*, 1 January 1874, 117.

22. Jeffrey R. Holland, "Safety for the Soul," *Ensign*, November 2009.

23. *History of the Church*, 6:600.

About the Author

Randal Wright has been fascinated by the study of families for many years. Seeking ways to raise righteous children led to his receiving a BS and MS with emphasis in the family area and then a PhD in family studies from Brigham Young University. He worked for many years as an institute director for the Church Education System and taught at BYU in the religion department.

He has written several books in the past on family topics including *Families in Danger: Protecting Your Family in an X-rated World, Building Better Homes and Families, Make Every Day Meaningful,* and *The Case for Chastity: Helping Youth Stay Morally Clean.* He has spoken across the United States, Canada, and England, and has been a frequent speaker at BYU Campus Education Week and the Especially for Youth program for many years. Randal and his wife, Wendy, live in Austin, Texas, and are the parents of five children and sixteen grandchildren.